Piaget:

Issues and Experiments

Guest editor

Peter Bryant

Watts Professor of Psychology, University of Oxford

The British Psychological Society

Published by The British Psychological Society
Headquarters St Andrews House, 48 Princess Road East, Leicester LE1 7DR, UK
Distribution Centre Blackhorse Road, Letchworth, Herts SG6 1HN, UK

First published, without an index, in *British Journal of Psychology*, volume 73, part 2, May 1982 – A
publication of The British Psychological Society

ISBN 0 901715 16 6

Printed in Great Britain at the University Press, Cambridge

Contents*

* Page numbers all refer to the numbering in square brackets at the head of every page.

3 Social and affective development

British Journal of Psychology (1982), **73**, 157–161   *Printed in Great Britain*

Editorial: Piaget's questions

Child psychology would have been a meagre thing without Piaget. During the long period when his work was largely ignored by most psychologists, the subject tended to treat children either as members of various remote and incomprehensible tribes or as slightly superior rats – 'somewhere along the biological continuum between rat and college student', to quote a famous behaviourist phrase of the time. It was a descriptive and a parasitic subject.

Piaget rescued us from that. He managed it in two ways. One was to develop a theory which was original and comprehensive. A paradox hovers around this theory. It is complicated, immensely complicated, and few people are bold enough to claim that they understand it entirely. Yet many of the most important ideas in it are simple and flexible and it is these ideas which give the theory its power. Take for example the notion of reversibility, a capacity which Piaget considered children to acquire somewhere beween the ages of five and eleven years. He meant that they begin to be able to manipulate perceptual representations and that, when they see a perceptual change, to be able to cancel out its effects by imagining the inverse change. It is an interesting idea but what is most impressive about it is the large number of very diverse aspects of child development to which Piaget managed to apply it. He used it of course in his account of the conservation experiment in which the child actually has to witness a perceptual change: but he used it too and as cogently in his research on social communication, on logical inferences, on the understanding of ordinal number, on the logic of classes and even on moral development. I cannot say that his use of reversibility was right in every case but I am impressed with the way Piaget managed to link such disparate topics with one simple idea and did so coherently. There are many other examples of the same flexibility in his theory.

The second main reason for Piaget's extraordinary influence on child psychology is perhaps a little less obvious. It is his skill and ingenuity as an experimenter. We are so used nowadays to hearing about the weaknesses in Piaget's experiments, about the controls which he left out and the alternative explanations which he forgot to exclude, that we easily forget that one of his greatest lessons was that it is possible to do simple and successful experiments on topics of great importance and apparent complexity in child development. It was Piaget who carried out the first systematic set of experiments on babies. It was Piaget who invented the conservation experiment, which by now is probably the most repeated experiment in psychology, and it was Piaget who thought of the experimental paradigms which still dominate most of the current work on cognitive and social development.

What can a single volume add in the face of this kind of achievement apart from demonstrating once again his pervasive influence? All the contributors in this issue do of course acknowledge his influence but taken together their papers perhaps do something more than this. All of them in different ways deal with the arguments that crowd round Piaget's work. The one uncontroversial thing about Piaget's theories is that they are controversial. Many child psychologists who are quite happy to recognize his unique contribution disagree very strongly with his conclusions about intellectual development. It is hardly ever his methods which worry these critics and indeed they themselves usually adopt these methods or variants of them. The trouble usually centres around the design of Piaget's experiments and around consequent questions about the conclusions which he draws from them.

To put it as bluntly as possible Piaget is criticized for neither considering nor trying to exclude alternative explanations to his own. The main purpose of his experiments is usually to demonstrate the curious and even surprising mistakes made by young children in various cognitive tasks, and he usually concludes from these mistakes that the young child lacks this or that ability. But negatives of this sort are notoriously difficult to prove, and there are usually half a dozen possible reasons why a child should get something wrong. It is often argued that Piaget tends to consider only one possibility. As this volume shows there have been many attempts to show that young children do possess the abilities which Piaget denies them and that they fail in his tasks for quite other reasons than those that he gives. However the argument goes both ways: there are as many psychologists who argue that Piaget's conclusions were right and that the critics managed to miss the main point. Smith's paper in this volume is a case in point.

I mention this sort of disagreement for a number of reasons. One is that these arguments have been remarkably productive. It is not just a matter of one side being hostile and the other defensive. On the contrary much of our most exciting information about intellectual development comes from experimenters whose starting-point was either a doubt about one or other of Piaget's conclusions or a desire to defend him against his critics. Secondly, bearing in mind that this is an issue of the *British Journal of Psychology*, a significant number of these experimenters have come from this country. (Members of the Genevan department have taken quite rightly but somewhat pejoratively to talking about the Anglo-Saxon approach.) But my third and main reason is simply that all the papers in this volume are concerned with these controversies in one way or another.

Let us consider how. One of the questions discussed is *object permanence* which is raised in the paper by Butterworth. He deals with the well-known $A\overline{B}$ error, a phenomenon which neatly demonstrates both Piaget's ingenuity and also the ease with which other people can produce quite different explanations for the same puzzling piece of behaviour. Piaget observed that at a certain age babies can successfully search for an object which they have seen hidden say under a cushion (A), but when later they see it hidden in another place (B) they continue to look for it in the first position. As Butterworth points out it must have taken a great deal of imagination on the part of Piaget to realize that this apparent perverseness was more than just a nuisance and that it might tell us something important about the child's understanding of objects. Piaget concluded that it meant that the baby did not have a proper understanding of an object's existence once it had disappeared. He argued that babies associate the object with a particular place and that they remember its position in terms of the response which they made to it before: they remember it, in other words, egocentrically. So at least two separate claims are involved, one about what the child thinks about objects which have disappeared and the other about how the child codes spatial positions.

It follows that at least one of these claims might not be right. The only reason for thinking that the error has anything to do with object permanence – that is with the child's understanding of what happens to things which he can see no longer – is that the object is typically hidden at A and B. But what would happen if it were plainly in view at A and then at B? Butterworth in an earlier paper has shown that the error still crops up and just as strongly in these conditions as when it is hidden in both places; this is a result which suggests that though the error may indeed tell us something about the baby's memory for spatial position it may have little to do with object permanence.

What then does it tell us about the baby's spatial codes? There is still the question, as Butterworth's paper in this volume points out, of the extent of the error. When they do make it there is some support for Piaget's idea that they are remembering spatial position egocentrically and possibly in terms of their own movements. But it is clear too that such egocentrism is not inevitable. There are several experiments in which the error virtually drops out in some conditions. It is impossible to resist the conclusion from experiments like these that babies have a variety of strategies at their disposal and use them differently in different situations.

Such a pattern is not on the whole part of Piaget's scheme. He was, it is true, happy to admit that children might solve a problem presented to them in one kind of material a long time before they managed the same moves with other kinds of material as well, and he even honoured this sort of unevenness with a theoretical label, horizontal décalage. Apart from this however he usually argued that at any stage the child would use one strategy to deal with a particular problem and that that strategy depended on his developmental level. Yet it is not only in work on object permanence that we find the same children failing dismally in one task and yet succeeding triumphantly in another which apparently makes the same logical demands as the first. This pattern is now a commonplace in research on cognitive development and especially in experiments which owe their inspiration to Piaget.

Transitivity, a problem which looms large in this volume, is a good example. The original observation of Piaget's is clear and undisputed. It also happens to have been his first experience of experimenting with children. He tried out a test devised originally by Cyril Burt in which children were given the premises A > B and B > C verbally and were then asked about the relationship between A and C. The question of course was whether they could combine the first two comparisons inferentially, and the answer was that when the problem is given in this form young children flounder. Piaget concluded that he had discovered a logical gap, and argued that it was a serious one because a child who does not understand transitivity will not be able either to measure or to understand measurement. To hammer home this last point he and his colleagues ran an experiment on measurement. They showed children a tower of bricks and asked them to build another tower of exactly the same height in a different part of the room. The question was whether the child would use a measure to make sure that he had got the right height. The answer was that younger children did not: they resorted to direct comparisons which tended to be rather unsuccessful.

Here are two definite failures, but besides them we can place successes which are at least as definite. There are now some very clear instances where young children do produce the correct answer to the AC question on the basis of being told that A > B *and* B > C (as the papers by Shultz, Pardo & Altmann and by myself show), usually when care has been taken to make them reasonably familiar with the premises before posing the inferential question. I cannot claim from these instances that young children do manage to make transitive inferences, because there are other ways of explaining children's successes in these tasks, but the contrast between the two sets of experiments is nevertheless quite sharp. Children fail in one version and succeed in another, and this contrast is as marked in experiments on measurement. Young children, who eschew measurement in Piaget's task, measure none the less in tasks in which direct visual comparisons are clearly out of the question. (See my paper in this volume.) Whatever else this kind of result means, it does at least demonstrate again that the same children use different strategies at different times. What exactly these strategies are and when and where they adopt them is still a matter of heated discussion.

Dramatic as the controversy over transitivity has been, it looks like a polite drawing room comedy in comparison to the Grand Guignol of the debate over *conservation*. It is fitting that such a large number of the papers in this volume deal with conservation because this is Piaget's best-known and most important experiment and because it has been repeated more often and argued over more strongly than any other of his techniques.

In essence the experiment is a simple one, and hardly needs describing. But since all the discussion about this experiment turns in the end on its design it is as well to get the details clear. The experiment is about the understanding of invariance, and asks the simple question whether the young child understands that changing the appearance of a quantity by spreading out, say, a row of counters or pouring liquid from a fat container into a thin one, does not affect the actual number of counters or the volume of liquid. The experiment is divided into two parts. In the first the child is shown two equal quantities (A and B) which also look alike – two rows of counters arranged alongside each other like two ranks of soldiers or two identical glasses holding the same amount of liquid. He is asked to compare A with B and usually judges them to be the same. Then the appearance of one of the quantities (B) is transformed, a transformation which we can describe as $B \rightarrow B_1$. One row for example is spread out or bunched up so that it is now a different length from the other. Once this is done the child is asked to compare the two quantities (A and B_1 now) again, and the question of course is whether the child will realize that the two quantities are still the same. Piaget considered this to be a test of the understanding of invariance because he thought that the child would have no other way of working out that A and B_1 are equal other than by using his knowledge that merely changing the appearance of B does not alter its quantity. So he concluded (1) that the younger children who typically fail in this task do not understand the principle of invariance and (2) that the older children who succeed do understand it.

It is as well to consider these two conclusions separately. First, does a negative result mean that children do not understand invariance? This is the more hotly disputed of the two conclusions. The strongest, current objection is the one made by Donaldson and her colleagues. Their standpoint, clearly described in Donaldson's paper in this issue, is that child and experimenter are on very different wavelengths. The child is misled into saying that there has been a change by the very fact that the apparently important adult experimenter has importantly changed one of the quantities.

This argument is largely based on the results of a well-known experiment (done with McGarrigle) which Donaldson describes in her paper. This experiment plays a large part in the work described in two papers here (Miller and Hargreaves, Molloy & Pratt). All the main features of the typical conservation task were preserved in this experiment apart from the transformation. In one condition this was done by a marauding teddy bear which was introduced at that point and which as though by accident transformed the appearance of one of the quantities during its cavorting. This change in procedure had a marked effect. Even four-year-old children who tended of course to fail in the normal conservation task managed, on the whole, very well in the teddy bear version. The authors concluded that young children do understand invariance, but are thrown off the track by the artificial nature of the traditional form of the conservation task.

The result is a powerful one, but there are some points for debate. One is some results which are difficult to explain in McGarrigle & Donaldson's terms. These are reported by Miller in this volume. His paper shows that children make the non-conservation error even with quite naturally occurring transformations (e.g. boats floating apart). No clumsy, egocentric experimenter misleading the child there, but plenty of failures none the less.

Another point is that the usual conclusion – that the right answer in a conversation task means that the child does understand invariance – is also a risky one. The trouble is that a child may give the right answer without even noticing the transformation and its results. He may be dimly aware that something has been done to one of the quantities without noticing what the perceptual changes are. In this case the task is not a proper test of invariance. It is only a proper test if the child notices the perceptual change as clearly as he noticed the pre-transformational display, and still is able to say that the two quantities are the same. It is strange but we have no guarantee that this is so. It would be very easy to include a check that children have attended to the display after the transformation, and the absence of a simple control of this sort discredits the whole conservation enterprise.

This is a soluble problem. Simply do the teddy bear transformation, and perhaps Miller's ingenious transformations as well, together with a measure of children's attention to the results of the perceptual transformation.

It is not so clear that the other two major problems covered in this volume can be solved so easily. One is the question of *necessity*, which is an important part of Piaget's scheme. He argued that to be logical a child must not only be able to produce the right answer to a logical problem. He must also know that answer and that answer alone is necessarily the right one. This requirement really does create an empirical problem. To rely, as Piaget did, on the child's own verbal justification of necessity is surely to court a thumping false negative, since it is quite possible that the child might understand that something is necessarily true but not be able to say so. On the other hand the common pattern of results in which children fail in one version of Piaget's tasks but succeed in another does invite the objection, as Smith's paper here shows, that the children's knowledge of the principle is so tenuous that they may not understand its necessity, even in the successful condition. Russell's paper is an interesting attempt to find an empirical test of necessity. There seems no reason why his methods could not be extended to the traditional problems of conservation, transitivity and class inclusion.

The last main problem is probably the most intractable. It is the question of the *causes of intellectual development*. Piaget's ideas about causes centre around his model of equilibration. The implications of this model are described in Boden's paper. Some of the model's consequences are explored in papers which touch on the role of conflict (Emler & Valiant, and my own). Recently as Emler & Valiant's paper shows a lot of interest has centred around the possibility that the main sources of conflict and hence of intellectual change might be social. This is indeed an interesting possibility, especially since one of Piaget's main, though often underestimated, interests was in children's social development and understanding of social rules (see the papers here by Siegal & Francis, by Macaskill and by Wright). But again we still await a satisfactory test of the effects of social conflict.

Most attempts to test the idea of conflict have involved training experiments, in which an experimental group is given added experience of conflict of one sort or another. But such experiments are worthless unless there is also a control group which is given exactly the same kind of experience (same material, same number of trials) except for the experience in question, e.g. conflict. Experiments of this sort are hard to find, and the result is that the causal side of Piaget's theory, despite a considerable body of research, remains untested. Yet there is no reason, in principle, why it should not be tested adequately.

In fact, one of the joys of working with Piaget's theory is that so many of his questions are answerable and seem very close to a solution. That they are is largely due to Piaget, partly because he raised so many provocative and important issues and partly through his ingenuity in thinking of ways of looking at these issues. He was indeed a very great man. I am glad that we have had the chance to show our gratitude and I hope that our enthusiasm for his achievement, which must be the one thing that all the authors of this volume have in common, shines through.

PETER BRYANT
University of Oxford

1
Origins and causes of development

British Journal of Psychology (1982), **73**, 165–173   *Printed in Great Britain*

Is equilibration important? – A view from artificial intelligence

Margaret A. Boden

The problem addressed by Piaget in terms of equilibration is the development of harmonious novelties, wherein genuinely new structures are created out of older ones without any impairment of the overall integration of the system. He posited a continuity between biological and psychological systems, such that structurally similar answers exist for embryological and cognitive development. 'Equilibration' differs from 'feedback' in stressing structural (not quantitative) parameters, and the self-maintenance of systems whose parameters are changing. Piaget did not specify the concept adequately, but he indicated important questions that might be better addressed later. Computational ideas (which are significantly consonant with Piaget's approach) provide a more rigorous specification of structural and procedural matters, and are in principle suited to the expression of the issues addressed in terms of 'equilibration'. As yet, however, learning and development are not understood in computational terms. Nor is it known whether there is some general, interdisciplinary, theory of structural development.

Piaget described equilibration as a 'development factor' of fundamental psychological importance, more general even than heredity, environment, or social education, since 'it intervenes in every hereditary or acquired process, and intervenes in their interactions' (Piaget, 1958, p. 836). He believed his account of equilibration not only to be of great value to psychology but also to have the potential to unify developmental psychology, theoretical biology, sociology, and epistemology. Although I shall challenge these assumptions, claiming that they must be rejected in their strong form, I shall argue that an important theoretical problem is marked (though neither clearly expressed nor solved) by the vocabulary of equilibration.

By 'equilibration' Piaget meant an adaptive interaction (consisting of simultaneous assimilation and accommodation) such that overall integration of the self-adapting system is maintained throughout any structural development taking place (Piaget, 1958). He described it as carrying the system from a state of 'disequilibrium' to one of relative 'equilibrium', meaning that the failure of the system in its earlier form to make appropriate (assimilatory and/or accommodatory) adjustments initiates a self-development such that in its later form its powers are adequate to meet new situational demands. It is because self-adapting systems are characteristic of life, whether at the biological or the psychological level, that Piaget hoped for an interdisciplinary unification in terms of a general theory of equilibration.

Many committed Piagetians regard this concept as Piaget's prime contribution to psychology. Such people use his terminology of equilibration and repeat his claims about it as though the former were crystal clear, the latter evidently true, and their union genuinely explanatory. However, even an admirer of Piaget has dismissed the concept as 'surplus baggage', contributing nothing useful to theory or experimental design (Bruner, 1959, p. 356). And hostile critics express especial exasperation at this use of polysyllabic terminology which, they say, is not just vague but pompously empty. In short, there is no general consensus that 'equilibration' is among the highest of Piaget's achievements: many psychologists asked to rank his contributions would award equilibration not the first prize, not even the consolation prize, but the booby prize.

Those who require precision above all else will have learnt long since not to seek it *chez* Piaget. But vague ideas can serve the heuristic purpose of keeping important questions alive, if empirically dormant, when better concepts do not exist for dealing with them.

They may engender a family of speculations some or all of which can eventually be given specific empirical content – 'eventually', because it may not be immediately apparent how one might map a given speculative vocabulary onto observable phenomena. One may have to await future conceptual and/or empirical advances in whose terms the initial speculations can be interpreted. If an idea is intended as a substantive unifying concept applicable to distinct theoretical domains, then parallel empirical specifications should eventually be possible in each field. For instance, the abstract concept of cybernetic 'feedback' (which Piaget saw as very close to that of equilibration) can be applied with varying degrees of rigour to many different phenomena, from warm-bloodedness to the political process.

These considerations prompt five questions: (1) Did Piaget identify a question of theoretical significance which is worth keeping alive in vague terms until better ones become available? (2) Does 'equilibration' offer anything over and above more familiar concepts, such as 'feedback'? (3) Did he provide the specifications necessary for his concept's fruitful application in all or any of the relevant disciplines? (4) Are there other (more recent) ideas which address the same range of questions more satisfactorily? (5) And if so, are these ideas so consonant with his approach that they may be seen as filling out his own account of equilibration, or are they totally unrelated to his work? The subsequent sections address these in turn.

The underlying problem

The prime theoretical problem addressed by Piaget in terms of equilibration is the development of harmonious novelties. In embryogenesis and histogenesis, for example, genuinely new structures are somehow created out of older ones, without any functional impairment of the working of the system as a whole. This sort of creativity, where structures arise *de novo*, differs from that wherein (possibly unique) phenomena are generated which are different from but of the same essential form as those existing previously, and of which an example is the sort of creativity attributed by Chomsky to language. It differs even more from the effecting of chaotic changes, that is, of changes which may arise in a principled fashion (in that they are caused rather than random events), but which have no tendency to cohere with the overall oganization of the system as a whole and so often lead to malfunction – of which the obvious example is genetic mutation. In general, when new structures are differentiated out of more primitive ones, we need to explain how overall integration can be maintained as the system develops from its more primitive to its more complex form.

As Piaget put it, speaking of both mental and physical life, we need to understand 'how the mechanism bringing about this continual construction may constitute at the same time a regulating mechanism ensuring coherence. In the field of the cognitive functions in particular, the problem is to understand 'how learning, discovery and creation may not only be reconciled with but take place at the same time as control and verification in such a way that the new remains in harmony with the acquired' (Piaget, 1958, p. 832). Other psychological (and biological) theorists, he said, discussed some of the novelties created but typically ignored the problem of how their creation could be harmoniously integrated. He claimed that his account of equilibration provided a solution to this problem.

Equally, he claimed thereby to have exhibited the continuity, or essential similarity, of cognitive and biological development. He even said that the 'true perspective' of the equilibrium factor 'is a biological and not a logical one, although the special equilibrium of logical structures is one of the finest achievements of living morphogenesis' (Piaget, 1958, p. 837). The term 'equilibrium' (like 'assimilation' and 'accommodation' too) originated in a biological context, wherein it refers to the maintenance of the internal environment. But Piaget saw embryological *homeorhesis* as even more like cognitive growth than is physiological *homeostasis*. That is, he saw the development of cognitive schemata and the morphogenesis of the embryo as two special cases of the same phenomenon, namely, the (largely autonomous) continuing increase of differentiation within a system whose overall integration is retained throughout.

Equilibration and feedback

As regards 'equilibration' and 'feedback', Piaget spoke of the former before Wiener identified the latter. So in so far as the two concepts are equivalent, this is a case of a later concept's clarifying an earlier, less well-defined, one. However, there is a significant difference between them. In classic examples of feedback, whether in biological homeostasis or control engineering, the central problem is how to arrive at and maintain a steady state by varying parameters whose potential relevance is already given. Even when the feedback controls a non-steady state (as in the braking of a large vehicle), the relevant constraints are explicitly allowed for in the design of the system. But Piaget's interest was in more complex cases, in which integrative control has to be maintained throughout a continuing process of structural differentiation. In differentiation, new parameters arise which solve, and also posit, problems of system-maintenance. Thus once liver and lungs appear, certain problems of overall control can be solved in ways not previously available to the organism; but, by the same token, new problems are posited concerning the mutual regulation of these organs themselves. Accordingly, different theoretical problems arise with regard to homeostasis and to homeorhesis. In so far as Piaget's 'equilibration' stresses the latter rather than the former it is not simply equivalent to 'feedback'. Indeed, as I have argued elsewhere (Boden, 1979, chapter 7), the concept of feedback (like algebraic concepts also) is inadequate to express complex structural changes of the sort that take place in cognitive and morphogenetic development.

The vagueness of 'equilibration'

Piaget was right to identify autonomous differentiation as a very important, very general, and profoundly problematic phenomenon. There are great difficulties in conceptualizing coherent, progressive, self-regulated change, whether it occurs within cognitive structures, biological organisms, social systems, or scientific knowledge. For instance, despite their many disagreements, Popper and Kuhn agree that scientific revolutions are not the result of any rationally reconstructable process of discovery. If they are right, their failure to conceptualize science as a harmonious self-generative process is of course no failure; but if they are wrong, we still await such a conceptualization (for an attempt to discover structural continuities in so-called scientific 'revolutions', see Krige, 1980). Within sociology, the difficulty of conceptualizing non-revolutionary social change is notorious. The orderly creation of new and functionally integrated forms in embryogenesis is acknowledged as an unsolved problem of theoretical biology, and some biologists (like Piaget) regard the origin of new genera and species in evolution as inexplicable by neo-Darwinism. And the development of cognitive structures, the increasing differentiation yet overall integration of knowledge and inferential power, is likewise obscure.

This last comment may seem strange, for Piaget devoted a lifetime's work to this very issue. Certainly, his discussions of cognitive change were more useful than his remarks on biological development. He suggested hidden complexities in the development of cognitive structures, and drew attention to many interesting empirical phenomena. But he did not clarify the equilibratory aspects of this development, because he failed to specify the concept of equilibration to any useful degree. His remarks about equilibration, suggestive though some of them may be, are of such extreme generality and abstractness as not to be even *prima facie* applicable to clearly distinct empirical phenomena.

For instance, he taught that equilibrium is a matter of degree: according to Piaget, all living structures are equilibrated, but some are more equilibrated than others. He claimed that complete equilibrium is reached with the (fully reversible) formal operations, whose structures and transformations he defined in terms of algebraic lattices. Prior to this stage, he said, 'equilibrium is only a compromise at the level of organic morphogenesis or variation of the species. With nervous organization and mental life... a twofold power of retroaction and anticipation considerably enlarges the field of this equilibrium and replaces fleeting compromises by actual syntheses' (Piaget, 1958, p. 837).

Again, he claimed to have distinguished three types of equilibration: between the subject's mental schemata and external objects; between the subschemes within a given overall scheme, some of which may have started life as independent schemes; and between the (hierarchically distinct) parts of knowledge and the totality of knowledge. About the latter, he said: 'Little by little there has to be a constant equilibrium established between the parts of the subject's knowledge and the totality of his knowledge at any given moment. There is a constant differentiation of the totality of knowledge into the parts and an integration of the parts back into the whole' (Piaget, 1975, p. 839). He insisted that in all cases of equilibration, 'the activities of the subject are always compensatory as well as constructive', and in a similar spirit spoke of 'the functional necessity of negations', saying that equilibration can involve processing as many negations as affirmations, implicit though these negations may be (Piaget, 1977, p. 11). And he often spoke of cognitive equilibration as being 'fed' by input from the outside world, as needing 'nourishment' much as organisms do.

None of these remarks is at all clear. Just *what* are the compensations, regulations, or negations involved in any particular case? And just *how* do they contribute to the overall control of cognitive function? Piaget's writing was not sufficiently precise to answer these questions, or even to state them adequately. In his lengthy discussion of what he called the 'how' of equilibration (Piaget, 1977), he struggled manfully with the vocabulary of 'positive' and 'negative disturbances', 'regulations', and 'regulations of regulations'. Disturbances are what trigger equilibration, being 'gaps that leave some requirement unfulfilled', gaps to be defined in terms of currently functioning cognitive schemata. Regulations are the adjustments made in response to disturbances, including disturbances that arise because of previous regulations. In describing the self-correcting action of a bicycle-rider, for example, Piaget said 'As for outside obstacles, these are avoided, which means compensating for the disturbances by a whole or partial negation, the latter corresponding to a differentiation of the scheme into subschemes which determine whether or not the goal can be attained by a direct itinerary' (Piaget, 1977, p. 26). But this is merely a roundabout way of saying that there are complex processes of problem solving going on, without specifying them or even clearly articulating the general sorts of complexity that might be involved.

However, if Piaget's own account of the mechanisms of equilibration does not do the job he set out to do, perhaps some other version of his theory might. This raises the final two questions listed above: Are there any recent concepts that can express the same phenomena more adequately, and if so are these wholly unrelated to Piaget's ideas or can his talk of equilibration fruitfully be interpreted in terms of them? The next section discusses these questions together.

Computational concepts in relation to Piaget's ideas

Concepts drawn from computer science and artificial intelligence are especially promising here (Boden, 1977, 1979). These ideas owe nothing in their provenance to Piaget, but it does not follow that Piaget's work cannot reasonably be interpreted in their terms. However, we must be careful not to cheat here, not to speak of 'interpretation' where we should rather speak of 'substitution'. We must not put words into the mouth of a reconstructed Piaget, which the unreconstructed Piaget would not have been prepared to accept. Even where there is some degree of conceptual affinity, so that straightforward *substitution* is not at issue, we must remember that it is one thing to say that he said something, another to say that he would (or might) have said it if he had been given the chance, and yet another to say that he could have said it without falling into incoherence.

I have argued elsewhere that Piaget's commitment to cybernetics, his formalism, his structuralism, and his semiotic mentalism all predisposed him to sympathy (which he occasionally expressed) for a computational approach to theoretical psychology (Boden, 1979, chapter 7). Similarly, I have argued that his vision of a cognitive biology is essentially consonant with recent developments in theoretical morphology, which are themselves influenced by computational ideas (Boden, 1979, chapter 6; Boden, 1981, chapter 4). So although Piaget did not use computational concepts, relying instead on algebraic and cybernetic formalizations (which as I said above are incapable of expressing a rich variety of structures and transformational processes), he probably would not have been averse to a computational interpretation of his work. Taking this as a licence, then, how might one use current computational ideas to clarify and elaborate his views on equilibration, views expressed in remarks like those quoted above?

Piaget described organizations in terms of 'part' and 'whole', but these concepts are problematic for computational systems involving recursion – such as many programs, and the human mind (Hofstadter, 1979). In recursive systems, a procedure functioning on a problem of one level can activate itself to solve a similar problem on a lower level. Likewise, procedure A can call on procedure B to solve a problem, and while B is dealing with this problem it can call on A to resolve a difficulty of its own. Is B part of A, or A part of B? Even within a single program, no sensible general answer can be given. However, if the particular processing-point and problem concerned are specified, one can distinguish between B's functioning under the control of A and A's being subordinated to B (one can specify the 'regulations of regulations' involved).

Piaget also erred in having an overly static view of organization. Despite his many reminders that the mind is a dynamic system, he represented it in essentially non-dynamic terms. For example, he relied on algebraic lattices to express properties of transformational systems, such as reversibility. This is not surprising, since computational concepts did not then exist with which to describe types of transformations and the relations between them. Such concepts are likely to be helpful here because they are expressly designed to represent dynamic processes and the organization of control within functioning systems.

Partly due to his lack of dynamic concepts, Piaget's notion of organization was simplistically hierarchical, and his understanding of integration limited accordingly. Much as biologists distinguish organism, organ-system, organ, cell, and organelle, so Piaget conceptualized cognitive hierarchies as systems wherein every member exists on a specific level, being clearly subordinate or superordinate to its neighbours. Computational work has given us a richer (though undoubtedly still primitive) sense of what sorts of organization there may be.

For example, hierarchy, in which control always passes either up or down between adjacent levels and has to follow fixed pathways, has been contrasted with heterarchy, in which control is much more flexible according to context (Winston, 1972). Hierarchy is likened to a rigid bureaucracy, while heterarchy resembles a committee of experts, each doing their own thing in their own way except when they recognize the need for help on a specific difficulty from some other expert. 'Production systems', too, have an organization very different from a hierarchy. These are sets of functionally independent rules, each of which performs a specific action when a particular condition pertains. The system is developed by the successive addition of independent rules. Yet the 'regulations' performed by such a system may be surprisingly coherent and intelligent overall. Indeed, Piagetian 'seriation' has been modelled in these terms (Young, 1976). Admittedly, as soon as a production system becomes really complex, additional organization has to be somehow introduced, which goes against the spirit of the initial philosophy (Davis & King, 1977). But although it is still unclear how different types of organization compare in their ability to carry out computations (equilibratory regulations) of various sorts, the sorts of questions that need to be asked about such matters are becoming clearer.

This is relevant to Piaget's notion of equilibrated coordination between subschemes. If two systems are to function in concert, information received by one (whether resulting from external events or from its own physical or computational actions) has to be made available to the other if it is likely to be relevant to its functioning. For instance, if grasping and looking are to be coordinated (and irrespective of whether some degree of coordination is present from birth, or whether they begin their development independently, then proprioceptive and visual information have to reach the cross-modal scheme in a coordinated fashion. One way in which information can pass from one system to another is by direct communication between them; another is via a central memory store, or 'blackboard', allowing messages to be written and read by both subsystems. These sorts of computationally distinct equilibratory regulation do not exhaust the possibilities (for instance, there could be a number of largely independent 'blackboards' – or memories – each communicating with a subset of the system's functions). And neither of them as just described explains how the need for or appropriateness of certain information is recognized by a system, on its own or on another's behalf. If a computer program is to function then these questions must be given provisional answers, but our ignorance about the specifics of coordination in the human case is still enormous.

We are even ignorant about the general question of how much coordination exists within the mind. Piaget's remarks often imply that adult human knowledge is a seamless robe, enjoying a degree of integration that allows of no inherent contradictions and provides for coordinate relations between every part. This seems to be implicit in his claim that 'little by little there has to be a constant equilibrium established between the parts of the subject's knowledge and the totality of his knowledge at any given moment'. This vision of knowledge is also commonly the epistemologist's ideal (which partly accounts for Piaget's own commitment to it). But work in artificial intelligence has suggested that knowledge may be modular, with limited opportunities of coordination between the various modules, and that potential contradictions can exist within a knowledge system without prejudicing its functioning. Considerations of computational efficiency show that both these features can afford positive advantages to a knowledge system, so they are of epistemological as well as psychological importance. Again, the dynamics of the system are crucial: whereas an actual contradiction (such as 'All birds can fly, but some can't') is no use to anybody, a potential contradiction (such as that between 'All birds can fly' and 'Emus are birds that can't fly') may cause no problem, provided that when remarks about emus are accessed or generated the system is somehow protected from being led into practical difficulties by the (false) over-generalization about birds present elsewhere within it.

To ask 'how much' coordination there is in the mind, as I did above, is itself problematic, for it implies that coordination can be measured. Certainly, gross comparative judgements can be made of the relative degree of coordination of different systems. This is done by the computer scientist in assessing the extent of communication between component modules of a system, by the psychiatrist in diagnosing 'dissociated' personality or consciousness, and of course by Piaget in speaking of more and less complete stages of equilibration. But we saw above that communication can be direct or indirect, which suggests that measurement of coordination is not a straightforward matter. Again, potential coordination has to be distinguished from actual (or normal) coordination. The development of a measure of coordination, or integration, is a matter for abstract computational logic, closely linked to the measurement of system complexity. But it seems most implausible that any useful notion of 'complete' coordination will be formulated, broadly equivalent to Piaget's 'complete' equilibrium.

If Piaget's talk of 'nourishment' is more than just a way of saying that minds (like organisms) are open systems affected by the environment, it is perhaps comparable to a remark made in computational circles, that 'the cheapest store of information about the real world is the real world'. This remark reflects the difficulty of providing programs with enough data and inferential power to compute the properties of the external world. Comparably, evolution apparently has not managed to produce cognitive systems that can function flexibly in the real world without taking in information from it. Even animals with a pre-programmed ability to behave in a given way usually rely on real-world input (the 'innate releasing stimulus') to tell them when to do so. On this view, that equilibration should be dialectical is a computational necessity.

It might be objected that all these computational reinterpretations of Piaget are irrelevant to the most interesting feature of his concept of equilibration. No one familiar with computational models, or even with Chomsky's grammar, would deny that finite sets of generative rules can give rise to historically novel phenomena sharing a certain structure. In so far as this is what Piaget was claiming in speaking of the creation of harmonious novelties, he was clearly right, although he did not specify any generative rules himself. But Piaget also emphasized systems where the structuring principles themselves change over time in an integrated fashion. What can the computationalist say about these issues?

At present, the computationalist can say very little. Adaptive learning is not well understood, and so cannot be clearly differentiated from (or, alternatively, identified as a special case of) development. In a well-known computational study of concept learning, the relevant parameters were both few and predefined by the programmer (Winston, 1975). The program had to learn that and how they were relevant, but did not have to define them for itself, nor distinguish them from myriad others which might have been relevant but were not. The program did use counter-examples as well as examples, but these had to be carefully presented in a particular order. Living organisms are not so constrained. Moreover, in real life, features which once were irrelevant may later become useful spurs to further improvement. For instance, studies of 'consolidation' in children's understanding of balance problems suggest that features are initially ignored as (Kuhnian?) anomalies which later come to be regarded as counter-examples enabling refinement of the child's current theory (Karmiloff-Smith & Inhelder, 1975). The computational basis of these changes is not understood: how is an exception (a 'disturbance') recognized as such, how is it classified as anomaly or as counter-example, and how is it used to guide development of the system?

These questions are addressed in some degree by another learning program, closer in spirit to Piaget's views on cognitive development. It uses meta-commentary and self-criticism to improve on its past performance, and generalizes its fresh insights so that they can be applied to many new problems of the same structural form (Sussman, 1975). Unlike the previous example, this program can perhaps be seen as relevant to differentiation, for the internal structure of its self-generated plans becomes increasingly complex, and it produces computational routines specifically designed to effect the coordination of newly generated subsystems. For instance, it not only generates distinct plans for achieving different subgoals, but it discovers that an extra step has to be inserted between the completion of one and the start of another (like taking the old cotton out of one's needle before trying to thread it with the new).

This program learns by reflecting on its mistakes, which it classifies according to structural principles. This is reminiscent of Piaget's dialectical view of development. But children drawing maps, for example, spontaneously improve their spatial representations even without the spur of failure (Karmiloff-Smith, 1979). Their increased computational efficiency enables them to solve problems later that they could not have solved before, but it was not forced on them by any earlier mistake. In general, it is not clear that differentiation is motored by incapacity (the foetus is a viable organism, and the ammonite a viable species). Accordingly, an adequate theoretical account of differentiation would presumably have to identify some autonomous tendency to (or, at least, potential for) self-improvement, irrespective of any response to the pressures of failure. While Piaget posited such a tendency, and even regarded the rise of logic and mathematics as an evolutionary inevitability, it cannot be said that he gave us any clear idea of how it might function.

Conclusion

A final caveat concerns Piaget's assumption that there can be a general theory of equilibration. Many computationally inclined psychologists share his faith, at least as regards cognitive phenomena. And some workers in artificial intelligence are seeking a theory applicable alike to machines, Martians, monkeys, and men. However, other such workers have abandoned their hopes that very general principles of reasoning might be found in terms of which to articulate all intelligent processes. Naturally, some general concepts, such as the distinction between depth-first and breadth-first search, are likely to have a widespread relevance. But many cases of intelligence seem to rely on large amounts of task-specific knowledge, which are sometimes specifically allowed for in the hardware [like early visual processing in the retina (Marr, 1976)], and sometimes have to be learnt. So while Piaget's faith in the possibility of a general theory of cognitive equilibration is not obviously mistaken, it is not obviously correct either. Still less is it obvious (though I have claimed that it is possible) that general principles of equilibration may be involved in all forms of development, whether cognitive, biological, or social.

But despite its vagueness, and the unclarity of its research implications, Piaget's theory of equilibration merits attention. It identifies an important theoretical problem – how the generation of harmonious novelties is possible – which is still highly obscure, despite some relevant scientific advances. These are situated within developmental biology, cybernetics, and artificial intelligence or computational psychology, which supports Piaget's claim that there are very general questions here, whose solution in different domains may be significantly similar. He was mistaken in thinking that as well as indicating the problem he had provided its solution. Understandably, many critics regard it as well-nigh devilish on his part to have tempted his disciples into the illusory faith that 'equilibration' provides an *explanation*. But to point out significant problems that are largely unrecognized by other theorists is no mean feat. Even the devil must be given his due.

References

Boden, M. A. (1977). *Artificial Intelligence and Natural Man*. Brighton, Sussex: Harvester.

Boden, M. A. (1979). *Piaget*. London: Fontana.

Boden, M. A. (1981). The case for a cognitive biology. In *Minds and Mechanisms: Philosophical Psychology and Computational Models*, chapter 4. Brighton, Sussex: Harvester.

Bruner, J. S. (1959). Inhelder and Piaget's *The Growth of Logical Thinking*. British Journal of Psychology, **50**, 365.

Davis, R. & King, J. (1977), An overview of production systems. In E. W. Elcock & D. Michie (eds), *Machine Intelligence*, **8**, pp. 300–334. Chichester: Ellis Horwood.

Hofstadter, D. (1979). *Godel, Escher, Bach: An Eternal Golden Braid*. Brighton, Sussex: Harvester.

Karmiloff-Smith, A. (1979). Micro- and macro-developmental changes in language acquisition and other representational systems. *Cognitive Science*, **3**, 81–118.

Karmiloff-Smith, A. & Inhelder, B. (1975). If you want to get ahead, get a theory. *Cognition*, **3**, 195–212.

Krige, J. (1980). *Science, Revolution, and Discontinuity*. Brighton, Sussex: Harvester.

Marr, D. (1976). Early processing of visual information. *Philosophical Transactions of the Royal Society, London*, **275** (942), 483–524.

Piaget, J. (1958). Equilibration processes in the psychobiological development of the child. In H. E. Gruber & J. J. Voneche (eds), *The Essential Piaget*. London: Routledge & Kegan Paul, 1977.

Piaget, J. (1975). Problems of equilibration. In H. E. Gruber & J. J. Voneche (eds), *The Essential Piaget*. London: Routledge & Kegan Paul, 1977.

Piaget, J. (1977). *The Development of Thought: Equilibration of Cognitive Structures*. Oxford: Blackwell.

Sussman, G. J. (1975). *A Computer Model of Skill Acquisition*. New York: Elsevier.

Winston, P. H. (1972). The MIT robot. In B. Meltzer & D. Michie (eds), *Machine Intelligence* 7, pp. 431–464. Edinburgh: Edinburgh University Press.

Winston, P. H. (1975). Learning structural descriptions from examples. In P. H. Winston (ed.), *The Psychology of Computer Vision*. Cambridge, MA: MIT.

Young, R. M. (1976). *Seriation by Children: An Artificial Intelligence Analysis of a Piagetian Task*. Basel: Birkhauser.

Requests for reprints should be addressed to Margaret A. Boden, School of Social Sciences, University of Sussex, Falmer, Brighton, Sussex, UK.

British Journal of Psychology (1982), **73**, 175–185   *Printed in Great Britain*

Piaget's stage 4 error: Background to the problem

George Butterworth and Nicholas Jarrett

Infants performed Piaget's stage 4 manual search task with an object hidden at successive locations (A and B) in the vertical plane. In the various studies, the initial location (A) either had an immediate background or the background was absent. The majority of infants in each experiment made persistent perseverative errors to the initial location (A) when the object was moved to a new location (B), if there had been no immediate background at A. When a background was available infants showed an equiprobable pattern of search to A and B. The results suggest that the typical stage 4 error, described by Piaget as characteristic of infants between eight and 11 months, may only occur when the baby is unable to monitor movements of the object with respect to a stable background as a visual frame of reference.

It is a tribute to Piaget's remarkable powers of observation that he should have recognized the significance of an apparently commonplace error that occurs when infants first search manually for a hidden object. He noticed that babies between the ages of approximately eight and 11 months pass through a stage in development when they will search correctly for an object hidden at an initial location (A), yet they continue to search at A even though they have seen the same object hidden at a new place (B). Piaget (1954) argued that these perseverative errors (sometimes known as stage 4 or $\overline{AB}$ errors) demonstrate incomplete development of the object concept; the infant experiences the object as if its spatio-temporal identity depends on the actions that have been made to it at the initial location. Lacking the 'object-concept', the infant fails to perceive the thing at its new location (B) as the 'self-same' object as was previously retrieved from A.

A great deal of research has been carried out on Piaget's stage 4 task and there is no doubt that babies make errors when searching for hidden objects. However, it has proved difficult to demonstrate that errors *inevitably* occur, as would seem to be required if the object is known as an extension of action, as Piaget maintains. It has usually been found that babies will search correctly at the initial location (A) but that they will search consistently *either* at A or at B (the final location) after the object is moved (Butterworth, 1974, 1975, 1977). That is, locations A and B are equiprobable after the object has moved, with babies searching at one place or the other. In longitudinal studies, the same infant may consistently perseverate to A or be consistently correct to B on successive occasions of testing (Bower & Wishart, 1972). Furthermore, passive observation of the object at its first hiding-place is sufficient to generate the same equiprobable search pattern after the object moves. This suggests that when errors do occur, the infant cannot simply be repeating a previously successful response (Landers, 1971; Butterworth, 1974; Bremner, 1978a, b). Instead, it seems as if movement of the object from A to B renders the old and new locations equally likely, as far as the baby is concerned. While this may still constitute evidence that young infants have difficulty identifying an object that moves from place to place, a different explanation may be required than that the object is known simply as an 'extension of action'.

In recent years, a number of studies have examined the role of spatial location cues in guiding infant manual search. A variety of effects on error rates have been observed, depending on the distinctive spatial characteristics of the occluder, the background and the manner of hiding the object (Bremner & Bryant, 1977; Lucas & Uzgiris, 1977; Bremner, 1978a, b, 1980). Indeed, when given distinctive spatial cues in the occluding covers babies

0007-1269/82/020175-11 $02.00/0 © 1982 The British Psychological Society

in the stage 4 age range can search correctly for an object they have seen hidden at successive places on a stable background (Butterworth *et al.*, 1982). It has proved difficult to establish whether, and under what conditions, babies actually show Piaget's typical pattern of persistent search to the initial location, which led him to characterize perseverative errors as a necessary stage in the child's developing object concept.

This investigation takes advantage of an asymmetry in infants' patterns of search in an attempt to elucidate the spatial conditions that lead infants persistently to err in Piaget's stage 4 task. The study was based on an earlier investigation (Butterworth, 1976), where it was discovered that infants at stage 4 made a greater number of errors when an object was moved from 'up' to 'down' with locations A and B arranged equidistantly above and below eye level than when the sequence was reversed (Fig. 1*a* shows the apparatus). Under these conditions, the significant majority of infants in the sample erred when A was at 'up'. They made the typical stage 4 error described by Piaget; all the infants searched 'where they had found the object first'. However, infants who started at 'down' either searched persistently at A or persistently at B after the object was moved; i.e. half the infants searched correctly and the other half erred. One aim of the experiments reported here was to establish what made the majority of infants err to 'up' when the object was moved from 'up' to 'down' since this information might be of interest in evaluating Piaget's claims about the stage 4 error.

The error pattern to 'up' is also of interest because it might be a precursor of a general spatial asymmetry that has been observed among both infants and adults (Sandstrom, 1951; Takala, 1951; Vereecken, 1961). All these authors showed that in a variety of spatial tasks arranged in the vertical plane 'up' locations seem to exercise a disproportionate effect on performance. Clark (1973) suggests that spatial asymmetries of this kind may have their origin in a natural asymmetry of perceptual space. He maintains that everything above ground level is perceptible, whereas everything below is not. Therefore, positions that are 'up' in the vertical plane tend to have a natural positive valence and act as spatial 'anchors'. From a theoretical point of view it would be of interest to establish whether errors observed in the vertical version of the stage 4 task may reflect a general asymmetry of the perceptual system.

General procedure

A series of experiments was carried out using the apparatus shown in Figs 1*a*, *b*, *c*, and *d*. To save space, those aspects of the apparatus and procedure common to all three studies will be outlined first.

The apparatus comprised a vertical stand to which were attached two oblong platforms (14 × 12 cm) with a different kind of background in each study. In Expt 1, the green baize background extended behind the lower platform only since it served merely to connect A with B (as in Butterworth, 1976, see Fig. 1*a*). In Expt 2, a green baize background of the same dimensions (19 × 12 cm) as in Fig. 1*a* extended behind the upper platform only, which was joined to the lower by transparent brackets (Fig. 1*b*). In the third experiment, the background was a vertical, circular board (36 cm in diameter) covered in green baize which extended symmetrically behind the upper and lower platforms (see Fig. 1*c*). The purpose of the apparatus therefore was to vary the properties of the immediate *background* from experiment to experiment.

In each experiment, infants were seated on a low chair with the platforms equidistant above and below eye level and at a distance of approximately 23 cm from the baby. Half the infants started first (A trial) at the upper platform while the remainder searched first at the lower. The same object was hidden throughout the experiment for any infant. Usually, a bunch of keys was used, although a toy car was sometimes hidden if the keys proved unattractive. The covers were two pieces of white cloth measuring 14 × 12 cm.

Each baby received two 'warm up' trials where the partially hidden object was retrieved from A. Then, depending on the particular experiment or condition within the experiment, infants received either one A trial, when the object was completely hidden at the initial location (A), or five A trials. The purpose of this comparison was firstly to replicate Butterworth (1976) (when five A trials were given) and secondly to establish whether differential experience of search at the initial location may contribute to error. The details of the hiding procedure were constant for each experiment and were as follows.

The object was placed on the platform at A and both platforms were simultaneously covered by the two white cloths. Following a three-second delay, the apparatus was pushed back into reach and the infant was allowed to search. Each infant was then given five trials at the second (B) location and the experimenter noted whether errors were made. An error was scored if manual search was directed at the wrong location and a correct response was scored if the infant removed only the correct cover and retrieved the object. A non-correction procedure was adopted, so that the apparatus was moved out of reach after the infant made his or her response.

Experiment 1

The aim of the first experiment was to replicate Butterworth's (1976) study which showed that infants made persistent, asymmetrical patterns of error in the stage 4 task arranged in the vertical plane. When an object was hidden at successive locations moving from 'up' to 'down' the majority of infants searched at the incorrect, initial location (A), whereas when the object was moved from 'down' to 'up' search at A and B was equiprobable to either location (i.e. half the babies searched persistently at A and half searched persistently at B).

Infants, apparatus and procedure

Forty-eight infants were seen. They were equally distributed by age groups eight, nine and 10 months, and sex. The mean ages were: eight-month group: ($\bar{X} = 254$ days, SD = 5·3), nine months: ($\bar{X} = 288·6$ days, SD = 10·3), 10 months: ($\bar{X} = 324$ days, SD = 10·5 days). A further eight infants failed to complete the study, either because they would not search or would not cooperate, and were excluded from the experiment. The apparatus comprised the vertical stand shown in Fig. 1 a, with the background behind the lower platform. The procedure was as outlined above, with half the infants in each age group receiving five trials at A and half receiving one trial at A. Half the babies started A trials at the upper location and half at the lower.

Results

None of the infants had any difficulty retrieving the hidden object on the first A trial in any of the conditions of the experiment.

Table 1 shows the number of infants making an error on the first B trial. On the assumption that the chance probability of a correct response to one of two locations is 0·5, a significant proportion of the infants searched at A on the first B trial when the object was moved from 'up' to 'down' (18/24, $P < 0·01$), whereas the number of infants making an error when the object was moved from 'down' to 'up' did not differ from chance (14/24, $P < 0·27$). That is, the 'up' location exercised a disproportionate effect on error and the data replicate those obtained by Butterworth (1976)—where the equivalent scores were 'up' 20/24 and 'down' 14/24 infants made an error on the first B trial.

The table also shows the data divided by age and by number of A trials. Significantly more than half the eight-month infants made an error on the first B trial (12/16, $P < 0·05$) whereas the number of infants in the nine-month and 10-month groups making an error did not differ from chance (11/16 and 9/16 respectively). Significantly more than half the infants made an error in the group receiving five A trials (17/24, $P < 0·32$) whereas the group receiving one A trial did not differ from chance (15/24, $P < 0·15$, n.s.). The data

(a)

Figure 1a. Experiment 1: Background behind 'down' location.

Table 1. Number of infants making an error on the first B trial; Expt 1 replication study

Subjects	n	No. of subjects erring		
Total	48	32**		
By sex	24	Males		Females
		16		16
By A trials	24	1A		5A
		5		17*
By starting location	24	Up to down		Down to up
		18**		14
By age	16	8 months	9 months	10 months
		12*	11	9

* $P < 0.05$; ** $P < 0.01$, binomial test.

were summed over sex of infant since this variable did not contribute significantly to error (males 16/24, females 16/24 infants made an error).

A series of chi-squared analyses was carried out to establish whether there were any significant differences between groups in the number of errors made on the first B trial but no significant differences emerged under any of the classifications 'up down', 1A vs. 5A, age or sex ($\chi^2 = 0.84$, d.f. = 1, n.s.; $\chi^2 = 0.09$, d.f. = 1, n.s.; $\chi^2 = 1.31$, d.f. = 2, n.s.; $\chi^2 = 0.0$, d.f. = 1, n.s., respectively).

Total error over five B trials. The patterns of responses over five B trials showed that infants were not searching randomly, even when the scores on the first B trial were at chance level. Of the 48 infants, 29 showed consistent search patterns (i.e. they made runs from one to five errors from the first B trial or searched correctly), while 19 were inconsistent (i.e. errors were mixed with correct responses). The distribution of consistent and inconsistent error patterns differed significantly from chance (χ^2 goodness-of-fit test = 76·49, d.f. = 1, $P < 0.001$).

Discussion

The major result was that there was an asymmetry of search patterns in the vertical plane. The $\overline{AB}$ error occurred among the significant majority of infants when the object moved from 'up' to 'down', but only among half the babies when the movement was from 'down' to 'up'. Although this asymmetry was slightly more probable after five A trials than after one A trial, there was no evidence that it was simply a function of the amount of experience at A, nor did the asymmetry vary systematically with the age or sex of the infants. The replication study therefore established the asymmetry of error to 'up' as an easily observable phenomenon.

The next question to be addressed was whether this asymmetry is general to tasks in the vertical plane, in order to establish whether it may reflect some general asymmetrical property of the perceptual system. Inspection of Fig. 1*a* shows that the apparatus itself was asymmetrical, in so far as the lower and upper platforms were joined by a green baize board that extended behind the lower location and not behind the upper. To establish whether this may have contributed to the pattern of errors, a second experiment was carried out, again with two platforms in the vertical plane but this time with the background behind the upper location and not the lower.

Experiment 2

Infants, apparatus and procedure

A new group of 24 infants served as subjects, equally distributed by age and sex. The mean ages were eight-month group: (263·25 days, SD = 10·1 days), nine-month group: (290·6 days, SD = 8·6 days), 10-month group: (320·125 days, SD = 9·21 days). A further five infants failed to complete the study and were excluded.

The apparatus comprised the vertical stand shown in Fig. 1*b* with a green baize background behind the upper location. The upper platform was joined to the lower by four thin strips of

(*b*)

Figure 1b. Experiment 2: Background behind 'up' location.

transparent perspex, so that the separation between platforms was identical to that in Expt 1 (19 cm). The procedure was identical to the 1A trial condition of Expt 1.

Results

As in previous studies, infants had no difficulty in retrieving the object on the first A trial. Only 3/24 infants made an error ($P < 0.001$, binomial test, 3 to 'up' 0 to 'down').

Table 2 shows the number of infants making an error on the first B trial. The significant majority of infants made an error when the starting location was 'down' (10/12 infants, $P < 0.02$), whereas infants who started A trials at 'up' were at chance level (4/12, n.s.).

Table 2. Number of infants making an error on the first B trial; Expt 2 background behind 'up' location 1A trial only

Subjects	*n*		No. of subjects erring	
Total	24		14	
By starting location	12	Up to down		Down to up
		4		10**
By age		8 months	9 months	10 months
		4	5	5

** $P < 0.01$, binomial test.

That is, the asymmetry of error patterns between starting locations was exactly the inverse of that found in Expt 1. In each case, the majority of infants in the sample made an error when there was no background behind the starting location. The data were summed over sex of infants (males 9/12 made an error, females 5/12, n.s.) since the probability of error was not different from chance in each group.

Chi-squared analyses for the first B trial showed no significant differences in the numbers of errors between boys and girls ($\chi^2 = 1.54$, d.f. = 1, n.s.) but the difference between starting locations was just significant ($\chi^2 = 4.29$, $P < 0.05$). Significantly more errors were made when the starting location was 'down' than 'up'.

Patterns of error over five B trials. Again, the patterns of responding over five B trials showed that infants were searching persistently at the initial or final location over repeated trials. In all, 17 infants made consistent patterns (runs of incorrect or correct responses from the first B trial) while seven made inconsistent patterns (i.e. patterns of response where errors were mixed with correct responses). The distribution of patterns of consistent and inconsistent responses differed significantly from chance ($\chi^2 = 42.74$, $P < 0.001$, goodness-of-fit test), thus demonstrating again that search was directed persistently to the chosen location and was not random.

Discussion

With the immediate background behind the upper location, the asymmetrical search pattern previously observed was reversed. Now the significant majority of infants made an error when the object was moved from 'down' to 'up', whereas only half the babies erred when the object moved from 'up' to 'down'. Thus, an asymmetry of the apparatus may have led to the asymmetry in the incidence of perseverative error to the initial location in both Expts 1 and 2.

However, this does not render the results any the less interesting since this suggests that persistent errors to the initial location, by the *majority* of infants in the sample (Piaget's typical stage 4 error) may be a *function of lack of an immediate background* at the initial location. As a test of the hypothesis that errors by the majority of infants may be associated with absence of an immediate background, a final experiment was carried out using an apparatus in which the background extended behind both the upper and the lower location.

Experiment 3

Infants, apparatus and procedure

A new group of 48 infants served as subjects, with equal numbers of babies of each sex in three age groups: eight months: ($\bar{X} = 252 \cdot 75$ days, SD = $5 \cdot 26$ days) nine months: ($\bar{X} = 288 \cdot 63$ days, SD = $10 \cdot 47$ days) 10 months: ($\bar{X} = 324 \cdot 13$ days, SD = $6 \cdot 78$ days). A further group of seven babies failed to complete the study and they were excluded from the experiment.

The apparatus is shown in Fig. 1c and comprised the circular background and platforms described earlier. The procedure of the experiment proper was identical to Expt 1. Infants received one A or five A trials with the experimental design fully counterbalanced for starting location at 'up' or

Figure 1c. Experiment 3: Background complete at 'up' and 'down'.

Figure 1d. Experiment 3: Apparatus in horizontal array for retest.

'down'. However, the experiment differed from the earlier studies in that a retest was incorporated, following the experiment proper, in which infants were given a second stage 4 task with A and B locations arranged in the horizontal plane. To accomplish this, the background and platforms were rotated through 90°, so that the platforms were aligned in the horizontal plane (background and platforms could be rotated independently) (Fig. 1d). On the retest, infants received one A trial and three B trials and they were randomly allocated to left/right starting locations with equal numbers of infants of each age and sex in each group. The purpose of this extra test was to establish whether there were any differences between the patterns of search in vertical and horizontal spatial planes.

Results

Infants had no difficulty retrieving the object on the first A trial. A total of 5/48 babies made an error distributed as follows: starting location 'up': 1A, 1/12, $P < 0 \cdot 003$, binomial test, 5A, 2/12, $P < 0.029$; 'down': 1A, 1/12, $P < 0.003$, 5A, 1/12, $P < 0.003$). That is, search was significantly correct under each of these classifications.

The results for the number of infants making an error on the first B trial in the experiment proper and in the retest are shown in Table 3. In this study there was no evidence for an asymmetry of error patterns whatever the starting location. The data for the 'down' to 'up' condition replicated Expt 1 (14/24 infants made an error, $P < 0.27$, n.s.) but now infants in the 'up' to 'down' condition were also at chance level (9/24, $P < 0.15$, n.s.). Furthermore, there was no evidence that the number of trials at A

Table 3. Number of infants making an error on the first B trial; Expt 3 background behind 'up' and 'down' locations

Subjects	n	No. of subjects erring		
Total	48		23	
By A trials	24	1A		5A
		10		13
By starting location	24	Up to down		Down to up
		9		14
By age	16	8 months	9 months	10 months
		10	7	6
Retest		Following Up to down	Down to up	
		9/24 n.s.	10/24 n.s.	

influenced performance since infants were at chance level following one A or five A trials (10/24 and 13/24 infants made an error in each case). The data were summed over sex of subjects since there was no evidence of any sex difference (males, 10/24 infants made an error, females, 13/24 infants).

A series of χ^2 analyses was carried out to compare performance under each of the following classifications: starting location (up vs. down), 1A vs. 5A trials, age and sex of infants, but no significant differences emerged ($\chi^2 = 1.34$, d.f. = 1, n.s.; $\chi^2 = 0.33$, d.f. = 1, n.s.; $\chi^2 = 3.19$, d.f. = 2, n.s.; $\chi^2 = 0.0$, d.f. = 1, n.s., respectively).

In summary, the major result of the data analyses for error on the first B trial was to show that the asymmetry of error pattern to 'up' locations was eliminated under the conditions of this study.

Patterns of error over five B trials. Analysis of the patterns of search over five B trials showed that 32 infants made consistent patterns (either an error on the first B trial followed by a run of up to five errors, or infants searched consistently correctly over five B trials) and 16 infants showed inconsistent patterns (errors and correct responses mixed in sequences other than runs). The distribution of these patterns of responding differed significantly from that which would be expected if infants were searching randomly ($\chi^2 = 72.34$, $P < 0.001$, goodness-of-fit test). Thus, although performance on the first B trial was at chance level, the overall pattern of responding shows that infants were not behaving randomly but searched equiprobably at the initial location (A) or at the final location (B) in a persistent fashion.

Retest

Following the experiment proper, infants were retested on a stage 4 task with the platforms arranged to left and right in the horizontal plane. The lower part of Table 3 shows the number of infants making an error on the first B trial of this retest. A total of 19/48 infants made an error and this distribution did not differ from chance in total or when subdivided according to previous condition (up 9/24, down 10/24 infants made an error). A McNemar χ^2 test for the significance of changes between the first B trial of the test and retest showed no significant association between performances in the two parts of the task ($\chi^2 = 0.5$, n.s.). That is, search at the initial or final locations was equiprobable in both the vertical and horizontal versions of the task and performance in the former did not determine the pattern of search in the latter. There was no evidence for asymmetrical search in the vertical or horizontal planes.

In summary, with the background behind A and B, there was now no evidence for an asymmetry of search patterns. Instead, infants showed the typical equiprobable pattern of search, where half the babies searched persistently at A and half searched persistently at B, just as in most studies where initial and final locations have been arranged in the horizontal plane (Gratch & Landers, 1971; Bower & Wishart, 1972; Butterworth, 1977; Butterworth *et al.*, 1982). Nor was there any evidence that the number of trials at A had any important effect on the incidence of error.

Discussion

This series of experiments had two main aims: first to establish whether persistent errors to 'up' may offer an insight into the spatial conditions responsible for the typical stage 4 error described by Piaget, and second, to establish whether the asymmetry of error to 'up' may reflect a general property of the perceptual system.

The major findings were that errors were not a function of the direction of movement (from 'up' to 'down' or vice versa) nor of the age or sex of the infants. It was possible to reverse the asymmetry of error to 'up' by removing the background from the lower location and placing it behind the upper and to eliminate the asymmetry altogether by using a circular background that extended behind upper and lower locations. With the circular background in place, the pattern of search in the vertical plane was similar to the equiprobable search pattern in the horizontal plane. Persistent search errors to 'up' in infancy do not provide evidence for a primitive asymmetry of the perceptual system in the vertical dimension but are a function of the conditions of testing.

What are the implications for Piaget's stage 4 error? One important result was that the experiments established a set of conditions associated with persistent, perseverative error by the *majority* of infants in the sample to the initial location (A). That is, stage 4 errors at above chance level, as Piaget described them, do occur, under conditions where there is no immediate background at the initial location (A). It might be objected that the general asymmetry of the apparatus was responsible for error, rather than absence of a background *per se*. For example, all the infants may have returned to the location without a background, simply because its absence caught their attention. However, several sources of evidence run against this interpretation. First, there was no asymmetry of search on A trials (before the object moved); infants had no difficulty retrieving the object whether the initial location was 'up' or 'down' or whether the background was present or absent. Second, in a series of experiments linked to the present study in which various cues had been deliberately introduced to make A and B locations visually discriminable from each other, it was found that patterns of search varied systematically depending on whether the cues were in the covers occluding the object or in the background behind the object, but in no case did the *majority* of infants in the sample search at the wrong location. Thus, the interpretation that errors to one location occur simply because it is discriminable from the other does not explain the *particular* form that the search pattern takes (i.e. whether the majority of infants err or whether the error is at chance level).

In previous papers by Butterworth, the theory was advanced that patterns of search may be influenced by the structure of the *perceived* space in relation to which the object moves. In particular, it was argued that the equiprobable pattern of search so often found in experimental investigations of Piaget's stage 4 task may reflect a dissociation between equiprobable spatial frames of reference, in relation to which the object is located. In brief, the argument is that an object is *simultaneously* located in relation to an *egocentric* spatial framework (e.g. to left or right of the body midline) and in relation to a stable, structured background (an allocentric spatial reference system). Where the background is structured with landmarks, these frames of reference are harmoniously coordinated and movements of object or observer are perceived appropriately as displacements within a multistable system (see Butterworth *et al.*, 1982, for a full account of the relevance of this theory to object identification and Butterworth & Cicchetti, 1978, for an account of the relevance to postural stability).

However, under the various conditions used to test infants in Piaget's stage 4 task, only some of the spatial cues necessary for the harmonious coordination of the spatial reference systems may be available and this has systematic effects on search and the perception of object identity. In the present study, the *majority* of babies perseverate to A when there is *no* immediate background at the initial location. It is as if they are forced to rely on an egocentric code for the initial stationary position, which they fail to update when the object moves. With a background connecting identical covers at A and B it is as if there is a dissociation between egocentric and allocentric spatial frameworks, perhaps because the identical successive locations can only be discriminated egocentrically. The consequence may be that search is directed *either* in relation to the egocentric code which is not updated *or* with respect to object movement coded in relation to the background. However, we have shown in other studies that where the background connecting A with B is structured with two different covers, the *majority* of infants will search *correctly* (Butterworth *et al.*, 1982). Under these circumstances, it is as if the covers act as landmarks that serve to coordinate spatial frames of reference and thus do away with the necessity to rely on the egocentric code to mark the successive positions. Taken as a whole, these studies show that persistent perseverative errors as Piaget described them do occur, but they need not indicate any absolute inability to identify an object that moves from place to place. Perseverative errors are a function of the spatial conditions under which the infant is tested.

The hypothesis that persistent search errors will be observed in infants in the stage 4 age range when the infant is unable *to perceive the path of movement of an object with respect to a stable background* may be useful in explaining a number of other phenomena in the literature on infant manual search. First, it may help to explain why Piaget consistently found perseverative errors in his tasks where the object was hidden by sliding it under a cushion or a large carpet (e.g. Piaget, 1954, Obs 40). Under these conditions the movement of the object from A to B may not occur with respect to a visible background since the large covers may occlude object and background simultaneously. Second, this may explain why quite subtle aspects of procedure sometimes have complex effects on the results obtained in manual search tasks. It has been suggested that the type of object used as the occluder may influence the pattern of search. For example, quite a different error pattern is observed when an object is hidden inside a succession of upright cups than in a succession of upside down cups. It has been argued that this reflects infant recognition of the canonical function of the cup as a container when in its upright orientation (Freeman *et al.*, 1980). However, an object hidden under a cup may also move in a different way with respect to the immediate background than an object hidden inside a cup. If the argument that has been advanced above is correct, it will be necessary to consider not only whether *presence* of certain types of spatial cues may affect patterns of search in young infants but also whether absence of a stable background under various conditions of testing may influence performance.

Finally, although the results did not support the hypothesis that there exists an asymmetry of the perceptual system in the vertical plane, the interpretation would be compatible with Clark's (1973) theory that there may exist a natural asymmetry of perceived space. This may be determined not by the visibility of objects above or below ground level but by the spatial extent of the ground in the total visual field.

Acknowledgements

This work was carried out with the aid of a grant from the Medical Research Council of Great Britain.

References

Bower, T. G. R. & Wishart, J. G. (1972). The effects of motor skill on object permanence. *Cognition*, **1**, 165–172.

Bremner, J. G. & Bryant, P. E. (1977). Place versus response as the basis of spatial errors made by young infants. *Journal of Experimental Child Psychology*, **23**, 162–177.

Bremner, J. G. (1978*a*). Egocentric versus allocentric spatial coding in nine-month-old infants: Factors influencing the choice of code. *Developmental Psychology*, **14** (4), 346–355.

Bremner, J. G. (1978*b*). Spatial errors made by infants: Inadequate spatial cues or evidence of egocentrism? *British Journal of Psychology*, **69**, 77–84.

Bremner, J. G. (1980). The infant's understanding of space. In M. Cox (ed.), *Is the Young Child Egocentric?* London: Concord Books.

Butterworth, G. E. (1974). The development of the object concept in human infants. Unpublished DPhil thesis. University of Oxford.

Butterworth, G. E. (1975). Object identity in infancy: The interaction of spatial location codes in determining search errors. *Child Development*, **46**, 866–870.

Butterworth, G. E. (1976). Asymmetrical search errors in infancy. *Child Development*, **47**, 864–867.

Butterworth, G. E. (1977). Object disappearance and error in Piaget's stage 4 task. *Journal of Experimental Child Psychology*, **23**, 391–401.

Butterworth, G. E. & Cicchetti, D. (1978). Visual calibration of posture in normal and motor retarded Down's syndrome infants. *Perception*, **7**, 513–525.

Butterworth, G. E., Jarrett, N. & Hicks, L. (1982). Spatio-temporal identity in infancy: Perceptual competence or conceptual deficit? *Developmental Psychology* (in press).

Clark, H. H. (1973). Space, time semantics and the child. In T. E. Moore (ed.), *Cognitive Development and the Acquisition of Language*, pp. 27–62. New York: Academic Press.

Freeman, N. H., Lloyd, S. E. & Sinha, C. G. (1980). Infant search tasks reveal early concepts of containment and canonical usage of objects. *Cognition*, **8**, 243–262.

Gratch, G. & Landers, W. F. (1971). Stage 4 of Piaget's theory of infants' object concepts: A longitudinal study. *Child Development*, **42**, 359–372.

Landers, W. F. (1971). Effects of differential experience on infants' performance in a Piagetian stage 4 object concept task. *Developmental Psychology*, **5** (1), 48–54.

Lucas, T. C. & Uzgiris, I. C. (1977). Spatial factors in the development of the object concept. *Developmental Psychology*, **13**, 492–500.

Piaget, J. (1954). *The Construction of Reality in the Child*. New York: Basic Books.

Sandstrom, C. I. (1951). *Orientation in the Present Space*. Stockholm: Almquist & Wiksell.

Takala, M. (1951). Asymmetries of the visual space. Soomalaisen/Tiedeakatemiantoimituksia/*Annales Academiae Scientiarum Fennicae Helsinki, Series B*, **72**.

Vereecken, P. (1961). *Spatial Development. Constructive Praxia from Birth to the Age of 7*. Gröningen: J. B. Wolters.

Requests for reprints should be addressed to George Butterworth, Department of Psychology, University of Southampton, Southampton SO9 5NH, UK.

Nicholas Jarrett is also at the above address.

References

British Journal of Psychology (1982), **73**, 187–195   *Printed in Great Britain*

Cognitive prerequisites to language?

P. L. Harris

The Piagetian hypothesis that there are cognitive prerequisites for language acquisition is examined. Two different formulations are distinguished: the hypothesis that the child interprets utterances in terms of what he knows about the world; and the hypothesis that the emergence of particular ideas leads the child to cast around for the linguistic means of expressing them. The second but not the first formulation implies that the sequence of cognitive development will influence the sequence and timetable of language acquisition. Evidence from three sources is reviewed and provides little support for this prediction. It is argued that the course of language acquisition is probably determined by three factors which are largely independent of level of cognitive development: (i) linguistic complexity, (ii) the likelihood that the non-verbal context will offer an unambiguous gloss of an adult utterance and (iii) the asymmetry between comprehension and production.

In a recent confrontation, Piaget and Chomsky debated whether or not language acquisition depends upon certain cognitive prerequisites (Piatelli-Palmarini, 1980). Piaget argued that the child's utterances do exhibit such a dependence, while Chomsky remained sceptical, preferring to invoke instead a faculty or mechanism specialized for the job of acquiring language.

One surprising aspect of the debate was that neither protagonist spent much time looking at the evidence concerning how children acquire language. Each defended their position on wider epistemological and biological grounds. Thus, Chomsky argued for the existence of several innate mechanisms, one specialized for face recognition, another for language acquisition and so forth. Piaget, on the other hand, reiterated his belief in the construction of multi-purpose cognitive structures. I shall ignore these wider considerations since I do not think that they help us to decide how children acquire language. It seems likely that there are both specialized and multi-purpose devices, and each type might be innate or constructed. So, we must examine each case, including that of language acquisition, on its merits.

Formulations of the cognitive prerequisites hypothesis

Piaget has always maintained that the development of language depends on the development of thought rather than vice versa (Piaget, 1967). His colleague Sinclair (1971) states the Piagetian view as follows:

> The infant brings to his language acquisition task not a set of innate linguistic universals, but innate cognitive functions which will ultimately result in universal structures of thought...since intelligence exists phylogenetically and ontogenetically before language, and since the acquisition of language structures is a cognitive activity, cognitive structures should be used to explain language acquisition rather than vice versa.

Piaget explicitly endorses this view in his debate with Chomsky: 'It is only at the sixth of these stages (of sensory-motor intelligence) – that is when the assimilation of objects to the schemes of action is able to be completed...that language begins' (Piaget, 1980).

Neither Piaget nor Sinclair is very explicit about the exact role that cognitive prerequisites play. If we look outside of the Piagetian school, we do find more explicit formulations. I shall mention two influential but different formulations. First, Pinker (1979) has discussed several formal models of language acquisition which invoke cognitive prerequisites as a means of narrowing down the range of candidate grammars. More

0007-1269/82/020187-09 $02.00/0 © 1982 The British Psychological Society

specifically, Pinker points out that if confronted with only a set of syntactically well-formed utterances there are an enormously large number of grammars which would be compatible with those sentences, even though such grammars would eventually generate deviant sentences. How then does the child manage to converge on an appropriate grammar so quickly? One possibility would be that the child is given feedback about what are and are not well-formed sentences. In this way, there would be two sources of information: a list of well-formed sentences and a list of improperly formed sentences. While such a double source of information would accelerate the elimination of incorrect grammars, there is little evidence that adults do provide feedback of this type (Brown & Hanlon, 1970). However, the cognitive prerequisites hypothesis offers an alternative source of feedback. Suppose that the child is able, on the basis of the non-verbal context in which an adult utterance takes place, to infer what the adult means by a given utterance without having to process the utterance as such. If the child now interprets the utterance according to his candidate grammar, but then discovers that he has assigned it a meaning which is different from the one that he believes to be intended on the basis of the non-verbal context, this is an indirect form of feedback to the effect that his candidate grammar is generating improperly formed sentences. Analogous assumptions have been made by recent formal models of language acquisition (Anderson, 1975).

This version of the cognitive prerequisites hypothesis states that various non-verbal concepts are necessary preconditions for selecting the appropriate interpretation of adult utterances; it does not imply that the order in which the child acquires particular non-verbal concepts will be reflected in the order in which relevant constructions appear in the child's language. Other factors, such as the linguistic complexity of the construction itself, will influence the ease with which an available concept can be expressed.

A second version of the cognitive prerequisites hypothesis, on the other hand, does imply that a common order of development for language and cognition is likely to be found. Thus, Slobin (1973) writes: 'the pacesetter in linguistic growth is the child's cognitive growth, as opposed to an autonomous linguistic development which can reflect back on cognition'. In fact, Slobin refines this position somewhat in the course of his paper. He distinguishes between two possible influences on the timetable for language acquisition. On the one hand, the child needs to have an idea of what he wants to say – what Slobin calls a 'semantic intention'. Second, the child needs to discover a linguistic means for expressing that intention in a given language. He points out that this may be more or less easy depending on the language. For example, locative relations can be easily expressed in Hungarian (by means of case inflections) but are harder to express in Serbo–Croatian (by means of both prepositions and case inflections). Not surprisingly, children bilingual in both languages can master locative relations in Hungarian earlier than in Serbo–Croatian. Thus, Slobin emphasizes the point made above that linguistic complexity will influence the speed of language acquisition because it determines the ease with which an idea can be expressed in a given language. Hence, we should not expect the timetable for language to be a direct reflection of the timetable for cognitive development. Nevertheless, Slobin (1973) goes further than Pinker (1979), since he argues that the development of a particular idea in the child will lead him or her to cast around for a means of expressing that idea. Thus, Slobin distinguishes between two aspects of language acquisition: a universal sequence with respect to the initial emergence of certain ideas or semantic intentions; and second, a more variable order among different languages, with respect to the order in which the child acquires mastery of the means of expressing particular semantic intentions. In Slobin's version of the cognitive prerequisites hypothesis therefore, cognitive development is the 'pacesetter' for acquisition, while linguistic complexity determines the time needed for complete mastery.

Evaluation of the evidence

Analogy and correlation

Evidence for the cognitive prerequisites hypothesis has been adduced in two different ways. First, Brown (1973) and others have looked for analogies between children's two and three word combinations and the putative structures of sensory-motor intelligence. For example, Brown (1973) suggests that the first sentences start with 'just those meanings that are most available...propositions about actions, schemes involving agents and objects, assertions of non-existence, recurrence, location and so on'.

It is conceivable that there is a link between what the child talks about and what the child understands at a preverbal level, but there are two major difficulties. In the first place, Piaget's account of sensory-motor development appears to be too rich to explain the rather rudimentary utterances which the child is able to produce. For example, the infant at 18 months has, according to Piaget, constructed a concept of depth and temporal succession. However, there is no reference in the child's early utterances to relative distance or to temporal succession. The second problem is that an analogy is, after all, no more than that. We might also be able to see analogies between the temporal organization of motor action and sentence production, since they both appear to involve the embedding of subroutines within a hierarchically organized plan (Bruner, 1973). However, it would be rash to assume that the ability to carry out a motor programme such as crawling to reach for an object constituted a prerequisite for the production of word combinations.

The second approach has attempted to move beyond the level of analogy by establishing a temporal link between the development of sensory-motor intelligence and the acquisition of language. Specifically, investigators have proposed that there ought to be a correlation in the rate of development across the two domains. Accordingly, they have assessed infants on two measures, one concerning their level of cognitive development and the other their level of language production, and looked at the correlation between the two measures. The assumption behind this methodology is that infants who are advanced in their cognitive development will as a result be advanced in their language development.

It is important to stress that such a prediction does not follow directly from the position adopted by Pinker (1979). It is reasonable to assert that there are cognitive prerequisites for language, such as the attainment of a given stage of sensory-motor intelligence, without going on to assert that the pace of development in cognition will affect the pace of development in language. Thus, this version of the cognitive prerequisites hypothesis is quite compatible with a finding of no correlation between measures of sensory-motor intelligence and language acquisition. As we have seen, however, Slobin (1973) does argue for a pacesetting function: variations in cognitive development will lead to variations in the development of 'semantic intentions'. Slobin, then, would expect a positive correlation between the two domains.

The correlational evidence that is currently available scarcely provides firm support for Slobin's claim. Corrigan (1978) found that although there was a correlation between the development of object permanence and language production, this disappeared once age had been partialled out. Even where substantial correlations have been found between some aspect of cognitive development and a measure of language acquisition (e.g. Moore & Meltzoff, 1978; Bates *et al.*, 1979), there are severe problems of interpretation. Such correlations might indicate that cognitive development causes language acquisition, but at least two other interpretations are possible. First, some third factor such as environmental stimulation might accelerate performance in both domains even though there is no causal link between them. Second, language production and the type of tasks which figure on scales of cognitive development both require certain common skills, such as the deployment of attention, the ability to produce an integrated series of motor acts, and the ability to store information. Variation in any of these skills would tend to produce a correlation between cognitive development and language production, whether or not any particular concept or idea is a prerequisite for language.

In conclusion, then, arguments from analogy and correlational evidence offer, at best, ambiguous support for the cognitive prerequisites hypothesis. Below, I examine two hitherto neglected sources of evidence: data on the development of comprehension, and the acquisition of language by bilingual children.

Language comprehension

When we examine language comprehension, we find that several of the milestones which investigators have linked to the emergence of various cognitive prerequisites appear considerably earlier in comprehension than in production. I shall examine two such indices: the rate of vocabulary growth, and the ability to combine words.

Taking up the rate of vocabulary growth first, Bloom (1973) argued that the spurt in productive vocabulary which she observed in her daughter was linked to the acquisition of object permanence. Likewise, Ingram (1978) re-examined various diaries of language development including that of Piaget (1951) and argued that the attainment of stage 6 of object permanence and the capacity for representation which is said to emerge at that stage provide a basis for the spurt in productive vocabulary. However, Benedict (1979), who traced the development of comprehension in eight infants between the ages of nine and 29 months, found that comprehension began at around nine months whereas production began at around 12 months. Moreover, the 50-word level was reached at about 13 months in comprehension but not until 18 months in production. The difference between these two time intervals – four months in the case of comprehension and six months in the case of production – strongly suggests that the rate of acquisition differs for comprehension and production. Hence, there are two problems for the cognitive prerequisites hypothesis. First, the spurt in comprehension vocabulary probably takes place before the attainment of stage 6. In addition, the cognitive prerequisites hypothesis offers no explanation for why the rates of acquisition should differ.

Further difficulties for the hypothesis emerge when we look at the ability to combine words. Ingram (1978) explicitly links this ability to stage 6 of object permanence, which has some plausibility given that stage 6 is typically reached at about 18 months and this is also the point at which word combinations begin to appear. However, Huttenlocher (1974), in a pioneering study of early comprehension, found that an infant of 14 months was able to understand sequences in which two items – the possessor and the possessed – were contrasted, for example: 'Where is your/mummy's nose/shoe?' A somewhat older child could even manage sentences in which three items were contrasted, so that the child had to select a particular action, perform it upon a particular object, in relation to a particular recipient. These findings have since been replicated by Sachs & Truswell (1978) who tested a larger sample of 12 children aged 16–24 months. Although none of these children had produced any two-word combinations, most exhibited comprehension of sentences in which two items varied. Even more striking was the finding that novel combinations, which the subjects would almost certainly not have heard before (e.g. 'kiss book'; 'pat candle') were also correctly interpreted. These latter findings parallel those obtained at later stages for production, when children generate word combinations that they have not heard. Thus, the precocity of comprehension relative to production cannot be explained by saying that the infant merely understands combinations that he has repeatedly heard, but produces entirely new combinations. Creativity is present both in comprehension and in production.

The above data on comprehension suggest that the cognitive prerequisites hypothesis, as it is currently formulated, ought to be revised. It can be saved by postulating that comprehension, despite its similarity of structure and content to production, is based on different cognitive prerequisites. This defence is unattractive precisely because there is such a marked overlap, notwithstanding the temporal lag, between what the child understands and what he talks about. The distribution of word types is also similar in the two vocabularies, being composed predominantly of nominals (words for people, animals or objects), to a lesser extent of action words, together with a small vocabulary for attributes and for social encounters.

A more plausible revision of the cognitive prerequisites hypothesis is to admit that search tasks, and spatial tasks, may not provide the most sensitive diagnosis of the infant's sensory-motor intelligence. If there are cognitive prerequisites for language development, they may well be present much earlier than the onset of production. Yet this still leaves the lag between comprehension and production unexplained.

Language acquisition in bilinguals

Bilinguals have often been studied in order to assess whether the acquisition of two languages helps or hinders cognitive development. A much more obvious question has rarely been asked. Children who acquire a second language frequently begin to acquire it well after their first language. Accordingly, they offer an opportunity to compare the process of language acquisition at different points in cognitive development. If we suppose, as does Slobin (1973), that cognitive development largely dictates the sequence for language acquisition, we should expect to find this sequence markedly altered in older children acquiring a second language. However, although the evidence is not completely consistent, a recent review (McLaughlin, 1977, 1978) indicates that first and second language acquisition are remarkably similar. This is a very puzzling finding in terms of Slobin's (1973) formulation of the cognitive prerequisites hypothesis. Presumably, many of the ideas or 'semantic intentions' which are assumed to dictate the sequence of linguistic development in the monolingual child, will be simultaneously present in the child of six or seven years who is setting out on the task of acquiring a second language. Accordingly, we should expect, on the basis of Slobin's hypothesis, dramatic differences in the sequence of development.

An alternative formulation

The data reviewed so far indicate three major problems. First, correlations between cognitive development and language acquisition are either non-existent or very difficult to interpret. Second, although the utterances that the child understands are similar to those that he produces, comprehension develops earlier and more rapidly than production. Third, many studies of bilingual children suggest that the process of language acquisition whatever the age, and by implication whatever the level of cognitive development of the child, proceeds along the same sequence.

We may account for these findings by admitting that whatever cognitive prerequisites there are have little impact on the timetable for language acquisition. This is not to deny the possibility raised by Pinker (1979) that children test grammatical hypotheses by comparing them with their conceptualization of the context surrounding the utterance. It does, however, call into question Slobin's (1973) hypothesis that the child's developing concepts lead him to look for a means of expressing those concepts in a more or less fixed order.

What then does account for the timetable for language acquisition? I believe that there are three major factors, each more or less independent of any particular level of cognitive development. First, as Slobin (1973) has pointed out by means of his observations on children simultaneously acquiring two languages, certain ideas are expressed in a more complicated way in one language than another. We can envisage that even within any particular language, there is a rank order of complexity, such that some constructions will be acquired early, and some late, irrespective of the age at which language acquisition begins. Second, if we take Pinker's (1979) hypothesis seriously, we can suppose that the non-verbal context provides an unambiguous gloss on some utterances but not others. To be more specific, if an adult comments on an action in which the child is engaged, the child is likely to infer that the adult is commenting on that action, whether the actual words are understood or not. However, if the adult comments on an event that happened the day before or will happen the next day, the child is unlikely to place the correct gloss on the utterance. It is important to underline the fact that this is likely to be the case, even if the child has a fully developed concept of past, present and future. Thus, the child acquiring a second language at six or seven years is likely to begin talking about the here and now even though he or she is perfectly capable of conceptualizing the not here and the not now. To take this point to its logical extreme, even an adult acquiring a second language 'in the field', i.e. by everyday listening and observation rather than the use of dictionaries and classroom methods, will begin by understanding and producing statements about the immediate situation. Thus, this second possible factor governing the timetable for language acquisition is not a reflection of the language acquirer's cognitive status; it is a reflection of the ease with which a listener can guess what is being said, without understanding all the actual words that are spoken. Nor is this second factor likely to be confined to the early stage of language acquisition. Admittedly, the non-verbal context will play a less important role as language acquisition progresses. However, the learner will continue to try to make sense of what is not understood in a sentence or utterance, in terms of the verbal context, i.e. in terms of what is already understood.

The third important factor governing the process of language acquisition is the asymmetry between comprehension and production discussed earlier. This asymmetry again illustrates the fact that what governs the timetable for language acquisition is not the emergence of ideas or 'semantic intentions' *per se*, but the ease with which such ideas can be mapped into words and vice versa. So long as we hypothesize that it is the emergence of ideas which dictates the course of language acquisition, we are at a loss to explain anything except a synchronous emergence of comprehension and production.

In order to throw more light on the lag between comprehension and production, we may take a closer look at a particular example: the phenomenon of over-extension.

Over-extension in early comprehension and production

Rescorla's (1980) description of one child's use of the 'clock' provides a simple illustration of over-extension in production. The child first used the word correctly for a picture of a cuckoo clock, and for an alarm clock. He then extended the word to many other clocks, but also extended it to other objects, including watches, dials and radios.

It is now quite firmly established that although young children in the second year of life over-extend a fairly large proportion of their production vocabulary — somewhere between 10 (Gruendel, 1977) and 33 per cent (Rescorla, 1980) depending on the exact criteria being used — the incidence of over-extension in comprehension is very small. Gruendel looked for over-extensions in comprehension but observed none. Rescorla found only a very small number. Nor can this asymmetry be attributed to the vagaries of naturalistic observation. Two experimental studies have recently confirmed that it can be found under experimental conditions (Thompson & Chapman, 1977; Fremgen & Fay, 1980). Thus, although young children will correctly select a picture of a dog rather than a sheep when asked to find a dog, they will still say 'dog' when shown a picture of a sheep.

How is this asymmetry to be explained? First, we may note that the asymmetry between comprehension and production rules out the missing feature hypothesis advanced by Clark (1973). If children over-extend words because they have not yet appended the full list of semantic features, over-extensions would be expected in both comprehension and production.

An alternative hypothesis, advanced by Fremgen & Fay (1980), is that although children may know that the word 'dog' applies to dogs and not to sheep or cats, as indicated by the comprehension data, they over-extend the word when an appropriate word is not available to them for some animal which resembles a dog. Such a lack of availability might be brought about either through simply not knowing the word or through being unable to retrieve it. Fremgen & Fay (1980) were able to show that retrieval failure rather than ignorance was a more likely explanation for at least some children since when they were asked to respond to a term that they had failed to produce (e.g. they had called a sheep 'dog'), they correctly selected the appropriate referent (e.g. they selected a sheep in response to 'sheep'). Thus the word could be recognized but not recalled.

If we accept Fremgen & Fay's explanation, we must conclude that the young child has a relatively well-organized category system. More specifically, the child is able to distinguish between cats and dogs, but can also group together various kinds of dog such as collies and terriers. This would reflect what Rosch and her colleagues have called the basic-object level of categorization (Rosch *et al.*, 1976). The child is thought to operate best at this level, rather than at superordinate (e.g. 'animal') or subordinate (e.g. 'collie') levels. Accordingly, when adults supply the term 'dog', it is understood to apply across the various types of dog, but is not extended, at least in comprehension, outside of the category. Thus, the child can be said to understand the correct extension of the term 'dog'. As experimenters, we are wrongly tempted into thinking the child does not grasp the correct extension, because the production task leads to retrieval difficulties and thence to over-extension.

My own interpretation of the available data is different. I do not think that the child grasps the correct extension of the term in either comprehension or production. The child's difficulty arises because he or she is engaged in constructing categories at several levels of abstraction, not just at the basic level, as suggested by Rosch. Therefore, supplied with a term of reference such as 'dog', the child does not know whether the adult is referring to the dog as a member of the category of collies, of dogs, or of animals, and therefore has difficulty in knowing the correct range of extension of the term.

If the child does not know the correct range of extension, how, it may be asked, does the child succeed on the comprehension task? Why does the child not pick out a cat or a dog in response to the term 'dog'? We know from recent work on preverbal categorization by young infants that they organize their categories around prototypical instances (Harris, in press). Thus, we may suppose that the child does not know the correct extension of the term 'dog' but still knows that any dog comes close to a prototypical instance of the animals that the term 'dog' has been applied to whereas a cat, for example, does not. This would permit the child to choose the correct examples in the comprehension test, whether or not the correct range of extension is known. The child's ignorance about the range of extension of the term as opposed to its most typical referent will, of course, reveal itself in production. Thus, I interpret over-extensions as indicating that the child has not worked out the meaning of the term, contrary to the claim made by Fremgen & Fay (1980).

How can these two hypotheses be distinguished? Let us suppose that the child fills in the gap in his vocabulary which Fremgen & Fay have seen as the cause of over-extensions. Thus, terms like 'sheep' and 'cat' are acquired alongside earlier terms like 'dog'. Once these are acquired, and the child can produce them appropriately, Fremgen & Fay (1980) must predict that over-extensions should cease. According to my hypothesis, however, the arrival of a new term should not necessarily lead to a circumscription of the old over-extended term. Let us suppose that the child believes that the term 'dog' is roughly equivalent to 'four-legged animal'; his acquisition of a new term such as 'sheep' should not necessarily lead him to narrow down the range of application of 'dog'. He may continue to treat the early term as a superordinate which subsumes the later term. Mervis & Canada (1981) have recently reported a child who exhibited this pattern: cars and trucks were initially included under the term 'car'. The subsequent emergence of a new term – 'truck' – did not lead to the circumscription of 'car'. Instead, cars and trucks continued to be included under the term 'car', while the term 'truck' was reserved for trucks.

Conclusion

The over-extension problem provides a microscopic illustration of a much wider problem facing the child. Even if he has the appropriate cognitive prerequisites, it is not obvious how those should be mapped onto the language he hears around him, and eventually comes to produce. It seems likely that it is this process of translation, in all its varieties, which will dictate the pace of language development, rather than the availability of the cognitive prerequisites as such. Moreover, even if there are cognitive prerequisites, it is quite conceivable that the translation of those prerequisites into language comprehension or language production is affected by the more specialized language acquisition devices which Chomsky envisaged. Ironically, then, Piaget and Sinclair may be right to postulate cognitive prerequisites, but we should not expect them to have any direct impact on the timetable for language development.

References

Anderson, J. (1975). Computer simulation of a language acquisition system: A first report. In R. Solso (ed.), *Information Processing and Cognition: The Loyola Symposium*. Washington: Erlbaum.

Bates, E., Benigni, L., Bretherton, I., Camaioni, L. & Volterra, V. (1979). *The Emergence of Symbols*. New York: Academic Press.

Benedict, H. (1979). Early lexical development: Comprehension and production. *Journal of Child Language*, **6**, 183–200.

Bloom, L. (1973). *One Word at a Time: The Use of Single Word Utterances Before Syntax*. The Hague: Mouton.

Brown, R. (1973). *A First Language*. London: Allen & Unwin.

Brown, R. & Hanlon, C. (1970). Derivational complexity and order of acquisition in child speech. In J. Hayes (ed.), *Cognition and the Development of Language*. New York: Wiley.

Bruner, J. S. (1973). Organization of early skilled action. *Child Development*, **44**, 1–11.

Clark, E. (1973). What's in a word? On the child's acquisition of semantics in his first language. In T. E. Moore (ed.), *Cognitive Development and the Acquisition of Language*. New York: Academic Press.

Corrigan, R. (1978). Language development as related to stage 6 object permanence development. *Journal of Child Language*, **5**, 173–189.

Fremgen, A. & Fay, D. (1980). Overextensions in production and comprehension: A methodological clarification. *Journal of Child Language*, **7**, 205–211.

Gruendel, J. M. (1977). Referential extension in early language development. *Child Development*, **48**, 1567–1576.

Harris, P. L. (in press). Infant cognition. In M. M. Haith & J. J. Campos, *Handbook of Child Psychology*, Vol. I. New York: Wiley.

Huttenlocher, H. (1974). The origins of language comprehension. In R. Solso (ed.), *Theories in Cognitive Psychology*. Hillsdale, NJ: Erlbaum.

Ingram, D. (1978). Sensori-motor intelligence and language development. In A. Lock (ed.), *Action, Gesture and Symbol*. London: Academic Press.

McLaughlin, B. (1977). Second language acquisition in childhood. *Psychological Bulletin*, **84**, 438–459.

McLaughlin, B. (1978). *Second Language Acquisition in Childhood*. Hillsdale, NJ: Erlbaum.

Mervis, C. B. & Canada, K. (1981). Child-basic categories and early lexical development. Paper presented at the Biennial Meeting of the Society for Research in Child Development, Boston.

Moore, K. E. & Meltzoff, A. N. (1978). Imitation, object permanence and language development in infancy: Toward a neo-Piagetian perspective on communicative and cognitive development. In F. D. Minifie & L. L. Lloyd (eds), *Communicative and Cognitive Abilities — Early Behaviour Assessment*. Baltimore, MD: University Park Press.

Piaget, J. (1951). *Play, Dreams and Imitation.* New York: Norton.
Piaget, J. (1967). Language and thought from the genetic point of view. In D. Elkind (ed.), *Six Psychological Studies.* New York: Random House.
Piaget, J. (1980). Introductory remarks: About the fixed nucleus and its innateness. In M. Piatelli-Palmarini. *Language and Learning.* London: Routledge & Kegan Paul.
Piatelli-Palmarini, M. (1980). *Language and Learning.* London: Routledge & Kegan Paul.
Pinker, S. (1979). Formal models of language learning. *Cognition,* **7,** 217–283.
Rescorla, L. A. (1980). Over-extensions in early language development. *Journal of Child Language,* **7,** 321–335.
Rosch, E., Mervis, C. B., Gray, W. D., Johnson, D. M. & Boyes-Braem, P. (1976). Basic objects in natural categories. *Cognitive Psychology,* **8,** 382–389.
Sachs, J. & Truswell, L. (1978). Comprehension of two-word instructions by children in the one-word stage. *Journal of Child Language,* **5,** 17–24.
Sinclair, H. (1971). Sensorimotor action patterns as a condition for the acquisition of syntax. In E. Ingram & R. Huxley (eds), *Language Acquisition: Models and Methods.* New York: Academic Press.
Slobin, D. (1973). Cognitive prerequisites for the development of grammar. In C. A. Ferguson & D. Slobin (eds), *Studies of Child Language Development.* New York: Holt, Rinehart & Winston.
Thompson, J. R. & Chapman, R. S. (1977). Who is 'Daddy' revisited: The status of two-year-olds' over-extended words in use and comprehension. *Journal of Child Language,* **4,** 359–375.

Requests for reprints should be addressed to P. L. Harris, Department of Experimental Psychology, University of Oxford, South Parks Road, Oxford OX1 3UD, UK.

2
Logical development

British Journal of Psychology (1982), 73, 199–207 Printed in Great Britain

Conservation: What is the question?

Margaret Donaldson

Success in a conservation task entails understanding that the transformation is irrelevant to the question. Much depends, however, on whether the question is treated as a set of disembedded words, in which case it is still 'the same question' when asked a second time, or as a unity of words-and-context, in which case it is not. There is now much evidence that young children tend to the latter mode of interpretation and, in effect, often fail to conserve the question.

Children are sensitive to indications of purpose and may try to make sense of the question by wondering about the purposes of the experimenter in asking it. Or they may have regard to purposes which are internal to the task structure, where these exist. Or they may concentrate on impersonal features of the array, as Piaget took them to do. What happens in a given instance will depend both on personal characteristics and on general developmental trends.

To find permanence in spite of change and reality in spite of illusion: these are human goals of great antiquity. Piaget set himself the task of showing how – in a limited way but, inside the limits, with complete assurance – the human intelligence achieves them. He set out to show in detail how we construct for ourselves mental systems that enable us to transcend the passage of time – even to reverse it.

There is an obvious sense in which the irreversible nature of time constrains us utterly. We live through a succession of acts and happenings which we can never undo. And yet we have contrived to achieve from this circumstance a perfect, if limited, mental freedom.

Suppose that one has a Ming vase and is careless enough to let it fall and shatter. What has happened is irreversible – the vase will never be the same again. But mentally one can reverse the entire series of events, return to the starting-point and find it unchanged. Thus one can arrive at the certainty that all the shattered pieces, if they were gathered together again, would have the same mass, weight and volume as the original whole.

In the context of the broken Ming vase this reads like an anticlimax and the knowledge would be small comfort. Yet Piaget argues that cognitive achievements of great significance underlie it. The heap of broken pieces will look different from the original. The direct perceptual evidence may suggest that mass and weight and volume have been altered. However, we *know* that they have been conserved. Thus we know invariance in spite of change. We know how things really are in spite of the illusion of difference.

The Ming vase is a very un-Piagetian example. But in some ways it is a good one, for it throws into sharp relief the contrast between what Piaget is talking about and what he is not talking about. The mental systems which, in his theory, make conservation possible – the operational systems as he calls them – are based on and concerned with *logico-mathematical experience*; not with *physical experience* – with such things as the form of the vase or the nature of the glaze; nor yet with *psychological experience*, which would include the experience of beauty.

Logico-mathematical experience, in Piagetian theory, is the experience of certain kinds of action, typical examples being the actions of dividing and bringing together again, sorting or arranging in series (see, for instance, Piaget, 1971). Strictly speaking, it is the experience we have, from early childhood onwards, of our own acts of this kind and of their outcomes. These acts, when they have been internalized and organized into systems, become operations. And it is when thought reaches the operational stage that conceptual 'invariants' arise and children become conservers.

0007-1269/82/0200199-09 $02.00/0 © 1982 The British Psychological Society

For direct evidence to support his account of the acquisition of conceptual invariants, Piaget relies mainly on results from the famous conservation test. These findings are of course backed up, as always in Piaget's work, by evidence bearing on other aspects of his singularly coherent and far-reaching theory. However, the issues raised by this indirect evidence are beyond the scope of a single paper. Here we shall focus on the conservation test itself.

In the standard task the child is first shown a two-part array where the parts are equal in some respect and where the equality is easy to judge on direct perceptual evidence. The two things look the same. The next step is to introduce an irrelevant transformation which destroys the obviousness of the equality. Finally the experimenter aims to discover whether the subject is able to discount the change and maintain the equality.

As is very well known, children of four or five regularly fail to do this. Thereafter, around the age of six or seven (in our culture), they begin to succeed on certain conservation tasks. We have therefore two questions to consider. Why do the young ones fail? And what developments lead on to the later success?

Piaget's answer to the first question rests on the claim that children who fail to conserve are those who take into account only certain features of the transformed array while neglecting others. Thus, for instance, when a row of objects is spaced out such children note that it becomes longer without noting that it also becomes less dense.

In much of his writing over the years Piaget has regarded this failure as one manifestation of a pervasive inability to decentre. More recently, however, without rejecting this idea, he has introduced a powerful new one: the idea that, in the early years of life, positive observations are strongly dominant over negative ones. The mind, he says, spontaneously concentrates on affirmations and on the positive characteristics of things (Piaget, 1975), which yields an initial imbalance or lack of equilibrium. Through time, however, this is corrected by processes of an autoregulatory kind to which Piaget gives the general name 'equilibration'. These processes are such as to ensure development through a succession of steadily improving or 'better' states of equilibrium.

This provides the core of Piaget's answer to the second question. It is of course far too brief a summary to do justice to his complex theorizing. However, if we now apply the general notion specifically to conservation, taking number as an example, then we may at least see the kind of progression he has in mind. The postulated sequence of events begins with the imbalance created by noting only the increase in length as a row of objects is extended. This is followed by a correction, attributable to equilibration, which leads the child to a first noticing of the negative change (decrease in density). There follows a realization that the negative change is bound up with the positive one. Finally comes the recognition of a necessary connection between the two, which leads to full conservation.

This ultimate recognition may manifest itself in various ways in the children's justifications for their judgements. The justifications may invoke what Piaget came to call 'commutability' (Piaget, 1975), by which he means the recognition that parts of the whole have merely been displaced; or they may make explicit reference to the way in which one aspect of the transformation is compensated for by the other; or they may rely upon the famous reversibility argument: 'You've only moved them apart and you could move them back again so it's still the same number'.

This last argument is particularly important since reversibility has long been regarded by Piaget as the hallmark of operational thought. And while he came to think of reversibility as the outcome of equilibration rather than as something which could itself account for development, it never diminished in significance for him as a criterion for the presence of operations.

It is instructive, then, to notice the limitations of the reversibility argument as a justification for a conserving response.

Consider the following bit of reasoning, parallel in form to the one cited above:

You've only added two and you could take them away again, so it's still the same number.

Clearly this does not work at all, as several authors have pointed out (cf. Berlyne, 1965; Wallach, 1969; Schultz *et al.*, 1979). So what is the difference between the two arguments, both of which invoke 'logical reversibility'? The difference is that in one case the action which is reversed is irrelevent to the question being considered, while in the other it is not. The act of adding is relevant, the act of moving apart is irrelevant. The conclusion has to be that it is the understanding of relevance that is fundamental. This conclusion does not imply that the ability to reason in ways that make use of reversibility is unimportant. And it does not imply that Piaget's general claims about the processes of equilibration are unfounded. It does imply that there is more to say.

One thing becomes evident as soon as relevance is given a central place: we have to take account of the fact that relevance is always relevance to a given question. What, then, if children do not understand that question? A persistent focus of doubt in the minds of Piaget's critics has been whether, sometimes, this might be so.

The Piagetian reply to this criticism is to say that of course the children do not understand but that this stems from deep reasons having to do with the entire structuring of their minds – with their inability to decentre, with their lack of logical reversibility, and so on: in short with the absence of operations. On a Piagetian view of the matter, the children *cannot* understand; but what prevents them is not lack of linguistic knowledge, except in so far as certain aspects of language can be mastered only when the prerequisite cognitive advances have taken place.

This kind of claim seems at first sight to lend itself to straightforward experimental test. The argument suggests a distinction between 'deep' cognitive difficulties and 'superficial' linguistic ones; and this in turn leads on to the notion that if the children are failing to conserve for linguistic reasons their difficulties should yield to linguistic training. Accordingly, Sinclair-de-Zwart (1967) carried out a series of studies designed to investigate this possibility.

Conservation tests make much use of words like *more* and *less*, *long* and *short*, *fat* and *thin*. Sinclair-de-Zwart wanted to find out if non-conservers understood these words; if not, whether they could be taught them; and, if so, whether they would then instantly become conservers. Her main finding was that linguistic training, even when it seemed to succeed in changing language, had little effect on conservation, although there were some words – words like *more*, *less*, *as much as*, *none* – which Sinclair-de-Zwart called 'operator-like' and which proved to be more closely linked than the others to the advent of conserving responses.

Sinclair-de-Zwart concluded that, in general, her results supported Piagetian claims. However, questions about the role of language are not so easily laid to rest. More recent research suggests very strongly that knowledge of single word-meanings – or even knowledge of constructions like 'longer but thinner', which Sinclair-de-Zwart also studied – is not all we have to consider. Indeed, we now know that studies of the comprehension of 'word meanings' in one context may grossly mislead if they are taken as evidence of what happens in another.

About 10 years ago my colleagues and I began to conduct a series of studies of which two had direct bearing on conservation. In the first of these (Donaldson & McGarrigle, 1974) two rows of toy cars were placed on shelves, one above the other, with or without enclosing garages, thus: or thus:

X	X	X	X	
X	X	X	X	X

X	X	X	X	
X	X	X	X	X

Always there are four cars in one row and five in the other and always the fifth car projected at the right-hand end of its row; but position was counterbalanced in the sense that the four cars might be either on the top or the bottom. Notice that the four cars were enclosed in four garages while the five were enclosed in six, leaving one garage empty.

The children were asked: *Are there more cars on this shelf or more cars on this shelf?* and, for each shelf separately: *Are all the cars on this shelf?* Each question was asked twice, first with garages present and then after the garages had been removed, or the other way round. Thus the questioning had the general characteristics of a conservation test: a question was asked, an irrelevant change was introduced, the question was asked again. We found that many children gave different answers to that repeated question. So how is this finding to be interpreted?

When children do not conserve number in the standard task, they appear to be confusing number with length. The number remains the same but the length of row alters and the child is deceived. In Piagetian terms, number and length are undifferentiated. Here, however, both number and length of row are unaltered; yet still the answer changes.

In the normal version of the test the children usually say that the longer row has more. In this experiment when the garages were absent they also usually said that the longer – and more numerous – row had more. But the presence of the garages changed this, so that now the 'non-conserving' answer to questions about which row had more was based not on attention to length but, apparently, on attention to fullness.

In the case of questions about *all*, the response patterns were more complex and harder to summarize, but the same tendency was evident. When the garages were present, 14 out of 21 children (mean age 4 years 4 months) said that the row which was full had 'all the cars' though they denied this for the more numerous row with the empty garage.

What is it, then, that is being conserved – or not conserved? In the case of *more*, we may speak of conservation of inequality of length and number, but the case of *all* is more perplexing. Yet the kinds of response given were so similar that we must look for a single unifying account of what is going on. This can be found in the notion that what the children may be failing to conserve is the meaning of the question – not the meaning of individual words, but the meaning of the utterance as a whole.

Literate adults in our kind of culture commonly conceive of language as having what Grice (1968) calls 'timeless meaning': meaning that is fixed and frozen, not liable to vary with the context of use, so that it is possible to speak of *the* meaning of an utterance. Within this conception, the existence of ambiguity is of course recognized but the ambiguities themselves are codified or codifiable. What is not allowed for on this view is a mode of thinking and behaving in which language is effectively embedded in the totality of the events among which it occurs, a mode in which meaning does not depend upon the words alone.

If language is treated as a formal isolated system, then it is possible to construct a sentence and ask: 'What does it mean?' Deciding what it means will entail precise consideration of the meanings of the separate words and of the ways in which these are combined. A student trying to interpret an examination question is expected to engage in just this kind of reflection, for example. But suppose that this is not what children commonly do – nor even what adults commonly do, except in certain formal modes of behaving. Suppose on the contrary that the normal thing is to take the language together with its context – physical and personal – and try to make sense of the whole. Suppose, further, that the younger the child the more likely it becomes that non-linguistic cues will outweigh linguistic ones if any trial of strength should arise. Now consider what happens in a conservation test. The experimenter sets up a special array, draws the child's attention to it, asks a question, receives an answer. Then he changes some feature of the array in a deliberate, calculated manner and asks the question again. Considered as a set of disembedded words this is the same question as before. But considered as a unity of words-and-context it is not. The experimenter by his action has introduced something new and highly salient, and if the child is trying to make sense not of the words alone but of the whole interaction then it is reasonable to regard the question as having changed.

Strong support for the notion that children – and adults much of the time – are indeed trying to make sense of the whole interaction comes from recent work by Freeman *et al.* (in press). They show how a topic may be systematically manipulated by non-linguistic means, both for adults and for children, and they conclude that the perceived purposes of the speaker are of central importance in determining interpretation. They point out that, while linguistic devices for topic-setting are well documented, the role of non-linguistic cues has been relatively neglected.

Notions of this kind help to account for the research findings which I have already described. They were put to a direct test in a further study (McGarrigle & Donaldson, 1974), the idea for which came from James McGarrigle. He postulated that, in a conservation test, the manner in which the transformation was carried out should make a difference. Specifically, he reasoned that the child should be sensitive to the agent and the purpose of the transformation, and he proposed a test of the hypothesis that if a 'naughty teddy bear' disarranged the array in order to 'mess up the game' children would produce more conserving responses than in the standard test.

This hypothesis was confirmed, and the initial study has since been replicated and extended (Light *et al.*, 1979; Dockrell *et al.*, 1980). At the same time, some of the implications of the work have been questioned.

McGarrigle & Donaldson described the intervention by 'naughty teddy' as effecting an *accidental* transformation, in contrast with the experimenter's intentional act. Light *et al.* devised an ingenious situation in which the transformation could be considered *incidental* to the rest of the task. They studied conservation of quantity using glass beakers which contained small pasta shells. These shells were to be used to play a competitive game and so both players had to have equal amounts of them. Once the subjects had accepted the initial equality, the experimenter made a pretence of suddenly noticing that one of the beakers had a badly chipped rim and might be dangerous to handle. Looking around the room, he found another beaker which, however, was not the same shape as the first two. After transferring the pasta shells from the chipped beaker into this one, he was then able to ask in a seemingly very natural way whether the competitors were satisfied that they still had the same amount and that the game would be 'fair'. In this way Light *et al.* obtained highly significant gains in conserving responses by comparison with the standard task. If we consider results for the first questioned child in each pair, only 5 per cent conserved in the standard condition whereas 70 per cent conserved in the incidental condition.

This is a dramatic difference. Light and his colleagues, however, express doubts about whether it is reasonable to conclude, as McGarrigle & Donaldson did on the basis of the 'naughty teddy' study, that the standard procedure seriously underestimates the child's knowledge. For they argue that, if the tester's action in the standard condition gives the child the implicit message: *this transformation is important*, then one may equally say that the intervention of 'naughty teddy' gives the implicit message: *this transformation is unimportant.* Thus while the one procedure may yield false negatives, the other may yield false positives.

There is some force to this argument. Curiously enough, however, the authors do not point out that it applies much more powerfully to the 'naughty teddy' study than to their own. Naughty teddy is explicitly a nuisance and an irrelevance, but the finding of a new beaker to replace a chipped one would seem to be fairly neutral as to importance. So far as one can tell from Light's account of the procedure there was little to constitute an implicit message either way. What there was, however, might rather have tended to suggest importance than the reverse. Light *et al.* report that, before asking the conservation question for the second time, the tester stressed 'the importance of equality for the game to be fair'. If anything, this might have suggested the possibility that the transformation *had* affected equality. It is hard to see how it could have suggested the opposite (*see* note at end).

Further, it is important not to consider the findings of these studies in isolation. There is now a good deal of other research which suggests that traditional conservation tests may underestimate children's competence. Notable among this is Gelman's work, particularly her well-known 'magic' experiments. These demonstrated that children as young as three are highly sensitive to alterations in number and not at all likely to confuse number with length (Gelman & Gallistel, 1978).

Gelman's results are not easy to reconcile with the claim that pre-school children lack a concept of number; nor is recent research by Hughes (1981) who reports a good basic grasp of the notions of addition and subtraction in children between three and five.

The conclusion to which all of this tends is that the conservation test is not a very good tool for studying *specific* conceptual developments. If we want to know what children understand about number – or weight, or volume, or whatever – there are better ways of finding out. However, this is not to say that the conservation test should be discarded. In a recent paper Sinha & Carabine (1981) argue that it serves a different purpose in an admirable way.

Sinha & Carabine used a test of conservation of inequality of liquid quantity having the following unusual characteristics. The child was shown two toy animals, a large horse and a small dog. In front of the animals were identical glass beakers containing 'juice' – a large amount for the horse, a small amount for the dog. The experimenter then poured the dog's drink into a narrower beaker so that the level was higher than that in the standard container. He also poured the horse's drink – but into another *standard* container – and said: 'Remember, the big horse likes a lot to drink, and the little dog only likes a little to drink; now give the animals their drinks'. In another variant of this task the words *more* and *less* replaced *a lot* and *a little*.

These studies yielded some intriguing results, among which one is specially relevant here: younger children gave more conserving reponses than older ones. In the first experiment there was a steady and significant decline in success rates over three groups with mean ages 3:5, 4:6 and 5:8, and this was true whichever pair of lexical items was used. The same trend was evident in a later study though this time it just failed to reach significance.

Age-trends of this kind are now known to be fairly common (Donaldson, 1971; Strauss, 1981). When they occur it usually appears that the children are beginning to take account of some information which they previously ignored, but that they are not yet quite able to handle it. Sinha & Carabine's explanation of their finding is that the youngest children's responses are 'function-based' – that is, the children attend primarily to the functions which the elements in the task fulfil and 'equivalence' is equivalence for a particular purpose, not equivalence in appearance. Specific perceptible attributes, like level of liquid, are simply neglected. Later, however – from about age four onwards – these attributes start to become a matter for concern: the children begin to take account of them. In a sense this is an advance, for these features are more isolable or 'abstract' and, in principle, more independent of context. However, the children do not at first succeed in integrating the earlier functional knowledge with this new attention to isolated features and their reliance on these features is too rigid and overgeneralized. Thus they make an increasing number of errors.

This analysis is cogent, though one might want to argue that the rigidity would have to entail a failure to notice *enough* specific attributes (that is, width as well as height) in which case, the account is reminiscent of the Piagetian emphasis on centration.

However, it is also important to notice that, although Sinha & Carabine mention the research on accidental transformations, they do not really take account of it in formulating their theory. Yet the results of this and related work are clearly relevant, for the 'animals' task is like the classic conservation task at least to the extent that the transformation is the deliberate act of the experimenter. In order to deal with findings about the nature of the transformation a somewhat different – though not radically conflicting – explanation of the Sinha & Carabine age trend may be proposed. This alternative explanation invokes a distinction which may prove to be of some general importance for developmental studies.

That young children are sensitive to purpose is clear. There are, however, two distinct ways in which this sensitivity may show itself in the context of a specific task, for there are two distinct kinds of purpose to which the child may attend. First, there may be purposes which are internal to the task – part of its very structure. For instance, in the 'animals' conservation task the purpose of giving each animal a drink appropriate to its size is built into the enterprise from the start. Another example may be found in the task that Hughes devised for studying decentration (Hughes & Donaldson, 1979), where the purpose is to find a place in which a boy can hide from a policeman. On the other hand, however, there are also *external* purposes, purposes which do not inhere in the task itself but have to do rather with the intentions of those who set the task or who intervene as it is being tackled. For instance, there is the naughty teddy's goal of 'messing up the game'; or in the study by Light *et al.* (1979), the experimenter's goal of preventing a child's hand from being cut; or the (supposed) purpose of the experimenter in the classic conservation task of signalling, by his action, the thing to which he wants the child to attend.

Now the Sinha & Carabine age trend might be explained by postulating that the very young children – the three-year-olds – are more likely to attend to the internal purposes, which amounts to saying that they would be less likely, once caught up in the game of providing the animals with their drinks, to ask themselves why the experimeter had taken the trouble to pour the juice from one glass into another. Older children, however, might be less wholly absorbed in the fiction and more likely to attend to purposes which are external to it.

The preceding argument may usefully be extended. It is of course the case that, as well as attending to purposes of either kind, children may attend also to impersonal, wholly non-purposive, features of task structure, though Sinha & Carabine may well be right in saying that very young children are less likely to do this than older ones, preferring to concentrate on functional or purpose-based criteria when these are available. However, some tasks have no internal purposes of any kind – and the classical conservation task (as distinct from the Sinha & Carabine version) is one of these. In such a task, then, there are two possibilities: either subjects focus on impersonal features, like level of liquid; or they focus on external purposes and wonder about the act of pouring water from one glass to another and why the experimenter did it.

The first of these patterns of attending is consonant with the Piagetian interpretation, whereas the second is not. But we do not necessarily have to choose between them, for both might occur. And both certainly might lead to failure on the standard task. The first would lead to failure if the child were overwhelmed by one salient feature and did not manage to take account of others which balanced it. The second would lead to failure if the emphasis on motive intruded sufficiently to mislead the child as to the meaning of the experimenter's question – that is, if the language was not interpreted in a sufficiently disembedded way. Clearly the use of 'accidental' or 'incidental' transformations greatly reduces the likelihood of errors of this latter kind. However, it is relevant to observe that the introduction of these transformations does not, in any of the studies so far published, come close to eliminating error entirely. Not even Light's ingenious version makes all children give conserving replies.

All of this suggests the possibility that some children at some points in development may tend to respond to impersonal, physical features while others – or the same children at other times – may tend to respond to interpersonal or social ones. Some may concern themselves with level of liquid and length of row, while others wonder about what the experimenter is up to. It is likely that many wonder about both and are apt to be swayed by each in turn. However, it seems reasonable to suppose that enduring personal characteristics will make themselves manifest. Nelson (1973) and others have observed that some children, from an early age, talk more about the physical world, while others talk more about people and their purposes.* This may well reflect general preoccupations relevant to many of the functions of the mind.

We are led to the general conclusion that the situation is more complicated than Piaget had supposed and that there are common sources of failure in conservation tests which his theory does not envisage. While this limits the value of the tests for some purposes – such as determining the state of a child's understanding of number – it suggests the possibility of using them in new ways. Sinha & Carabine (1981) argue that they provide an excellent instrument for studying the manner in which language is related to context and in particular for revealing how those features which a child selects as the 'significant context' are subject to developmental change.

References

Berlyne, D. E. (1965). *Structure and Direction in Thinking*. New York: Wiley.

Dockrell, J., Neilson, I. & Campbell, R. (1980). Conservation accidents revisited. *International Journal of Behavioural Development*, 3, 423–439.

Donaldson, M. (1971). Preconditions of inference. In J. K. Cole (ed.), *Nebraska Symposium on Motivation, 1971*. Lincoln, NB: Nebraska University Press.

Donaldson, M. & McGarrigle, J. (1974). Some clues to the nature of semantic development. *Journal of Child Language*, 1, 185–194.

Freeman, N., Sinha, C. & Stedmon, J. A. (in press). All the cars — which cars? From word-meaning to discourse analysis. In M. Beveridge (ed.), *Children Thinking Through Language*. London: Edward Arnold.

Gelman, R. & Gallistel, C. R. (1978). *The Child's Understanding of Number*. Cambridge, MA: Harvard University Press.

Goodenough, D. R. (1977). Field dependence. In H. London & J. E. Exner (eds), *Dimensions of Personality*. New York: Wiley.

Grice, H. (1968). Utterer's meaning, sentence meaning and word meaning. *Foundations of Language*, 4, 225–242.

Hughes, M. (1981). Can pre-school children add and subtract? *Educational Psychology*, 1, 207–219.

Hughes, M. & Donaldson, M. (1979). The use of hiding games for studying the coordination of viewpoints. *Educational Review*, 31, 133–140.

Light, P., Buckingham, N. & Robbins, A. H. (1979). The conservation task as an interactional setting. *British Journal of Educational Psychology*, 49, 304–310.

Nelson, K. (1973). Structure and strategy in learning to talk. *Monographs of the Society for Research in Child Development*, 38 (1–2) (Serial No. 149).

McGarrigle, J. & Donaldson, M. (1974). Conservation accidents. *Cognition*, 3, 341–350.

* It may also be relevant to note that a relationship has been found between responsiveness to social cues and field dependence. (See, for instance, Goodenough, 1977.) However, it is clear that a child who is misled by salient *physical* cues in a conservation test is showing dependence on the immediate 'field' too, even if it is a physical field and not a social one.

Piaget, J. (1971). *Biology and Knowledge*. Edinburgh: Edinburgh University Press.
Piaget, J. (1975). *The Development of Thought*. Oxford: Blackwell.
Shultz, T. R., Dover, A. & Amsel, E. (1979). The logical and empirical bases of conservation judgements. *Cognition*, **7**, 99–123.
Sinclair-de-Zwart, H. (1967). *Acquisition du Langage et Développement de la Pensée*. Paris: Dunod.
Sinha, C. & Carabine, B. (1981). Interactions between lexis and discourse in conservation and comprehension tasks. *Journal of Child Language*, **8**, 109–129.
Strauss, S. (ed.) (1981). *U-Shaped Behavioral Growth*. New York: Academic Press.
Wallach, L. (1969). On the bases of conservation. In D. Elkind & J. Flavell (eds.), *Studies in Cognitive Development*. New York: Oxford University Press.

Requests for reprints should be addressed to Margaret Donaldson, Department of Psychology, University of Edinburgh, 7 George Square, Edinburgh EH8 9JZ, Scotland.

Note added in proof

On the other hand, Bovet *et al.* (1981) (in an article which I had unfortunately not seen until this paper was in press) report further work on Light's task. They argue that large numbers of correct responses are given in this situation because the children are so eager to get on with the game that they do not seriously attend to the effects of the transformation.

Reference

Bovet, M. M., Parrat-Dayan, S. & Deshuss-Addor, D. (1981). Peut-on parler de précocité et de régression dans la conservation? I Précocité. *Archives de Psychologie*, **49**, 289–303.

British Journal of Psychology (1982), **73**, 209–220   *Printed in Great Britain*

Accessing one-to-one correspondence: Still another paper about conservation

Rochel Gelman

When given experience designed to highlight the fact that the specific cardinal values of sets in one-to-one correspondence are the same (or different), three- and four-year-old children pass the standard number conservation tasks of equivalence and non-equivalence. The initial training involved set sizes of three and four items; the conservation transfer trials involved set sizes of eight and 10 items. Even where success was defined as being able to give a correct judgement *and* explanation on at least one task in the small-set range *and* one task in the large-set range, children did well. In Expt 1, 75 and 88 per cent of the three- and four-year-olds, respectively, met this criterion. In Expt 2 (run by an experimenter who was naïve to the hypotheses and results of Expt 1) 58 and 75 per cent of the respective age groups met the same criterion. It is concluded that the children must have accessed an available, albeit implicit, ability to use one-to-one correspondence. Otherwise they could not have passed the large set-size tasks which are beyond the range they count accurately. The paper ends with a defence of Rozin's (1976) accessing account of cognitive development.

Yes, the focus of this paper is on Piaget's number conservation task. Specifically, I confront seemingly contradictory results: preschool children do not conserve number. Yet, as revealed on the magic task (e.g. Gelman, 1977) they know that the operations of addition and subtraction alter set size whereas a change in the length of an array is number-irrelevant. I have *avoided* writing that the young children who pass the magic studies can conserve, this for the obvious reason that they would fail Piaget's task. Instead, I have granted them a *number-invariance scheme* wherein the operations of addition and subtraction are classified as number-relevant and others like displacement as number-irrelevant. Still, if they know that a length change is number-irrelevant how can they possibly fail to conserve?

I shall argue that preschoolers fail the number conservation task because they lack an *explicit* understanding of the principle of one-to-one correspondence. Despite an implicit understanding of one-to-one correspondence, this understanding is inaccessible under most circumstances. The proof of the argument is that there are some circumstances which yield successful performance on the Piagetian task. By successful, I mean that an explanation is given for a correct judgement – even on set sizes too large to permit accurate counting.

To begin, it helps to contrast the magic paradigm with the conservation task. In the former, young children are shown two sets of objects on separate trays placed side by side. Over a period of covering, shuffling and uncovering the displays to find 'the winner' (so designated by the experimenter), children come to expect that each tray will have a specific number of items, e.g. 'The winner has two; the loser has three'. Then unexpected variations, such as a rearrangement of the display or removal of items, are surreptitiously introduced. When children encounter the unexpected changes, they react with surprise, ask how the change came about and tell us whether the numbers have changed or not, e.g. 'Not four, only one-two-three; took one', 'Still three; just moved them'. As evident in these examples, there is a tendency for the children to use a counting algorithm to figure out answers.

In the magic experiment: the displays are placed side by side; the set sizes are small ($n \geqslant 5$); and counting behaviours are observed. In contrast, in the conservation experiment the two displays are one above the other; set sizes are seldom smaller than six; counting behaviours are seldom observed and, when they are, they are discouraged. In both tasks

0007-1269/82/020209-12 $02.00/0

the child has to judge the effects of relevant and irrelevant transformations. A young child in the magic study can (and often does) do this by comparing the *specific* expected values with the ones encountered. There is no requirement that she use the principle of one-to-one correspondence. Indeed the magic task does not lend itself readily to this end since the displays are side by side. And since small sets are used, the young child's tendency to count single arrays serves as a reliable algorithm (Groen & Resnick, 1977; Gelman & Gallistel, 1978).

Piaget (1952) placed a premium on the ability to use one-to-one correspondence to judge numerical equivalence. He assumed that one-to-one correspondence is the psychologically primitive basis for a judgement of equivalence—a position that is congruent with many formal definitions of number (see Kline, 1972; and Greeno *et al.* (unpublished), for further details).

Gelman & Gallistel (1978) accepted Piaget's view that a child who conserves uses the operation of one-to-one correspondence. However, they maintained that the use and understanding of one-to-one correspondence is a later achievement, one which indexes the ability to reason about *non-specified* values. For Gelman & Gallistel, preschoolers' understanding of whether two sets are numerically equal rests on their ability to determine whether they yield the same particular cardinal value when counted. Hence, preschoolers are granted the ability to reason about specified values but not non-specified ones. Since, as Piaget pointed out, a true test of the use of one-to-one correspondence should rule out the tendency to count and thereby achieve a specific numerical representation, success on the standard conservation task should be beyond the very young child. (Parenthetically, it should be clear why Piaget insisted children not be allowed to count and small set sizes be avoided.)

A strong form of the Gelman & Gallistel hypothesis would have it that preschoolers are *never* able to reason about non-specified numerical values and thus should be unable to reason about equivalence judgements derived from an understanding of one-to-one correspondence. Since we first presented the argument in this strong form, I have come to question it.

Despite Bryant's critics (e.g. Katz & Beilin, 1976; Starkey, 1981), his conclusion that preschool children can and do use one-to-one correspondence to judge equivalence relations (Bryant, 1972, 1974) is probably correct. Brush (1972), Cooper *et al.* (1978), and Starkey (1978) all studied the preschooler's understanding of addition and subtraction with a method that first required the use of one-to-one correspondence. Children watched as an experimenter placed one object in each of two separate containers; then another pair in each, etc. In all three sets of experiments, some tasks involved set sizes beyond the counting range of their subjects. Even three-year-olds were able to indicate whether the containers had the same number of items. This done, the children then continued with a series of addition (and subtraction) trials with either one or both of the covered displays. For example, having established an equivalence relation, Cooper *et al.* (1978) placed another object in one container and then asked the child about the numerical relation. Since the three- and four-year-old children could participate in these experiments, they must have used one-to-one correspondence to judge equivalence and the subsequent effects of addition and subtraction. Still, there was no clear evidence that very young children could conserve—until Markman's (1979) results appeared.

Markman distinguishes between concepts that are organized as *classes* as opposed to *collections* (Markman & Siebert, 1976; Markman, 1979). The difference between concepts of *trees* and *forests* illustrates the distinction. Given a particular instance of a tree, one can answer whether or not it is a member of the class *trees*. However, given the same instance of the same tree, one cannot answer whether it is a member of a forest. There must be other trees nearby, i.e. the instance *tree* is a member of a forest only if it is in proximity with other trees. Markman contends that class terms focus attention on the particular members of a display, whereas collection terms focus attention on the overall characteristics of the display. She hypothesized that were young children induced to think of the rows in a conservation task as collections, their attention would be drawn to the emergent properties such as numerical value. Hence, she assessed the ability of four- and five-year-old children to conserve as a function of whether they were tested with the standard (class) or modified collection question. As an example, one group of children was asked the collection question, 'Does your army have as many as my army?' The other group was asked the standard question, 'Do you have as many soldiers as I do?' The exact same displays were used; except for the substitution of collection terms for class terms, the two conditions followed the standard conservation procedure.

Children in the class condition correctly answered about one and a half of four conservation trials. Children in the collection condition answered twice as many correctly. In addition they were able to give explanations. Given the explanation data, it is hard to deny that Markman's subjects conserved numbers. Presumably then, they accessed a quantitative use of the principle of one-to-one correspondence.

If a preschool child can access the principle of one-to-one correspondence, what might be the source of this ability? A clear candidate is the ability to count since counting involves the use of one kind of one-to-one correspondence: a unique count tag must be assigned to each and every object in an array. However, when counting a young child need not recognize the equivalence relation between the number of count tags and number of items in a display; after all only one set can be seen, the other is represented within the child. Thus, although the competence model for preschool counting grants the implicit use of one-to-one correspondence, it does not follow that the child has ready access to the knowledge (see Gelman, 1982; and Greeno *et al.*). A similar argument is made to distinguish between rule-governed sentence use and metalinguistic knowledge. A young child's ability to produce and understand language is rule-governed (e.g. Clark & Clark, 1977). Despite this, access to these rules on metalinguistic tasks will be beyond him for some time to come (e.g. Gleitman *et al.*, 1972).

How to make explicit the principle of one-to-one correspondence to children who can count but not conserve? We showed children pairs of rows of objects in one-to-one correspondence that represented either equal or unequal values. A child was first asked to count one of the rows and then indicate its cardinal number. Then she was asked to count the other row and then give its cardinal value. This done, she was asked if both rows had the same number. Note the judgement of equivalence was not solicited until the child had already achieved a specific cardinal value for both rows. This was done here and on other trials intentionally. We wanted to show the role of one-to-one correspondence in the definition of cardinal number by pointing out and making explicit the fact that displays which are (or are not) perceptually in one-to-one correspondence yield the same (or different) specific cardinal values when counted.

The proposed training had to be done with set sizes young children could count, i.e. around three to four items. In contrast the conservation post-tests had to include set sizes beyond the range young children count reliably. Should transfer occur, but be restricted to small set sizes, the findings would support the strong version of the Gelman & Gallistel hypothesis; should transfer also occur on large sets, the hypothesis would have to be revised.

Experiment 1

Children

Seventy-nine children participated in the study. Three three-year-olds failed to follow instructions. The remaining 38 three- and 38 four-year-olds were randomly assigned to the experimental group ($n = 16$), the cardinal-once group 1 ($n = 12$) and the no cardinal group ($n = 8$). The mean age and range for the respective three-year-old groups were 42 months (37–47 months); 43 months (39–47 months) and 42 months (37–47 months). The comparable figures for the three four-year-old groups were 55 months (49–59 months); 54 months (49–58 months); and 54 months (50–59 months).

Children were in attendance at one of two day-care centres or one nursery school. They came from heterogeneous socio-economic and racial backgrounds. Overall the group tended towards a middle middle-class background.

Procedures and rationale

The design of the study included two age groups (three- and four-year-olds) and three training groups. Each group participated in a two-phase experiment which lasted 10–15 minutes. In the first phase, children were given the treatment for the group they were in. In the second phase all children were treated alike. They were tested on conservation of equals and non-equals in both the small and large set size ranges.

Since, in our experience, the children in the target age ranges from the schools involved almost never conserve, we did not run a control group of children who were simply given conservation tests during phase 1. It was presumed that the random assignment of children yielded comparable abilities across groups.

Phase 1

The experimental condition: Experience with two rows. The children were shown two rows of equal (4–4) or unequal numbers of items (4–3) placed horizontally and in one-to-one correspondence. Half the children were first shown two equal rows of equal lengths; half were first shown the two unequal rows of different lengths. Objects here and elsewhere were blue toy turtles measuring 2·5 cm in diameter.

A child was first asked to count the number of items in one of the rows. That row was then covered by the experimenter's hands and the child was asked 'How many are under my hands?' This was repeated for the remaining row. The child was then asked to judge whether the uncovered rows contained the 'same number or a different number' of items. All children answered these questions correctly.

Next, the child watched as the length of one row was transformed and then was asked to judge whether the specific number of items in that row had changed. For example, after lengthening or shortening one of the rows, the experimenter pointed to the altered (or unaltered row) and asked 'Are there still four (three) there?' If the child's response was 'Yes' a comparable question was asked for the remaining row. The child was then asked to judge whether the rows had the same number or a different number of items and to explain his judgement. The order of transformation types was randomized. Transformations on unequal trials yielded rows of the same length; equal trials involved rows of different lengths.*

One three-year-old responded 'No' to the initial question on the transformation trials. He was asked to count the array and judge again whether it still contained four items. Then he agreed to the numerosity of the array and the procedure continued as above.

Control conditions: There were two control conditions. In the first, children counted only one row and answered the 'how many' question. Children in the second condition were also asked to count one row; but they were not asked for the cardinal value. These groups are referred to as the *cardinal-once* and *no cardinal* controls.

Children in the cardinal-once control condition were shown single rows instead of pairs of rows.

---

* Gréco (1962) used a similar procedure with older children. However, he first solicited an initial equivalence judgement and then had children count one row. Also, it is not clear whether the same children had experience with both equivalence and non-equivalence relations.

They first counted one linear row (of three or four items); stated its cardinal value after the experimenter covered it; watched as that array was transformed (lengthened or shortened); and then judged whether the array still had three (or four) items. Each row was altered four times to provide a comparable number of trials across pretest conditions. The presentation order of set size was counterbalanced; that for transformation type was randomized.

In the cardinal-once condition, children had no experience with rows in one-to-one correspondence. Thus, unlike those in the experimental group, they had no opportunity to note that rows in one-to-one correspondence were assigned the same (different) cardinal values. Still, given that the pre-test could have set them to consider the specific value before and after a transformation, some transfer might occur.

The second control group—no cardinal—was asked to count single rows of three or four items for as many trials as the first control group. They were not, however, required to indicate the cardinal value rendered by a count. We expected the children in this group to behave as if they had no conservation-relevant experience. They received no explicit cardination experience and no equivalence experience. We anticipated they would fail to conserve, as three- and four-year-olds typically do.

Phase 2

Conservation tests. Conservation tests were administered immediately after phase 1. All children were given four conservation tasks representing two set sizes (large and small) and two types of number conservation (equivalence and non-equivalence). In these conditions two transformations (lengthening and shortening) were performed.

The small-set tasks used two rows of five toy turtles on the *equal* task and one row of five versus four turtles on the *unequal* task. The respective displays for the large set-size tasks were 10 and 10 and 10 versus eight.

The order of presentation of large and small set sizes was counterbalanced as was the order of conservation of equality and inequality tasks within a set-size range. The equal arrays were equal in length prior to the transformation and unequal in length after being transformed. The reverse was true for the non-equivalent arrays: before being transformed they were unequal in length and then equal in length after the transformation.

The conservation trials were run in the standard way older children are tested and *included requests for explanations*. Likewise, children were discouraged from counting. Tape-recordings were obtained here as well as during training.

Results and discussion

Training: Phase 1. As expected, children had no trouble counting the small set sizes. There were no errors in response to the initial request to count the number of items. In the experimental and cardinal-once conditions, requests of 'how many' were also answered correctly.

When experimental subjects initially saw the effect of transforming one of the displays they were simply asked whether 'that row still has four (or three)'. In the three-year-old group 50 per cent counted *before* they answered this question: the same result obtained for 4–4 and 4–3 displays. By the second transformation the respective figures were down to 31 and 19 per cent. The four-year-olds' tendency to recount before saying a transformation was irrelevant was not as striking. Thirty-eight and 25 per cent recounted on their first transformation; 31 and 13 per cent did so on their second transformation. Not too surprisingly, when these same children were asked why the two displays still had the same number, they made reference to their specific values and/or recounted again. There were only a few children who appealed to the irrelevance of the transformation or the absence of addition and subtraction.

Children in the cardinal-once group were less inclined to recount their single array when asked if it still had three (or four) after the first transformation. The respective three- and four-year-old figures were 25 and 6 per cent. The greater tendency to count on the part of experimental children presumably reflects an initial hesitation about the equivalence of set-size value when they first encountered a conflict between perceptual cues and numerical values of the two arrays.

Conservation: *Phase 2*. Table 1 presents the overall proportion of correct conservation judgements as a function of set sizes and condition. Three- and four-year-old children did very well; a full 68 and 74 per cent, respectively, were correct responses. Inspection of the table reveals no obvious effect of set size for the experimental group, i.e. the experimental children did about as well on the larger set sizes as on the smaller ones.

Table 1. Overall proportion correct judgements on conservation tasks in Expt 1

Values of displays and age group	Condition		
	Experimental ($n = 16$)	Cardinal-once ($n = 12$)	No cardinal ($n = 8$)
4 and 5			
3 yr	0·73	0·08	0·19
4 yr	0·75	0·58	0·19
5 and 5			
3 yr	0·69	0·13	0·06
4 yr	0·75	0·58	0·13
8 and 10			
3 yr	0·68	0·08	0·00
4 yr	0·66	0·29	0·13
10 and 10			
3 yr	0·75	0·08	0·00
4 yr	0·63	0·38	0·13
Overall			
3 yr	0·68	0·09	0·06
4 yr	0·74	0·46	0·15

Both control groups did poorly compared to the experimental one. In neither three-year-old control condition is there much evidence of conservation. More than half of the four-year-olds in the cardinal-once condition transferred on small set sizes. In contrast to their experimental counterparts they did not show much transfer on the larger set sizes.

Explanations of incorrect judgements were as expected. They made reference to irrelevant perceptual variables, contained fabrications or made no sense.

Explanations of correct conservation judgements were coded as *unacceptable* if a child counted *before* answering the same or different questions. Likewise, so were answers which stated the obvious (e.g. 'they both have a lot'). This left as *acceptable* explanations which included: references to irrelevant transformations (e.g. 'they just moved'); references to addition or subtraction ('you need to put another to make them the same'); references to the initial equality or inequality of number; appeals to one-to-one correspondence arguments; and counts that *followed* a correct judgement, e.g. 'They're still the same number because...well, you see there's 1, 2, 3, 4, 5 here and 5 there'.

Two independent raters coded the explanations. They agreed on 97 per cent of their judgements. The overall conditional probabilities that correct judgements were backed up by adequate explanations were 0·82 and 0·93 for the three-year-olds and four-year-olds, respectively. Given these high rates of explanations, the conclusion that children in the experimental group did conserve is on firm ground. When four-year-olds in the cardinal-once group gave correct judgements, they too tended to provide explanations

Table 2. Proportion of each type of explanation of correct judgements in Expt 1

	Explanation's focus				
Group	Addition–subtraction	Irrelevant transformation	1–1 Correspondence	Number	No explanation
Experimental: 3 yr	0·04	0·34	0·21	0·23	0·18
Experimental: 4 yr	0·04	0·53	0·09	0·24	0·07
Cardinal-once: 4 yr	0·10	0·20	0·15	0·35	0·20

although not quite as often as their experimental counterparts. The conditional probability was 0·77.

Table 2 shows a breakdown of the explanations which followed a correct judgement. Even if we exclude references to number, 63 and 67 per cent of the three- and four-year-olds gave adequate explanations. If we do the same for the four-year-olds in the cardinal-once control group, they again look worse than the experimental groups of either age: still 45 per cent of their explanations would qualify under this more stringent criterion.

Table 3 provides information regarding an individual child's tendency to conserve, i.e. give a correct response and explanation, on at least one of the tasks with small sets *and* one with large sets. Again, children in the experimental group look very good. Seventy-five and 88 per cent of the respective three- and four-year-olds pass this criterion. In contrast no three-year-olds in either control group do and a smaller percentage of the four-year-old cardinal-once controls do. Still a respectable level, 50 per cent of the four-year-olds in the first control group did pass this criterion.

In the analyses presented above, there is a slight tendency for the three-year-olds in the experimental group to do worse than the four-year-olds. This reflects a tendency for them to conserve less consistently. Whereas half of the four-year-olds in the experimental condition gave correct judgements on all of their trials, only 25 per cent of the three-year-olds did. The younger children were more shaky conservers, despite their ability to provide explanations.

In sum, three- and four-year-old children benefited from a brief session (5–7 min) wherein the emphasis was on their using specific cardinal values to make judgements of equivalence. Since the children transferred what they learned to small-item *and* large-item conservation tests and since they also provided explanations, two conclusions follow. First, they accessed an ability to conserve. Second, although preschoolers are biased toward reasoning about specific numerosities, they are not restricted to just this avenue. Under certain conditions, they can be induced to solve conservation tasks they would fail if they

Table 3. Percentage of children in Expt 1 who conserved with explanations on at least one small and one large set-size test

Condition	Age of children	
	3 years	4 years
Experimental	75	88
Cardinal-once	0	50
No cardinal	0	25

had to count. I was startled with the strength of the above effects and decided a replication study was needed to assess their stability.

Experiment 2

The experimenter (E.M.) who ran the first study was experienced in doing research with preschoolers, familiar with the hypotheses and very skilled at interviewing children in conservation tasks. Hence the decision to use a naïve experimenter (P.P.) in the second study; someone who did not know the hypotheses, was unaware of the initial results, and had very little experience with conservation tasks. This meant that we used someone who was also new at testing preschoolers since others who were experienced knew the hypotheses and results from Study 1.

This experiment was run as a replication of the first except: the experimenter obtained no explanations during training; and the sessions were shorter because, as revealed in transcripts, there was less time spent on obtaining explanations.

Children

Thirty three-year-olds and 30 four-year-olds participated in this study. They came from a comparable sample of children as above. There were 12 children in each experimental group; 12 in each of the cardinal-only groups and six in each of the no cardinal groups. The respective mean age and range of age for the three three-year-old groups were: 43·5 months (38–47 months); 43 months (36–47 months) and 45 months (42–47 months). The comparable figures for the four-year-old groups were 53 months (49–56 months); 53 months (48–59 months); and 52 months (49–54 months).

Results

In the main, the second study replicated the first. Strong results were obtained again, although the children in the experimental group in this study did not do quite as well. The overall proportions of correct conservation judgements were 0·63 and 0·79 for the three- and four-year-old subjects. In this study there was some effect of set size; still the experimental children did quite well on the large-item tasks. The proportions of correct response for the small and large tasks were 0·71 and 0·54, respectively. The comparable figures for four-year-olds were 0·88 and 0·71. These as well as the control groups' data are summarized in Table 4.

Children in the experimental groups were able to explain correct conservation judgements. Adequate explanations were provided on 0·45 and 0·76, respectively, of the three-year-olds' and four-year-olds' correct trials. Further, as in the first experiment, many of the experimental subjects conserved (with explanations) on at least one small set-size and one large set-size task. The respective figures are 58 and 75 per cent of the three- and

Table 4. Proportion correct conservation judgements in Expt 2

Set-size range and age	Condition		
	Experimental	Cardinal-once	No cardinal
Small			
3 yr	0·71	0·46	0·16
4 yr	0·81	0·46	0·04
Large			
3 yr	0·54	0·23	0·21
4 yr	0·71	0·08	0·04

four-year-old groups. The same was true for only 25 per cent of the four-year-olds in the cardinal-once condition and even fewer children in the three remaining control conditions.

In sum, levels of transfer performance were down somewhat from those obtained in the first study. Still, three-quarters of the four-year-olds and over half of the three-year-olds in the experimental condition did conserve on both large and small set-size tasks. I conclude that the training procedure reliably induces number conservation in preschool children.

General discussion

The training studies presented here do not support the strong form of the Gelman & Gallistel account of why preschoolers fail the standard number conservation task. Children in the experimental group were given experience designed to bring them to recognize that the specific cardinal values of two displays represented either the same or different number(s). The three- and four-year-old subjects were trained with small set sizes so as to ensure their being able to count and determine the cardinal values. When then tested on conservation tasks, three- and four-year-olds conserved on both small (4, 5) and large set sizes (8, 10). Since most children of this age cannot count accurately set sizes greater than four or five, the only way they could have conserved is on the basis of one-to-one correspondence. Hence it cannot be that preschoolers are never able to use this principle of numerical equivalence. Obviously, under certain circumstances even three-year-olds can.

I interpret the above transfer findings in terms of an accessing account of cognitive development. Rozin (1976) proposed that part of cognitive development involves an increasing ability to access the structures underlying early cognitive and perceptual abilities (cf. Fodor, 1972). What are early and possibly innate abilities, are used in restricted (or even just one) situation(s). But with development these are used in wider and wider settings because of a growing general ability to gain access to underlying competences. For Rozin, development also involves an increasing ability to access components of some of the structure used in specific settings and combine the accessed structures to serve a new ability. Consider the case of reading. I know of no claims that the ability to read is innate. Many have argued that a child has to access the phonetic speech-stream if he is to master the sound–sight correspondence rules (see Rozin & Gleitman, 1977, for a review). But the ability to do this develops relatively late, e.g. Liberman *et al.* (1977). In Rozin's terms, this is because the ability to produce speech only embeds an implicit ability to use the phonetic code. This ability is not an explicit one. With development, there is an increase in the ability to access the phonetic code and put it to work in the service of acquiring a new ability – to read.

In my accounts of counting (e.g. Gelman & Gallistel, 1978) the principle of one-to-one correspondence is an integral component of the counting scheme which is used in the service of counting. When I say that the above training results support an accessing account of development, I mean that the implicit ability to use one-to-one correspondence when counting was brought out and made explicit by the training procedure. Genevan reports of precocious number conservation lend support to the general idea that later developing number concepts often involve the accessing of implicit knowledge embedded in the structures which characterize early number concepts.

Piaget's initial treatment of number conservation focused on the child's understanding of transformations. More recently (e.g. 1975, 1977) he turned his attention to the conditions that a child must recognize before she can deal with transformations. She must first discover the correspondences between two states in order to make comparisons and this 'has to precede any transformations, any working of changes on these fixed states'. First, the child can determine correspondences without being able to apply the rules of transformations. Second, the use of transformations *relies* on the use of correspondences.

Finally, the child understands the system of transformations as it generally applies to quantity.

Following from Piaget's recent account, Inhelder *et al.* (1975) succeeded in producing 'precocious' number conservation. In their experiments four- and five-year-olds were shown displays in one-to-one correspondence and then a series of item removal and replacement transformations. For example, one item in an array was removed and the child was asked if the number of items in both rows was the same; then that item was put back into the array but at a different position and again the child was asked about equivalence. The idea in these experiments was to highlight the 'commutability' of items in a discrete set, i.e. that conservation holds when the act of adding an item at one point in space is undone by the taking out of an item from another point in space. Note that tasks like these require the child recognize that permuting the positions of items within set does not alter the number therein. This is akin to what a child does understand about counting, i.e. that the order of objects is irrelevant to the counting procedure (the order-irrelevance principle in Gelman & Gallistel's model). Inspection of the procedural details of the Inhelder *et al.* task makes it clear that children were also counting and using the resultant cardinal values. Hence the Inhelder *et al.* procedures could very well have worked because they made explicit, or pulled forward, the already implicit knowledge of one-to-one correspondence and cardinal number in the counting-principle structure.

I end up by focusing on access theories of development because they offer a potential setting within which to capture the picture of early cognitive development that I see emerging in the literature. I focus on Rozin's and not Fodor's position mainly because the former offers a potential account of whence new knowledge in development – a problem that was central to Piaget's objections to Fodor's and Chomsky's nativist positions (Piatelli-Palmarini, 1980).

As regards early cognitive development, it used to be commonplace to characterize preschool cognition in terms of how it was not like that in later years. White (1965) catalogued a variety of findings – from outside as well as from inside the Piagetian view – to support the idea that a major leap forward occurred between the ages of five and seven years. Given the subsequent research activities on the part of many, it is now possible to talk as well about the common abilities (e.g. Donaldson, 1978; Gelman, 1978). Under certain conditions, preschoolers can reveal competence in these and other domains. Indeed, it begins to look as though infants can be shown to have more competences in the perceptual and conceptual domains (e.g. Gibson, 1980; Cohen & Younger, 1981; Spelke, in press) than once presumed. One can even demonstrate that they are sensitive to numerical properties (e.g. Starkey *et al.*, 1980).

Despite the long list of what the old and young can both do, preschool children nevertheless are at a disadvantage. There are many occasions where their potential brilliance fails them. Theirs is a competence that is fragile, that can be on-again, off-again, that is used only in restricted settings, that does not generalize readily. In other words they have limited access to their competences. In retrospect, from the perspective of Rozin's version of accessing theory we have ended up with the characterization of preschool thought that we should have found. The theory leads one to expect pockets of competence which only reveal themselves under 'appropriate' circumstances.

If development involves, in part, increased access, the younger the child the more difficult it should be to show a capacity. Similarly, variations in tasks – even simple ones – should have more effect on the younger child than an older one. It should also take more to show a competence on their part. In this regard, the fact that it was only the four-year-olds in the cardinal-once control who conserved during the post-tests makes sense.

As we continue to show capacities at an earlier and earlier age, it is hard to resist the idea that there are foundations for cognitive development that are innate and specific to a particular domain. Although Piaget has allowed that the processes of assimilation, accommodation, and equilibration are innate, he has steadfastly held out against the idea that cognitive structures are innate. In a debate with Chomsky and others (Piatelli-Palmarini, 1980) on this matter Piaget defended his view that structures are constructed and not inherited. He said ' ... I am satisfied with just a functioning that is innate' (p. 157). Chomsky and Fodor argued that structure begets structure and it is logically necessary to assume a nativist position like theirs.

One of Piaget's reasons for resisting the nativist's arguments of Chomsky and Fodor was his concern for the problem of new knowledge. If we say that it is logically required that one can only know what one already is capable of knowing (to be sure in an unexpressed form), then Piaget's position that development brings new knowledge and more mental power is hard to defend. However, new abilities, i.e. other than those which are programmed in the genetic code, can develop from what is innately given. Recall the Rozin account of the ability to read, a new ability which surely brings with it new mental power. Rozin's notions about accessing by themselves do not constitute a solution to the developmental problem, i.e. how to account for new concepts within a nativist frame of reference. But it points to the form such a solution might take.

Acknowledgements

The research reported here and the preparation of the manuscript were supported by grants from the National Science Foundation. I thank the parents, children and schools involved for their cooperation; Patricia Pitt who was second experimenter; Diane Evans who served as a second coder; and Elizabeth Meck who ran the first experiment and did the data analyses.

References

Brush, L. R. (1972). Children's conceptions of addition and subtraction: The relation of formal and informal notions. Unpublished PhD thesis, Cornell.

Bryant, P. E. (1972). The understanding of invariance by very young children. *Canadian Journal of Psychology*, **26**, 78–96.

Bryant, P. E. (1974). *Perception and Understanding in Young Children: An Experimental Approach*. New York: Basic Books.

Clark, H. H. & Clark, E. V. (1977). *Psychology and Language: An Introduction to Psycholinguistics*. New York: Harcourt Brace Jovanovich.

Cohen, L. B. & Younger, B. A. (1981). Perceptual categorization in the infant. Paper presented at the Jean Piaget Society, Philadelphia.

Cooper, R., Starkey, P., Blevins, B., Goth, P. & Leitner, E. (1978). Number development: Addition and subtraction. Paper presented at the symposium of the Jean Piaget Society, Philadelphia.

Donaldson, M. (1978). *Children's Minds*. New York: Norton.

Fodor, J. A. (1972). Some reflections on L. S. Vygotsky's thought and language. *Cognition*, **1**, 83–95.

Gelman, R. (1977). How young children reason about small numbers. In N. J. Castellan, D. B. Pisoni & G. R. Potts (eds), *Cognitive Theory*, vol. 2. Hillsdale, NJ: Erlbaum.

Gelman, R. (1978). Cognitive development. *Annual Review of Psychology*, **29**, 297–332.

Gelman, R. (1982). Basic number abilities. In R. J. Sternberg (ed.), *Advances in the Psychology of Human Intelligence*, vol. 1. Hillsdale, NJ: Erlbaum.

Gelman, R. & Gallistel, C. R. (1978). *The Child's Understanding of Number*. Cambridge, MA.: Harvard University Press.

Gibson, E. J. (1980). Development about intermodal unity: Two views. Paper presented at the Jean Piaget Society, Philadelphia.

Gleitman, L. R., Gleitman, H. & Shipley, E. F. (1972). The emergence of the child as grammarian. *Cognition*, **1**, 137–164.

Gréco, P. (1962). Quantité et quotité. In P. Gréco & A. Morf (eds), *Structures Numériques Élementaires. Études d'Épistémologie Génétique*, vol. 13, pp. 1–70. Paris: Presses Universitaires de France.

Greeno, J. G., Riley, M. S. & Gelman, R. (Unpublished). Young children's counting and understanding of principles. Under review.

Groen, G. & Resnick, L. B. (1977). Can preschool children invent addition algorithms? *Journal of Educational Psychology*, **69**, 645–52.

Inhelder, B., Blanchet, A., Sinclair, M. & Piaget, J. (1975). Relations entre les conservations d'ensembles d'éléments discrets et celles de quantités continués. *Année Psychologique*, **75**, 23–60.

Katz, H. & Beilin, H. (1976). A test of Bryant's claims concerning the young child's understanding of quantitative invariance. *Child Development*, **47**, 877–880.

Kline, M. (1972). *Mathematical Thought from Ancient to Modern Times*. New York: Oxford University Press.

Liberman, I. Y., Shankweiler, D., Liberman, A. M., Fowler, C. & Fischer, F. W. (1977). Phonetic segmentation and recoding in the beginning reader. In A. S. Reber & D. L. Scarborough (eds), *Toward a Psychology of Reading: The Proceedings of the CUNY Conference*. Hillsdale, NJ: Erlbaum.

Markman, E. M. (1979). Classes and collections: Conceptual organization and numerical abilities. *Cognitive Psychology*, **11**, 395–411.

Markman, E. & Siebert, J. (1976). Classes and collections: Internal organization and resulting holistic properties. *Cognitive Psychology*, **8**, 561–577.

Piaget, J. (1952). *The Child's Conception of Number*. London: Routledge & Kegan Paul.

Piaget, J. (1975). On correspondences and morphisms. Presented at the Jean Piaget Society, Philadelphia.

Piaget, J. (1977). Some recent research and its link with a new theory of groupings and conservations based on commutability. *Annals of the New York Academy of Sciences*, **291**, 350–358.

Piatelli-Palmarini, M. (ed.) (1980). *Language and Learning: The Debate between Jean Piaget and Noam Chomsky*. Cambridge, MA: Harvard University Press.

Rozin, P. (1976). The evolution of intelligence and access to the cognitive unconscious. In J. M. Sprague & A. D. Epstein (eds), *Progress in Psychobiology and Physiological Psychology*, vol. 6. New York: Academic Press.

Rozin, P. & Gleitman, L. R. (1977). The structure and acquisition of readings, II. The reading process and the acquisition of the alphabetic principle. In A. S. Reber & D. S. Scarborough (eds), *Toward a Psychology of Reading: The Proceedings of the CUNY Conference*, Hillsdale, NJ: Erlbaum.

Spelke, E. S. (in press). The development of intermodal perception. In L. B. Cohen & P. Salapatek (eds), *Handbook of Infant Perception*. New York: Academic Press.

Starkey, P. (1978). Number development in young children: Conservation, addition and subtraction. Unpublished doctoral dissertation, University of Texas at Austin.

Starkey, P. (1981). Young children's performance in number conservation tasks: Evidence for a hierarchy of strategies. *The Journal of Genetic Psychology*, **138**, 103–110.

Starkey, P., Spelke, E. & Gelman, R. (1980). Number competence in infants: Sensitivity to numeric invariance and numeric change. Paper presented at the International Conference on Infant Studies, New Haven.

White, S. H. (1965). Evidence for a hierarchical arrangement of learning processes. In *Advances in Child Development and Behaviour*, vol. 2. New York: Academic Press.

Requests for reprints should be addressed to Rochel Gelman, University of Pennsylvania, 3813–15 Walnut Street, Philadelphia, PA 19104, USA.

British Journal of Psychology (1982), **73**, 221–230   *Printed in Great Britain*

On the generalizability of conservation: A comparison of different kinds of transformation

Scott A. Miller

Three studies are reported which examined the generalizability of experimentally elicited conservation or non-conservation of number in kindergarten and first-grade children. In the standard conditions of all three studies the transformations were the usual ones in conservation research, i.e. adult-produced, intentional, explicit. In the modified conditions the transformations occurred in a more ecologically natural, less adult-mediated fashion, e.g. boats floating apart, cars running downhill, children moving closer together or farther apart. In Expts 1 and 2, performance was equivalent in the standard and the modified conditions. In Expt 3, performance was significantly better on the modified trials, which utilized accidental/incidental changes, than on standard trials. It is suggested that one important determinant of the child's response to conservation problems is the extent to which the perceptual change and subsequent question are embedded in some natural ongoing activity, as opposed to being the sole focus of attention.

In the child's everyday environment there are numerous examples of collections of objects which undergo natural perceptual transformations. Leaves blow from a tree and scatter in the wind; people move closer together or farther apart; coins are dumped onto a table or scooped into a purse. From Piaget's work on conservation of number (Piaget & Szeminska, 1952) it is clear that young children often believe that number changes when perceptual appearance changes. Does this work imply that the young child must experience apparent non-conservation many times daily in his natural environment?

That there may be limits on how readily the experimental results can be generalized to more natural contexts is suggested by a comparison of the stimuli and transformations found in the two settings. In a typical experimental study, the stimuli are inanimate objects (e.g. poker chips) whose power of movement is completely dependent on the actions of the experimenter. The experimenter begins by carefully establishing the equality of two collections, after which he performs a deliberate perceptual transformation of one of the collections. The transformation in this case is thus human-mediated, intentional, and attention-drawing; its sole purpose, in fact, lies in the possibility that it may alter the number. Clearly, most real-life transformations do not have these qualities. It may well be that the usual experimental procedure elicits a kind of erroneous responding that is less likely in the child's daily dealings with numbers.

This article reports three studies in which the generalizability of experimentally elicited conservation or non-conservation of number was examined by means of a comparison between standard conservation trials and modified trials which utilized different forms of transformation. The attempt in the first study was to sample a variety of kinds of stimuli and natural transformations of those stimuli. These included: animate objects which rearrange themselves; inanimate objects which are moved by natural forces such as gravity; human-produced changes which are incidental to some other goal; and human-produced changes which are apparently accidental. The latter manipulation was derived from a similar transformation in McGarrigle & Donaldson (1974). These authors included trials on which a naughty teddy bear displaced the conservation stimuli in the course of running amok on the table. They reported significantly better performance when the conservation transformation occurred in such an apparently accidental manner than when it was produced in the usual fashion for conservation studies.

Experiment 1

Children

The subjects were 80 kindergarten and first-grade children (mean age = 6:6), half of whom were randomly assigned to the modified condition and half of whom were assigned to the standard condition. There were 20 boys and 20 girls in each condition.

Procedure

Verbal pre-test. The stimuli for the pre-test were 5 cm square wooden blocks. On the first trial two rows of two blocks were presented; on the second trial, a row of two and a row of three. The question was, 'Do the two rows have the same number of blocks, or does one row have more blocks than the other?' (the order of phrases was alternated from trial to trial). If an error occurred on the blocks, two similar trials with pennies were given; if an error occurred with the pennies, the trials with blocks were repeated. Had any child failed at this point he or she would have been rejected; no child failed, however.

Modified condition. There were five problems in the modified condition, with the order of problems balanced across subjects. The conservation question was, 'Do the two rows have the same number of ———, or does the one row have more ——— than the other?' (on half the trials the order of phrases was reversed). The child was also asked to explain his or her judgement.

On the *boats* trial the child was shown two rows of five toy boats floating in a tub of water. Once the child had agreed to the equality, the experimenter pulled a hidden switch, releasing an underwater wire that was holding one row together. The boats in that row then floated slowly apart.

The stimuli for the *cars* trial were two rows of five toy cars. The cars were initially presented in one-to-one correspondence facing downward on two inclined boards. The experimenter then removed a braking peg on one board, causing the cars on that board to run downhill and assume a more spread-out appearance.

The stimuli for the *crickets* trial were live crickets. The crickets in the two collections were presented in identical glass containers. At the start of the trial there were 11 crickets in each container, all bunched in one of the two compartments within the container. Once the child had agreed that the numbers were equal, the experimenter removed the dividing wall in one container, thus allowing the crickets in that collection to spread throughout the entire container. Note that on this trial and the cars trial, in contrast to the boats trial, the child was able to see the experimenter's action that initiated the transformation.

There were two trials with candies as stimuli. On both, the trial began with two rows of five candies lined up in one-to-one correspondence. A small doll was placed next to each row and introduced as that row's 'owner'. On the *candies-spread* trial, the experimenter made one doll chase the other in and out of the rows, the result being an apparently accidental spreading of one row. On the *candies-bunch* trial, the experimenter explained that one doll wanted to 'take his candies home' and therefore was going to 'put them in a bag'. The candies in one row were then scooped up and placed in a transparent plastic bag.

Standard condition. There were seven trials in the standard condition. The first five paralleled the five trials in the modified condition. The stimuli were identical to those on the modified trials, with the exception of the crickets trial, on which artificial crickets were substituted for the live ones. Both the initial and the final stimulus arrangements were similar to those on the modified trials; on the boats and cars trials, however, the stimuli were simply laid out on the table rather than presented in the tub or on the inclined board. The conservation question was identical to that in the modified condition.

The primary difference between the modified and standard conditions concerned the manner in which the conservation transformation was performed. In the standard condition the transformations were performed in the usual manner in conservation studies, i.e. by the experimenter's explicit spreading or bunching of one of the rows.

The last two trials used poker chips as stimuli. On both trials there were two rows of five chips; in one case a row was spread and in the other case a row was bunched. The purpose of these trials was to test for possible stimulus effects *per se*, that is, for the possibility that the use of interesting stimuli such as candies and toys might in itself facilitate performance.

Results and discussion

The percentage of correct judgements was 51 per cent in the modified condition and 43 per cent for the first five trials of the standard condition. A 2 (condition) by 2 (sex) analysis of variance revealed no significant difference between conditions, $F < 1$, d.f. $= 1, 76$. The effects of sex and condition by sex were also non-significant. These conclusions remain the same if an adequate explanation is made part of the criterion for conservation. In this case the percentage of correct responses was 42 per cent in the modified condition and 41 per cent in the standard condition.

Comparisons were also made, via chi-square tests, between the parallel trials in the two conditions (e.g. crickets in the modified condition vs. crickets in the standard condition). Again, no significant differences were found. There also were no significant differences in difficulty among the five trials of the modified condition or the seven trials of the standard condition, nor were there any significant effects of order of trial. McNemar's test of change was used for these within-subject comparisons.

Although performance was slightly better in the modified than in the standard condition, the difference was small and far from significant. The transformations of the modified condition appeared to elicit the same degree of erroneous responding as that found on typical conservation tests. The non-conservation errors on the modified trials appeared despite the fact that the transformation occurred in an ecologically natural manner and the role of the experimenter was minimized. This finding suggests that the standard conservation tests may indeed be relevant to the question of how children conceive of numbers in the natural environment. Clearly, however, this conclusion can be only tentatively advanced on the basis of a single study, especially a study in which so many different kinds of transformations are examined simultaneously. The purpose of the next two experiments was to probe further the issue of naturally occurring transformations, concentrating in each case on subsets of the types of stimulus objects and transformations sampled in the first study.

Experiment 2

The second experiment focused on one particular form of transformation examined in the first study, namely, the case in which animate objects change their position in space. Although the crickets trial of Expt 1 falls within this category, both the specific stimuli used and the manner in which they were presented may have militated against the familiarity and naturalness that were sought. The stimuli for the present study were undoubtedly familiar, since they consisted of other children from the subject's classroom. The transformations which they underwent were quite natural, resulting from the children's movements in the course of a game. The spatial rearrangement of one's peers is, of course, an everyday occurrence in the lives of young children – certainly much more common than the transformations typically examined in conservation research. The question now is whether young children who fail the typical conservation test really believe that the number of children changes as they watch their peers move closer together or farther apart.

Despite the ubiquity of such transformations in the child's natural environment, very few conservation studies have examined natural changes of animate objects. Curcio *et al.* (1971) reported significantly better (although still poor) performance on conservation-of-number tests using the child's own fingers as stimuli than on tests using pipe cleaners as stimuli. Macready & Macready (1974) obtained better performance on conservation of weight when the subject's or an adult's body was changed from a standing to a fetal position than when a doll was similarly transformed. Murray (1969), however, reported exactly the opposite result: better performance on tests of mass, weight, and volume with inanimate stimuli than with the child's own body as stimulus.

It should be noted that the new form of conservation test devised here, in which movements of other children constitute the transformation, differs from the standard tests in several ways in addition to the self-produced nature of the transformation. Of these differences, perhaps the most important is the fact that other children are not only familiar stimuli but *specifically* familiar stimuli – i.e. the child knows that the row consists of Johnny, Billy, Susie, etc. It seems quite possible that this knowledge of the specific identity of each stimulus might contribute to the recognition that the total number of stimuli is conserved in the face of perceptual change. As a test of this possibility, the standard condition in this study included four trials: two with identical poker chips as stimuli and two with five distinct Sesame Street dolls as stimuli. The latter stimuli approximated the children of the modified condition in distinctiveness and familiarity, without, however, possessing the quality of self-produced movement.

One difference between this experiment and Expt 1 should be mentioned. In the first study the focus was on equivalence conservation, i.e. the realization that two initially equal sets remain equal in the face of perceptual change. In the present study the focus was on identity conservation, i.e. the realization that the number of objects in a single set is not affected by a perceptual change.

Children

Fifty-three kindergarten children received the verbal pre-test described below. Of the 43 children who passed the pre-test, 18 boys and 18 girls (mean age = 5:5) were chosen for the main experiment.

Procedure

Each child participated in three experimental sessions: the verbal pre-test, the standard assessment, and the modified assessment. The pre-test was always the first session, with the order of the two experimental conditions balanced across subjects. The average time between the first and second session was five days; that between the second and third session was six days. Different experimenters administered the two experimental conditions for a given child.

Verbal pre-test. The stimuli for the pre-test were the same as those in Expt 1: blocks for the first two trials, pennies for the next two (if an error occurred with the blocks), and blocks for the last two (if an error occurred with the pennies). The specific procedure was different from that in Expt 1, since in this case the goal was to test the child's understanding of the wording to be used on problems of identity conservation. Each trial began with a row of two objects. The experimenter then slid a book next to the objects and lifted them onto the book. On half the trials a third object was already in place on the book, and on half the book was empty. The question was, 'Is the number of blocks now (gesture toward the book) the same as when we started (gesture toward the table) or is the number different?' (the order of phrases was alternated from trial to trial). Only children who could eventually respond correctly on both the 'same' and 'different' trials were retained for the study.

Modified condition. Children were brought in groups of six to an unused classroom in the school. The groups always contained three boys and three girls drawn from the same class. Two experimenters were used, one (experimenter 1) to ask the conservation questions of each child individually and the other (experimenter 2) to play a Simon Says game with the remaining five children.

At the start of the session the children were told that they would be playing two games: one in a group with experimenter 2, and the other seated individually at a table with experimenter 1. Five of the children were lined up in a row, with about two feet separating adjacent children. The rules for Simon Says were reviewed, and various examples of possible commands and appropriate responses were given. Experimenter 2 explained that in the course of the game Simon would give three commands that were especially important: 'go to your starts', which would mean to go to the places in which they were now standing; 'spread out', which would mean to move far apart, with the children at the ends of the rows moving to opposite ends of the room; and 'bunch together', which would mean to move close together so that their shoulders touched.

Once the instructions had been given, the remaining child was seated at a table about 4 m from the row of children, and the Simon Says game began. In the course of the game a variety of commands were given; the only ones of importance, however, as well as the only ones involving a change in the length of the row, were the three indicated above. The game began with the children remaining in their start positions for about 10 seconds. During this time, experimenter 1 drew the attention of the child at the table to the way 'the children look in their starts'. The spread-out command was then given. Once the row had reached its maximum length, the child was asked, 'Is the number of children now the same as when they were in their starts, or is it different?' (on half the trials the order of phrases was reversed). The row remained spread until a clear judgement had been given and an attempt made at eliciting an explanation. The children then returned to their start positions, remained there for about 10 seconds, then bunched together in response to the bunch command, at which time the second conservation question was asked.

Following completion of both the spread and bunch trials, the tested child took a place in the row and another child sat down to be tested. In this way eventually all six children were tested. Both the use of background music and the general noise level prevented children in the row from hearing the conservation questions or answers.

Standard condition. There were four trials in the standard condition, two with poker chips as stimuli and two with Sesame Street dolls as stimuli. The order of the chips and dolls trials was balanced across subjects.

Each trial began with the experimenter laying down a row of five objects. As in the modified condition, the objects were left in place for a few seconds and the child's attention was drawn to the initial appearance. On the first trial for a given material the objects were spread, and on the second trial they were bunched. Since a verbal label was necessarily applied to the transformations in the modified condition, a similar label was used in the standard condition (e.g. 'Now I spread them out'). The conservation question was, 'Is the number of chips (or "friends" for the Sesame Street dolls) now the same as when we started or is it different?' (on half the trials the order of phrases was reversed).

Results and discussion

Preliminary analyses revealed no significant differences as a function of sex. Results for the two sexes are therefore combined in the analyses that follow.

As noted, explanations as well as judgements were elicited in both the modified and the standard conditions. The practical constraints of the Simon Says game, however, precluded probing of unclear explanations to the extent that was possible in the standard condition. For this reason, the condition comparisons that follow utilize a judgements-only criterion.

The percentage of correct judgements was 57 per cent in the modified condition and 53 per cent in the standard condition – 51 per cent on the trials with chips and 56 per cent on the trials with dolls. There were no significant differences between performance in the modified condition and that on the chips trials, the dolls trials, or both kinds of standard trial combined (here and throughout, the test statistic was the Wilcoxon signed ranks test unless otherwise noted). There were also no significant differences between performance on the chips trials and performance on the dolls trials.

Various other possible determinants of performance were examined. There were no significant differences between performance in the first experimental session and that in the second session (within sample $t < 1$). There were no significant differences between performance on the first trial for a given stimulus and that on the second trial (which also means, in this particular case, no difference between the spread and bunch transformations). Finally, it was thought possible that responses in the modified condition might be affected by the extent to which the child had had experience as a member of the expanding or contracting row prior to being tested. Performance was therefore examined as a function of ordinal position of testing. There was no indication that this variable had any effect.

As in the first experiment, children were no more likely to recognize the invariance of number in the modified than in the standard condition. This equivalence of performance occurred despite several factors that might have been expected to facilitate performance on the modified trials: the naturalness and familiarity of the type of transformation, the very great familiarity and interest value of other children as stimuli, and the child's specific knowledge of each of the other children as a distinct individual. Despite these seemingly conducive factors, children responded in the same way to other children moving about a room as they did to chips being spread on a table.

Experiment 3

The focus in Expt 3 was on transformations that occur either accidentally or incidentally. As noted, McGarrigle & Donaldson (1974) reported substantially better performance when the conservation transformation occurred in an apparently accidental manner, via the machinations of the naughty teddy bear. This finding has since been replicated by both Light *et al.* (1979) and Dockrell *et al.* (1980), although in both studies the differences between the accidental and standard conditions were less marked than in McGarrigle & Donaldson. In addition, Light *et al.* found that an incidental transformation – that is, a change produced intentionally but in a casual manner in the context of some other activity – also led to better performance than did the standard test.

The accidental and incidental transformations examined in Expt 1 (the two candies trials) did not result in superior performance. The comparable manipulations in the present study differed in two ways from those in Expt 1. First, the transformations were not embedded in a series of other sorts of trials; rather a given child received only accidental or only incidental changes. Second, each child received two such trials. One trial was a virtual replication of the manipulation used in either McGarrigle & Donaldson (for the accidental condition) or Light *et al.* (for the incidental condition). The other trial was a new accidental or incidental manipulation not examined before. The new trial in the accidental condition involved a change that was made to appear literally accidental, in contrast to changes brought about by a teddy bear or doll operated by the experimenter. This study is the first to examine such a literally accidental change.

Children

The subjects were 120 kindergarten children (mean age = 5:6), 40 of whom were randomly assigned to the accidental condition, 40 of whom were assigned to the incidental condition, and 40 of whom were assigned to the standard condition. There were 20 boys and 20 girls in each condition.

Procedure

Both the accidental and the incidental conditions were presented in the context of a 'Halloween game'. The stimuli for the game were candies of various sorts and two toy pumpkins with openings at the top. One pumpkin was designated as the child's and placed about 1 m in front of him or her; the other was designated as the experimenter's and placed about 1 m in front of her. The experimenter explained that the object of the game was to see who could succeed in throwing more candies into his or her pumpkin. She stressed that it was important that the game be fair and that the two players therefore always start with exactly the same number of candies.

Accidental quantity. Two conservation problems (balanced for order) were presented within the accidental condition, one for conservation of quantity and one for conservation of number. On quantity trials the experimenter and child began with 12 candies each, dropped in a paired fashion into two identical transparent cups. The experimenter began by asking 'Do we have the same number of candies or does one of us have more candies than the other?' and the game proceeded only once the child had agreed to the equality. On the first trial the experimenter and child simply played the candy-throwing game. The second trial began in a similar manner with the establishment of initial equality. Before the candies could be thrown, however, the experimenter, while reaching out, knocked over her cup in an apparently accidental manner, the result being that her candies spread across the table. After verbalizing the fact that an accident had occurred, the experimenter went on to say, 'Let me be sure that it's still fair. Do we have the same number of candies, or does one of us have more candies than the other?' If the child indicated that the numbers were the same the game proceeded. If the child indicated that one player had more he or she was asked how to make the numbers equal, and the game proceeded only once the correction had been made.

Accidental number. The first number trial began with five candies already in place as the experimenter's row, next to which five candies were laid down as the child's row. In addition to the instructions about fairness and the establishment of initial equality, the lead-in in this case included one additional element: the introduction of a 'Halloween witch'. The witch (a 14 cm high wax figure) was presented in a manner identical to that used for McGarrigle & Donaldson's teddy bear: as a naughty figure who was kept in a box but who might at some time escape and try to spoil the game. The first candy-throwing trial then proceeded without incident. On the second trial, however, the witch did escape, running around the table (just as did McGarrigle & Donaldson's teddy bear) and spreading out the experimenter's candies. Once the witch had been captured and returned to her box, the experimenter said, 'Let me be sure that it's still fair. Do we have the same number of candies, or does one of us have more candies than the other?' Again, the candies were adjusted prior to the throwing game if the child so requested.

Incidental quantity. The incidental condition also included one quantity problem and one number problem, again balanced for order. As in the accidental condition, the first quantity trial was used simply to introduce the candy-throwing game. After establishing the initial equality on the second trial, the experimenter suddenly noticed that the cup holding the child's candies was chipped. Expressing concern about possible injury, she decided to transfer the candies to a new container. The new container turned out to be lower and wider than the original one, thus resulting in a lower level of candies. The procedure from this point on – the verbalization about fairness, the conservation question, and the opportunity for adjustment of the stimuli – was identical to that in the accidental condition.

Incidental number. The incidental number problem was preceded by two trials on which the candy-throwing game was played in a manner identical to that described for the accidental condition (without, however, any mention of a Halloween witch). After the second trial, the experimenter indicated that the child was finished with this portion of the game, but that she would appreciate his or her help in fixing the game for the next child. Two rows of five candies were laid down, and the child verified that the numbers were equal. The experimenter then suddenly remembered, however, that when the child had played the game only the experimenter's candies had initially been in place, the child's candies being subsequently taken from a bag and laid down next to the experimenter's. Indicating that the game should start in the same way for all the children, the experimenter scooped up the candies that had been designated for the next child and placed them in a transparent plastic bag. With the bunched-up candies next to the experimenter's still spread-out row, the experimenter then indicated the need to check on the fairness of the game and went on to ask the conservation question.

Standard condition. There were four trials in the standard condition, two for quantity and two for number. The stimuli were identical to those in the accidental and incidental condition, as was the wording of the conservation question. Both the initial and the final appearance of the stimuli paralleled the appearance of the stimuli on the four accidental and incidental trials. The difference between conditions lay in the manner in which the transformation was performed. In this case there was no Halloween game; rather the experimenter transformed the stimuli in the deliberate, explicit manner typical in conservation research. Thus, on one quantity trial the experimenter poured the candies onto the table and on the other she poured them into a wider container; on one number trial she spread the candies and on the other she bunched them. The order of quantity and number problems was balanced, as was the order of trials within a concept. The standard conservation explanation was not elicited; as in the other two conditions, however, the child was asked how to make the numbers equal whenever a non-conservation judgement was given.

Results

The percentages of correct responses for the three conditions and six kinds of trials are shown in Table 1. Preliminary analyses indicated no significant differences as a function of sex; this variable is consequently omitted in the subsequent analyses.

This study examined four new methods of presenting conservation trials. In each case, the interest was in whether the new version resulted in better performance than a comparable standard test. Specific planned comparisons were therefore deemed more appropriate than an overall analysis of variance. Four planned t tests were carried out, each one comparing one of the modified tests with its parallel standard test. In three of the four cases the new test resulted in significantly better performance: accidental quantity better than standard quantity, $t = 2.13$, d.f. $= 78$, $P < 0.05$; incidental number better than standard number, $t = 3.72$, d.f. $= 78$, $P < 0.01$; incidental quantity better than standard quantity, $t = 2.42$, d.f. $= 78$, $P < 0.05$. The only test that failed to elicit superior performance was the accidental number test, $t = 1.10$, d.f. $= 78$, $P > 0.10$.

Table 1. Percentage of correct responses for the three experimental conditions

	Type of problem		
Condition	Number	Quantity	Total
Accidental	73	78	75
Incidental	93	80	86
Standard	61	56	59

Although the usual conservation explanation was not elicited, the child was asked how to make the collections equal whenever a non-conservation judgement was given. Suggestions to add or subtract candies occurred on 51 per cent of the non-conservation trials, suggestions to restore the initial perceptual appearance occurred on 45 per cent of the trials, and 4 per cent of the responses were uninterpretable.

General discussion

The results of Expt 3 stand in contrast to those of the first two studies. In this case, three of the four modified tests led to better performance than the comparable standard test. The only exception was the accidental number trial, on which a modest mean difference fell well short of statistical significance.

It should be noted that the accidental number trial used here, while quite similar to McGarrigle & Donaldson's procedure, did differ from it in several ways. The changes that were made, however, would seem likely to enhance rather than reduce any superiority of the modified assessment. Specifically, the major such changes were the use of a single trial rather than the four 'accidents' engineered by McGarrigle & Donaldson, and the use of a between-subjects rather than within-subjects design for comparing conditions. It might be expected that producing the transformation in an apparently accidental manner would work best on first occurrence and would diminish in plausibility and effectiveness as repeated 'accidents' occur. It might also be expected that the accidental manipulation would work best if the child had not previously been exposed to the standard transformations and standard questioning. The basis for the discrepancy between the present results and those of McGarrigle & Donaldson thus remains unclear.

One conclusion that does seem clear from the studies reported here is that adoption of a more natural form of conservation transformation does not necessarily lead to better performance by children. As suggested in the discussion of Expt 1, this finding provides an important extension with respect to the external validity of standard Piagetian assessment. The fact that children believe that the number of chips changes when an adult spreads them on the table is both well validated and remarkable. The fact that they believe that the number of other children changes as the children move about is a new finding that is in some ways more remarkable still.

Although the tests utilized here may have increased the naturalness of conservation assessment, it must be noted that most of the modified transformations still provided only a partial analogue of the real-life situations of interest. In particular, most of the tests retained an explicit focus on number and on the operations that may affect number that is clearly not found in most of the child's real-life dealings with objects. Consider the procedure just discussed, the Simon Says game of Expt 2. Although children may often see other children move about, they do not usually have their attention explicitly drawn to the movement, and they are not usually explicitly asked about the number of children before and after the change. Or consider the witch trial of Expt 3. The witch was introduced, following McGarrigle & Donaldson, as someone who might 'spoil the game', and indeed the only apparent purpose of her actions, and of the experimenter's subsequent question, was the possibility that spreading the candies might in fact change the number and thereby ruin the game. When the context for the conservation task retains such an explicit focus on number and the possibility of change in number, the exact manner in which the transformation is produced may have little effect on the child's judgement.

This discussion raises a possible explanation for the superior performance elicited by three of the four modified trials in Expt 3. In this case, the Halloween game provided a natural context for the experimenter to ask about the number of candies both before and after the perceptual change. In addition, the transformation was not the sole focus of attention that it usually is in conservation studies, but rather occurred in a casual manner in the course of playing the game. The procedure was such that the child was still required to attend to the change and make an explicit judgement about number following it. Nevertheless, the peripheral nature of the transformation may have made it less likely that the possibility of a change in number would even occur to the child. If so, the superior performance in the modified conditions might be more accurately described as an avoidance of non-conservation than as an explicit avowal of conservation.

The fact that different methods of assessing conservation can lead to different levels of performance has long been clear (e.g. S. Miller, 1976; P. Miller, 1978). What sense can be made of this diversity in performance? As Light *et al.* argue, there is little warrant in designating any single method of assessment as *the* best test of conservation, or in automatically relegating results from other methods to the categories of false positives or false negatives. Both the wrong answers on Expt 3's standard trials and the right answers on its modified trials can be defended as legitimate measures of the child's ability to conserve. More generally, it is a long-established (thought still little understood) fact that for a period in development children's ability to express certain kinds of knowledge, or to avoid certain kinds of errors, depends very much on the immediate context. The new contexts examined here indicate that the phenomenon of non-conservation is by no means limited to the kinds of stimuli and transformations typically utilized in laboratory studies. They also indicate, however, that non-conservation may be less likely in a more natural context that places less emphasis on number and the possibility of a change in number. And among all the different methods of assessing a concept, certainly special attention must be given to those that come closest to the real-life situations of interest.

Acknowledgements

I am grateful to the staff and children of Glen Springs, Lake Forest, Littlewood and P. K. Yonge Elementary Schools, Gainesville, Florida for their generous cooperation. I also thank Dan Zehler for his collaboration on Expt 1, Lynn Woodward for her assistance with the testing in Expt 2, and Carla Stubbs for her assistance with the testing in Expt 3.

References

Curcio, F., Robbins, O. & Ela, S. S. (1971). The role of body parts and readiness in acquisition of number conservation. *Child Development*, **43**, 1641–1646.

Dockrell, J., Campbell, R. & Neilson, I. (1980). Conservation accidents revisited. *International Journal of Behavioral Development*, **3**, 423–439.

Light, P. H., Buckingham, N. & Robbins, A. H. (1979). The conservation task as an interactional setting. *British Journal of Educational Psychology*, **49**, 304–310.

Macready, C. & Macready, G. B. (1974). Conservation of weight in self, others, and objects. *Journal of Experimental Psychology*, **103**, 372–374.

McGarrigle, J. & Donaldson, M. (1974). Conservation accidents. *Cognition*, **3**, 341–350.

Miller, P. H. (1978). Stimulus variables in conservation: An alternative approach to assessment. *Merrill-Palmer Quarterly*, **24**, 141–160.

Miller, S. A. (1976). Nonverbal assessment of Piagetian concepts. *Psychological Bulletin*, **83**, 405–430.

Murray, F. B. (1969). Conservation in self and object. *Psychological Reports*, **25**, 941–942.

Piaget, J. & Szeminska, A. (1952). *The Child's Conception of Number*. New York: Humanities Press.

Requests for reprints should be addressed to Scott A. Miller, Department of Psychology, University of Florida, Gainesville, FL 32611, USA.

British Journal of Psychology (1982), **73**, 231–234   *Printed in Great Britain*

Social factors in conservation

David J. Hargreaves, Colleen G. Molloy and **Alan R. Pratt**

This study is a partial replication, with variations, of the experiments of McGarrigle & Donaldson (1975) and Light *et al.* (1979). Sixty-four 5-year-old children were tested on traditional Piagetian tests of conservation of number under a standard control condition, and one of two experimental conditions: one (*M*) in which the task materials were apparently accidentally transformed by a mischievous monkey manipulated by a second experimenter, and another (*I*) in which the transformation was made to appear irrelevant to the main purpose of the task. The frequency of initial conserving responses was higher in the two experimental conditions than in the control, and this effect was strongest for the *I* condition. All groups of children but one appeared to exhibit a response set such that initial judgements were preserved in the second test condition. These results are discussed in relation to those of the other two studies, and their implications for Piagetian theory are considered.

One of the central features of the newly emerging field of social cognition is an interest in the social context of cognitive test situations, and several studies (e.g. Rose & Blank, 1974) have concentrated upon Piaget's classic conservation tasks (e.g. Piaget, 1952). McGarrigle & Donaldson (1975) contrasted 4–6-year-old children's performances on standard tests of number and length conservation, in which the experimenter's transformation of the materials is explicitly *intentional*, with conditions in which the transformation appeared to the child to be *accidental*; a 'naughty' teddy bear, manipulated by the experimenter, 'spoilt' the conservation 'game'. There was a substantial rise in the frequency of conserving responses under these latter conditions; this result calls into question the view that pre-operational children cannot understand the invariance principle, and suggests that it is vital to take extra-linguistic aspects of the test situation into account when assessing cognitive abilities.

Light *et al.* (1979) carried out a partial replication of McGarrigle & Donaldson's experiment, and found that although there was a higher 'success rate' for conservation responses in the accidental than in the intentional condition, the overall level of conserving judgements was much lower. They also carried out a second study in which the transformation of stimulus materials was made to seem incidental to a competitive game; this proved even more effective than the accidental condition in increasing the proportion of conserving responses. This may partly arise from the fact that the experimenter openly manipulated the teddy bear in the latter condition; it seems very likely that children would link the actions of the bear with the intentions of the experimenter, such that the validity of this as an 'accidental' transformation must be called into question. In Light *et al.*'s 'incidental' condition, however, no such link can be made, and conservation rates were correspondingly higher.

The present study is in two parts. The first is a further partial replication of McGarrigle & Donaldson's (1975) experiment, with an important variation. In order to eliminate any possibility of the child linking the actions of the disrupting agent with the questions of the tester, two experimenters were used to carry out each part of the accidental condition procedure independently; we predict that this should increase the effectiveness of this condition in producing conservation responses. A further minor variation is that a glove puppet monkey (approximately 9 in tall) was used in place of the teddy bear; monkeys are traditionally regarded as being more mischievous than teddy bears, and this may add to the realism of this condition. The second part of the study involves an experimental

0007/1269/82/020231-04 $02.00/0

condition that resembles Light *et al.*'s 'incidental' condition in that the transformation is made to appear irrelevant to the main activity of the child. In this condition a second experimenter (E_2) interrupts the testing session at an appropriate stage and attempts to remove the test materials; when instructed to return them by the first experimenter (E_1) s/he complies, but leaves them in a transformed state.

Method
Children

Participants were 64 normal children from two primary schools serving the same (predominantly middle-class) geographical area of a Leicester suburb. They ranged in age from 5·0 to 5·11 years, with a mean of 5·5 years, and there were approximately equal numbers of boys and girls in the sample.

Design

Each child was tested on conservation of equality and of inequality of number under *control* conditions, and under either one of the two experimental conditions, *monkey* or *interruption*. Children were randomly assigned to one or the other of these such that the age distribution and composition by sex of each group were approximately the same. Within each group, half the children were given both tests in the experimental condition before being tested on the control condition, while for the other half the order was reversed. The order of appearance of the equality and inequality tasks was counterbalanced within each of these subgroups. One of the experimenters was male, and the other female; in order to avoid any experimenter sex effects, the roles of E_1 and E_2 were enacted by each for half the children in each subgroup.

Procedure

In the *control* condition (C), the procedure, wording of questions and task materials were identical to those in McGarrigle & Donaldson's intentional transformation condition, with E_1 carrying out the transformation as well as eliciting both pre- and post-transformation judgements.

In the *monkey* condition (M), the test materials and wording of questions were identical to those in McGarrigle & Donaldson's accidental transformation condition, though the procedure was modified in order to include E_2. E_1 first introduced the child to E_2 and to 'Micky', the mischievous monkey. The child was told that Micky was being held captive under the table by E_2 because he was very naughty, and likely to attempt to escape and 'spoil the game'. E_1 arranged the materials, and elicited the pre-transformation judgement. E_2 then 'lost control' of the monkey, expressed surprise at having done so, and the monkey appropriately transformed the materials. After 'regaining control', E_2 ticked off the monkey for his misdemeanours, and returned him under the table to be held still so that the game could proceed. At this point E_1 elicited the post-transformation judgement from the child.

In the *interruption* condition (I), E_2 first explained to the child that s/he was 'busy next door' with a similar game, and went away into a play area that was divided from the rest of the classroom by a large screen displaying the children's art work: in this way the interaction between E_1 and the child could be heard. After E_1 had elicited the pre-transformation judgement, E_2 interrupted the task on the pretext of borrowing some counters, and picked up one row with the intention of taking them 'next door'. At this point E_1 pointed out that the counters were still in use, and suggested that E_2 should look for more in the cupboard next door. E_2, satisfied with this, returned the counters to the table, transformed appropriately, and E_1 elicited the post-transformation judgement.

Although all three experimental situations were closely scripted in order to standardize the procedures, they were staged in such a way as to make the interactions appear as natural and spontaneous as possible. Slight modifications to the wording were required for the second task (either equality or inequality) in the M and I conditions, in order to maintain this spontaneity.

Results

Children's responses were judged, following McGarrigle & Donaldson, as conserving or non-conserving without justifications being required; all results are summarized in Table 1. As a check that the base-line level of conservation ability was the same in the two groups of children, a χ^2 test was carried out to compare the number of children in each group

Table 1. Number of conservers and non-conservers in each condition in the two groups of children, on both tasks

	Monkey group (*M*)				Interruption group (*I*)			
	$M \rightarrow C$ (*n* = 16)		$C \rightarrow M$ (*n* = 16)		$I \rightarrow C$ (*n* = 16)		$C \rightarrow I$ (*n* = 16)	
Equality task								
Conservers	9	9	5	5	15	9	9	7
Non-conservers	7	7	11	11	1	7	7	9
Inequality task								
Conservers	9	10	6	6	13	10	6	6
Non-conservers	7	6	10	10	3	6	10	10

giving conserving versus non-conserving judgements *in the control condition when this came first*, for the equality and inequality tasks combined: this was $\chi^2 = 1\cdot04$, d.f. = 1, $P > 0\cdot05$. This value is well below that required for statistical significance, and so we can confidently assert that the two groups start with equivalent levels of ability.

In order to compare the overall proportions of conserving responses in the three conditions, χ^2 tests were carried out on the number of children giving conserving vs. non-conserving judgements *on their first response only* in each condition: these were $\chi^2 = 11\cdot14$, d.f. = 2, $P < 0\cdot01$ for the equality task, and $\chi^2 = 8\cdot28$, d.f. = 2, $P < 0\cdot05$ for the inequality task. Further inspection of Table 1 reveals that by far the highest 'success rate' for conservation responses was that in the *I* condition: 15/16 and 13/16 subjects conserved in the equality and inequality tasks respectively. The equivalent figures for the *C* condition were 14/32 and 12/32, and for the *M* condition, 9/16 and 9/16.

To investigate the significance of changes in frequency of conserving responses between the two conditions of testing within each group of children, it was intended to apply the McNemar test for the significance of changes (Siegel, 1956). This proved to be impossible as the overall number of changes between conditions was so slow that the expected frequencies for the test were very small. It was therefore decided to combine results from the equality and inequality tasks; this seemed to be justifiable since children's patterns of response in the two tasks appeared to be similar in the previous analysis, and Light *et al.* (1979) had followed a similar course in their study. Expected frequencies were still too small for the McNemar test to be applied, so the binomial test was used for each of the four testing orders ($M \rightarrow C$, $C \rightarrow M$, $I \rightarrow C$ and $C \rightarrow I$). The only result to reach significance at the 0·05 level, using either two-tailed or one-tailed tests, was that nine children changed from conserving responses in the *I* condition to non-conserving responses in the subsequent *C* condition, with no children changing in the reverse direction (binomial $P = 0\cdot004$). There were no significant changes when *I* followed *C*, nor for any of the children in the *M* group (all binomial *P*s $\geqslant 0\cdot5$).

Discussion

The findings from the analysis of children's first responses, which are free from any transfer effects, demonstrate that the *I* condition was more effective than *M* in producing conserving responses (approximately 88 and 56 per cent of children respectively, for the equality and inequality tasks combined). Approximately 41 per cent of children conserved on their first response under *C* conditions, which indicates that the difficulty level of the task was appropriate for our experimental children. This latter figure is higher than the equivalents in the studies of McGarrigle & Donaldson and Light *et al.*, and may explain why the 'success rate' in our *I* condition is even higher than that in Light *et al.*'s 'incidental' condition. It is therefore rather surprising that our prediction that our *M* condition should be *more* effective in producing conserving responses than McGarrigle & Donaldson's accidental transformation condition was not confirmed. Light *et al.*, who found a similar discrepancy between their own and McGarrigle & Donaldson's results, speculate that differences in the socio-economic backgrounds of the samples may be an important factor. Despite these discrepancies, however, our findings are consistent with those of both studies in indicating that the overall frequency of conserving responses is greater in both experimental conditions than in the control.

The results from the analysis of changes within groups suggest that, with the exception of one group, most children show a response set; having settled on a particular response in the first condition, they are unlikely to change it in the second. This is in line with Rose & Blank's (1974) notion that 'the implicit contextual cues which the child first encounters play a large role in determining the response he will employ on... all subsequent related tasks' (p. 502). The implication is that repeated measures designs introduce their own social constraints, and should therefore presumably be complemented by the use of independent groups designs in this research area. The one group that did not exhibit a response set effect was that in which the *I* condition was followed by *C*: a significant proportion of children changed from conserving to non-conserving responses.

Whilst the broad pattern of our results lends support to the view that pre-operational children are more likely to conserve when the transformation of the task materials is made to seem accidental, or incidental to the main purpose of the interaction, this latter, exceptional result suggests that conspicuously high 'success rates' obtained in this way may be followed by normal, lower levels of conservation responses when the task is repeated on the same children under standard conditions. The most likely explanation of this is that whilst pre-operational children may exhibit an understanding of the principle of number invariance when the conditions of assessment are optimal, under 'normal' circumstances they do not. The vital question posed for Piagetian theory is whether or not this leads to the generalization that many instances of conservation failure in young children reflect some kind of performance deficit, rather than a lack of operational competence. Social and interpersonal aspects of the test situation are fundamental to our understanding of the child's response, and should not be regarded merely as surface phenomena; Piaget realized this long ago, when expressing the view that 'the decentering of cognitive constructions necessary for the development of the operations is inseparable from the decentering of affective and social constructions' (Piaget & Inhelder, 1969, p. 95).

Acknowledgements

We should like to thank the heads, teachers and children of Launde Infants School and Sandhurst Infants School, Oadby, Leicester, for their cooperation. We are grateful to Professor P. E. Bryant and an anonymous reviewer for some valuable editorial suggestions.

References

Light, P. H., Buckingham, N. & Robbins, A. I. (1979). The conservation task as an interactional setting. *British Journal of Educational Psychology*, **49**, 304–310.

McGarrigle, J. & Donaldson, M. (1975). Conservation accidents. *Cognition*, **3**, 341–350.

Piaget, J. (1952). *The Child's Conception of Number*. London: Routledge & Kegan Paul.

Piaget, J. & Inhelder, B. (1969). *The Psychology of the Child*. London: Routledge & Kegan Paul.

Rose, S. & Blank, M. (1974). The potency of context in children's cognition: An illustration through conservation. *Child Development*, **45**, 499–502.

Siegel, S. (1956). *Nonparametric Statistics for the Behavioral Sciences*. New York: McGraw-Hill.

Requests for reprints should be addressed to Dr D. J. Hargreaves, Department of Psychology, The University, Leicester LE1 7RH, UK.

British Journal of Psychology (1982), **73**, 235–241   *Printed in Great Britain*

Young children's use of transitive inference in causal chains

Thomas R. Shultz, Seymour Pardo and **Esther Altmann**

Mediate causal transmissions are those in which the transmission between an initial cause and an eventual effect is mediated by a third event. The concept of causal mediation is seen as analogous to that involving use of a middle term in non-causal transitive inference problems. Contrary to some previous research, both three- and five-year-olds understood mediate causal transmission as portrayed in simple, three-term causal chains. Children of both ages chose to activate a cause which could produce an effective causal mediator over an alternative cause which could produce an ineffective causal mediator. The five-year-olds in addition correctly identified the impossibility of producing the effect without an appropriate causal mediator and often mentioned the causal mediator explicitly in verbal justifications of their responses. Relations between the present experiment and previous literature on causal reasoning and transitive inference are discussed.

In his latest work on causal reasoning, Piaget (1974) maintained that pre-operational children (below about seven to eight years of age) were incapable of understanding mediate causal transmissions. Mediate causal transmissions are those in which the transmission between initial cause and eventual effect is mediated by some third factor. The results of several different experiments were used to support this conclusion. In one, the intermediary was a row of marbles, the last of which started rolling after the first had been hit by an active marble. In another, the red liquid originally in one glass was exchanged (behind a screen) with the green liquid originally in a second glass, using a third glass as the intermediary. The child was asked to explain how each effect could have occurred, and it was reported that children younger than seven to eight years failed to do so. Piaget linked these failures with the young child's difficulties on non-causal transitive inference problems, in which relations (usually of length) between a common term and each of two others imply a certain relationship between the two others. However, a number of experiments have shown that children as young as four years of age can solve such problems if memory for the premises is ensured (Bryant & Trabasso, 1971; Bryant, 1974). Whether these successful performances actually involve transitive deductive inference is controversial (Deboysson-Bardies & O'Regan, 1973; Trabasso, 1975; Thayer & Collyer, 1978; Breslow, 1981).

   The purpose of the present investigation was to determine whether young, *pre-operational* children could employ transitive inference in reasoning about simple causal chains. A causal chain is the simplifying hypothesis that one event (say X) causes a second (Y) which, in turn, causes a third (Z), etc. (Bunge, 1979). For such a chain, if an observer believes that event Z can be produced by the activation of event X, then presumably it is because s/he understands that event Y functions as a causal mediator. To control for the possibility that the observer activates X simply because of a lack of alternative responses, the present experiment allowed responses to either X (which led to Y and thus to Z) or X' (which caused Y' which failed to cause Z).

Method

Children

Ten girls and 10 boys at each of two age levels, three and five years, were recruited from a day-care centre and a kindergarten class in urban Montreal. The mean ages of the two groups were 3·5 and 5·3 years, respectively. The children were from either working-class or middle-class families. Five of the three-year-olds spoke French as a first language and were

0007-1269/82/020235-07 $02.00/0 © 1982 The British Psychological Society

tested in French. The remaining children spoke English as a first language and were tested in English.

Apparatus and procedure

An apparatus was constructed to illustrate each of two different causal chains. A schematic top view of each of the problems is presented in Fig. 1. The so-called *lanes* problem, illustrated in Fig. 1a consisted of two lanes which started in parallel at points X and X', narrowed at points Y and Y', and then converged at point Z at an angle of 38°. The parallel sections were 25·4 cm long and the converging sections were 42·2 cm long. The lanes were 6·4 cm wide in their parallel sections and 5·1 cm wide in their converging sections. The lanes were banked with walls 3·8 cm high and the entire platform was tilted 6° towards the Z position. A tennis ball could be placed at positions X or X' and rolled down its respective lane. Two golf balls were placed at positions Y and Y' on either side of a plexiglass arch which blocked the progress of any of the balls. The experimenter demonstrated the effect by pushing a light plastic ball positioned at Z so that it rolled 10·2 cm from its position. She explained that the child was to make the Z ball fall from its position but only by placing the tennis ball at X or X' and rolling it down its respective lane. Since the tennis ball could not pass through the plexiglass arches or the narrow converging lanes, the position of the causally mediating Y and Y' golf balls was critical. Position Y was on the far side of the arch and thus could roll to position Z after being struck by ball X through the arch. In contrast, position Y' was on the near side of the arch and so was prevented from rolling even if struck by ball X'. Each child received 10 trials, five of which had Y on the left and Y' on the right and five of which had the reverse. The order was randomized separately for each child to control for any left–right orientation preferences. Choices were recorded for each of these 10 trials. One the 11th trial, *both* intermediate balls were placed on the near side of the arch (position Y') and the child was asked if s/he could still produce the effect. After both the 10th and 11th trials, the child was asked to verbally justify his/her decision, and these justifications were recorded in writing.

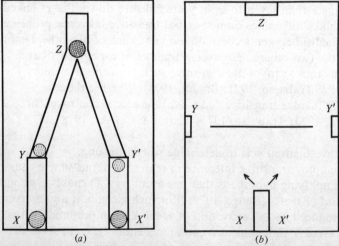

Figure 1. Schematic top view of the *lanes* (*a*), and *light* (*b*) problems. (See text for further explanation.)

The second causal chain, illustrated in Fig. 1*b* involved the transmission of *light*, by reflection off a mirror onto a target. The experimenter demonstrated the effect by shining a 20·3 cm long flashlight directly onto a 12·7 cm square (position Z). Then she mounted the flashlight on a swivel 69·6 cm away from the target, explaining that the child was to turn the flashlight either to the left or to the right in order to make the light hit the target. The direct path to the target was blocked by a 42·5 cm long wooden barrier positioned 31 cm from the flashlight. A small mirror was placed on the side walls 7·6 cm from each end of the barrier, one with the reflecting surface exposed (Y) and the other with the non-reflecting surface (Y') exposed. When the flashlight was directed towards the exposed reflecting surface of the mirror (X), the light reflected off the mirror (Y) hitting the target (Z). When the flashlight was directed towards the non-reflecting surface (X'), no light could be seen to hit the target. Each child received 10 trials, five of which had the reflecting surface exposed at the left side of the barrier and the non-reflecting surface at the right side of the barrier, and five of which had the reverse. As in the other causal chain, the order was randomly determined separately for each child. On the 11th trial, the non-reflecting surfaces were exposed at both sides of the barrier, and the child was asked if s/he could still produce the effect. Verbal justifications were solicited and recorded as above.

Results

Correct choices on each of the first 10 trials were coded as 1 and incorrect choices were coded as 0. Lunney (1970) has shown that analysis of variance can be appropriately applied to dichotomous data if there are sufficient degrees of freedom in the error terms. These data were subjected to an analysis of variance in which age and gender served as between-subjects factors and apparatus and trial served as within-subject factors. The analysis yielded main effects of age ($F = 13\cdot91$, d.f. $= 1, 36$, $P < 0\cdot001$) and trial ($F = 5\cdot19$, d.f. $= 9, 324$, $P < 0\cdot001$).

The mean proportions of correct choices for each age and trial are shown in Table 1. Five-year-olds obtained a greater proportion of correct choices ($\bar{X} = 0\cdot862$) than did three-year-olds ($\bar{X} = 0\cdot688$). By chance alone, the most likely mean proportion of correct responses would be $0\cdot50$. The mean number of correct choices for both three-year-olds and five-year-olds was found to exceed this theoretical mean using a modification of Dunnett's (1955) procedure for comparing treatment means with a control mean, $P < 0\cdot005$. Thus, both three- and five-year-olds, as groups, could be said to have solved these mediate transmission problems.

Table 1. Mean proportion of correct choices on trials 1–10

	Age	
Trial	3 years	5 years
1	0·500	0·600
2	0·675*	0·775**
3	0·575	0·850**
4	0·750**	0·925**
5	0·675*	0·900**
6	0·675*	0·800**
7	0·725**	0·925**
8	0·775**	0·900**
9	0·775**	0·975**
10	0·750**	0·975**

Note. Means marked with * differ from the theoretical value of $0\cdot50$ at $P < 0\cdot05$; those marked with ** differ from $0\cdot50$ at $P < 0\cdot005$.

The modification of Dunnett's technique was also applied to the means for the two age groups on each of the 10 trials. For the five-year-olds, each mean except that for trial 1 was found to exceed $0\cdot50$, $P < 0\cdot005$. For the three-year-olds, each mean except that for trials 1 and 3 exceeded $0\cdot50$; five means at $P < 0\cdot005$, and three means at $P < 0\cdot05$. Thus, both age groups solved these problems by the second trial; three-year-olds lapsed on the third trial but then recovered on trials 4–10.

The numbers of correct choices were also analysed on an individual basis. Obtaining eight or more correct choices out of 10 would be considered to reach the conventional level of significance by the sign test, $P = 0.055$. The proportions of three-year-olds reaching this criterion were 0·60 on the lanes problem and 0·35 on the light problem. The analogous proportions for five-year-olds were 0·80 and 0·85.

Responses to the 11th trials were coded as 0 if the child incorrectly asserted that s/he could produce the effect or if s/he attempted to produce it and as 1 if the child correctly said that the effect could no longer be produced. These data were subjected to an analysis of variance in which age and gender served as between-subjects factors and apparatus served as a within-subject factor. This analysis yielded a main effect for age, $F = 7.64$, d.f. = 1, 36, $P < 0.01$, reflecting more correct responses from the five-year-olds ($\bar{X} = 0.725$) than from the three-year-olds ($\bar{X} = 0.400$). By chance alone the most likely proportion of correct answers would be 0·50. Again, the modification of Dunnett's procedure was used to compare the two obtained means to this theoretical mean. The results indicated that the five-year-olds scored significantly higher than 0·50, $P < 0.005$, and that the three-year-olds did not score significantly below 0·50.

Verbal justifications solicited after the 10th and 11th trials were coded according to the following scale: *3* for citing the connections of a causal mediator with both its effect and initial cause, *2* for mention of a single connection between a causal mediator and either its effect or initial cause, *1* for mention of a causal mediator alone, and *0* for none of the above. The proportion of agreement between two independent raters on cases in which some justification was given was 0·97. Justification scores were subjected to an analysis of variance in which age and gender served as between-subjects factors and trial and apparatus served as within-subject factors. This analysis yielded a main effect of age ($F = 36.12$, d.f. = 1, 36, $P < 0.001$) indicating more complete justifications by five-year-olds ($\bar{X} = 0.150$) than by three-year-olds ($\bar{X} = 0.362$). The frequencies of each type of justification are presented in Table 2, separately for each age group. Complete justifications were rare, but mention of the critical mediator was quite common, especially among five-year-olds, and in a sizable minority of three-year-olds. There was also an effect of trial ($F = 8.25$, d.f. = 1, 36, $P < 0.01$) indicating that justifications were more complete after trial 10 than after trial 11.

Table 2. Frequencies of justification types

Justification types	Age	
	3 years	5 years
3—mediator and links to cause and effect	1	2
2—mediator and link to cause or effect	5	20
1—mediator alone	17	44
0—none of the above	16	8
0—no response	41	6

Discussion

The present results demonstrated that both three- and five-year-olds are capable of understanding mediate causal transmission. This was revealed most clearly in their attempts to produce a terminal effect by activating a cause which could produce a causal mediator which could, in turn, bring about the terminal effect. They avoided activating an alternate cause which could produce an event which was not capable of causing the terminal effect. This conflicts with Piaget's (1974) findings that pre-operational children did not understand causal mediation. The discrepancy can partly be accounted for by contrasting the present behavioural methodology with Piaget's reliance on the child's verbal explanation of the mediation process. Consistent with this interpretation is the fact that three-year-olds in the present experiment gave less complete verbal justifications than did five-year-olds. In addition, it may be the case that the problems used by Piaget (1974) were too complicated for young children. There are undoubtedly many causal chains that even adults do not understand and consequently would be of limited value in diagnosing the ability to deal with causal mediation. It is clear from the present results that a methodology combining simple problems with behavioural measures can be used to provide evidence of the causal mediation concept in children as young as three years.

As such the present findings are consistent with other research indicating successful solution of non-causal transitivity problems by preschool children (Bryant & Trabasso, 1971; Bryant, 1974). The traditional deductive inference explanation of successful performance on these problems holds that the relation between two terms ($_xR_Z$) is logically deduced from premises specifying that each term is related to another, common term ($_xR_Y$ and $_YR_Z$) (Piaget *et al.*, 1960). A subject reasoning in this way would conclude, for example, that, if X is longer than Y and Y is longer than Z, then X must be longer than Z. The present results fit this transitive deductive inference model quite well, with the relation R being specified as *causes*. Children in the present study may have reasoned that, if X causes Y, and Y causes Z, then X can cause Z.

Three alternate models proposed to account for successful solution of non-causal transitivity problems do not appear applicable to the present experiment. One model hold' that the subject integrates the terms of the premises into a linearly ordered spatial representation during training and then accesses this representation during testing to make direct comparisons among the terms (Trabasso, 1975; Trabasso & Riley, 1975; Trabasso *et al.*, 1975). While the spatial representation strategy may well apply to experiments on transitivity of length as an aid to learning the relations contained in the premises, it would not be useful in the present experiment where memory difficulties were precluded by giving subjects continuing visual access to the entire apparatus. Moreover, forming a spatial representation of the apparatus or even examining the actual apparatus would not ensure success unless the distinction between effective and ineffective causal mediators was grasped.

Similar limitations exist for Breslow's (1981) spatial representation model. His model assumes the construction of a linear order based, not on the specific relation involved, but rather on sequential contiguity among the terms described in the premises. Stick X is contiguous with, and thus related to, stick Y, etc. An analysis of the spatial contiguities observed in the present experiment would fail to yield correct answers for the light apparatus since the transmission there occurred without spatial contact between the X, Y and Z objects. There were, or course, temporal contiguities between causes, mediators, and effects but these contiguities alone would not provide immediate solutions. Children using contiguity information would undoubtedly require numerous trials to sort out whether object, direction, or position was the critical contiguous cue. The rapid solutions obtained are more consistent with the idea that subjects insightfully discovered the causal relationships involved. Research on children's understanding of direct causal transmission has likewise demonstrated the priority of identifying the causal mechanism over analysing spatial and temporal contiguities (Shultz, 1982).

A third model proposes that extreme and adjoining terms are labelled (e.g. as *long* or *short*) whereas intermediate-sized terms remain unlabelled (Deboysson-Bardies & O'Regan, 1973). References to such labels are considered to provide correct comparisons among tested terms. The labelling model would not apply to the present experiment since the critical distinctions between effective and ineffective causal mediators were never verbally described by the experimenter. Any spontaneous labelling by the child of initial causes, mediating objects, or sides of the apparatus would fail to yield consistent success unless such labelling focused on the conceptual distinction between effective and ineffective causal mediators. Thus, the present results are consistent with only one of the available models for solving transitivity problems, that based on transitive deductive inference.

The present data are also consistent with evidence that children as young as three years possess considerable knowledge about direct causal transmission (Shultz, 1982). Children of three years know, for example, that an object must be transmitting a relevant type of energy in order to produce an effect and that this transmission, to be effective, must not be blocked or directed away from the effect. The present research shows that three- to five-year-olds understood not merely direct, but mediate, causal transmissions.

It is possible that transitive reasoning may emerge somewhat earlier in the causal realm than in the logical or non-causal realm. There is analogous evidence that children understand concepts of necessity and sufficiency earlier in a causal context than in a non-causal, but equally logical, context (Bindra *et al.*, 1980). Such findings are consistent with the view that the child comes to abstract purely logical structures from more primitive causal frameworks (Shultz, 1979). Whether this would also be the case for the concept of transitivity could only be established by future research, drawing explicit comparisons between causal and non-causal transitive problems. In this context, it is noteworthy that Halliday (1977) obtained evidence of transitive inference in three-year-olds using a causal problem, albeit one in which the causal mechanism was not completely evident. In that experiment, children chose a geometric form from one of two cupboards and inserted it in a third panel to obtain pieces of candy. They may not have known how the inserted geometric form caused the piece of candy to appear, but they could easily learn that one shape was an effective causal mediator.

In the present experiment, three-year-olds experienced considerable difficulty in identifying the impossibility of producing the terminal effect without an effective causal mediator. This may suggest that their understanding of casual mediation in these problems was not complete. However, it is conceivable that they might have easily learned about these impossibilities if they had been given more than just a single trial of that type.

Acknowledgements

This research was supported in part by a grant from the Natural Sciences and Engineering Research Council Canada.

References

Bindra, D., Clarke, K. & Shultz, T. R. (1980). Understanding predictive relations of necessity and sufficiency in formally equivalent 'causal' and 'logical' problems. *Journal of Experimental Psychology: General*, **109**, 422–443.
Bryant, P. E. (1974). *Perception and Understanding in Young Children*. London: Methuen.
Bryant, P. E. & Trabasso, T. (1971). Transitive inferences and memory in young children. *Nature, London*, **232**, 456–458.
Bunge, M. (1979). *Causality and Modern Science*, 3rd rev. ed. New York: Dover Publications.
Breslow, L. (1981). Re-evaluation of the literature on the development of transitive inferences. *Psychological Bulletin*, **89**, 325–351.
Deboysson-Bardies, B. & O'Regan, K. (1973). What children do in spite of adults' hypotheses. *Nature, London*, **246**, 531–534.
Dunnett, C. W. (1955). A multiple comparison procedure for comparing several treatments with a control. *Journal of the American Statistical Association*, **50**, 1096–1121.
Halliday, M. S. (1977). Behavioral inference in young children. *Journal of Experimental Child Psychology*, **23**, 378–390.
Lunney, G. H. (1970). Using analysis of variance with a dichotomous dependent variable: An empirical study. *Journal of Educational Measurement*, **7**, 263–269.

Piaget, J. (1974). *Understanding Causality*. New York: Norton.
Piaget, J., Inhelder, B. & Szeminska, A. (1960). *The Child's Conception of Geometry*. New York: Basic Books.
Shultz, T. R. (1979). Causal and logical reasoning. Paper presented at the International Congress of Psychology of the Child, Paris.
Shultz, T. R. (1982). Rules of causal attribution. *Monographs of the Society for Research in Child Development* (in press).
Thayer, E. S. & Collyer, C. E. (1978). The development of transitive inference: A review of recent approaches. *Psychological Bulletin*, **85**, 1327–1343.
Trabasso, T. (1975). Representation, memory, and reasoning: How do we make transitive inferences? In A. D. Pick (ed.), *Minnesota Symposium on Child Psychology*, vol. 9. Minneapolis, MN: University of Minnesota Press.
Trabasso, T. & Riley, C. A. (1975). On the construction and use of representations involving linear order. In R. L. Solso (ed.), *Information Processing and Cognition: The Loyola Symposium*. Hillsdale, NJ: Erlbaum.
Trabasso, T., Riley, C. A. & Wilson, E. G. (1975). The representation of linear order and spatial strategies in reasoning: A developmental study. In R. J. Falmagne (ed.), *Reasoning: Representation and Process in Children and Adults*. Hillsdale, NJ: Erlbaum.

Requests for reprints should be addressed to Thomas R. Shultz, Department of Psychology, McGill University, 1205 Docteur Penfield Avenue, Montreal, Quebec H3A 1B1, Canada.
Seymour Pardo and Esther Altmann are also at the above address.

British Journal of Psychology (1982), **73**, 243–251   *Printed in Great Britain*

The role of conflict and of agreement between intellectual strategies in children's ideas about measurement

Peter Bryant

Four experiments tested the hypothesis that it is agreement and not conflict between strategies which produces intellectual change in young children. The argument behind the hypothesis is that conflict tells the child that something is wrong but not what it is, and certainly not what is the right strategy. On the other hand if one strategy consistently produces the same answer as another, the child can be reasonably sure that both are right. In the first experiment it was demonstrated that children measured more after seeing that measurement agreed with direct comparisons. In the next two experiments experience of conflict failed to have any effect on children's willingness to measure. The final experiment looked at the effect of telling children that their measurements were right. This did not increase measurement either. Together these experiments provide support for the idea that children learn when strategies agree rather than when they conflict.

Measurement plays an important part in any child's education and it also involves a central logical principle, the transitive inference. This combination of educational relevance and logical demand guaranteed Piaget's interest in the question. His main experiment on measurement is well known. He and his colleagues (Piaget *et al.*, 1960) showed children a tower of bricks perched on a high table and asked them to build another tower of exactly the same height from top to bottom on a much lower table. Because the towers were placed at different levels it was difficult to make a direct visual comparison between them which had any chance of being consistently accurate. The experimenters also provided a measure in the form of a stick whose length was the same as the height of the first tower. Younger children tended not to use the measure and resorted instead to comparing the two towers directly. Older children, on the other hand, did measure. Piaget concluded that younger children do not understand the principles of measurement, a deficit which he attributed to an inability in these children to make transitive inferences.

Over the last 10 years immense interest has centred, albeit rather inconclusively, around the question of whether young children can or cannot make transitive inferences (Bryant & Trabasso, 1971; Trabasso, 1977; Thayer & Collyer, 1978; Breslow, 1981; Shultz *et al.*, 1982). Rather surprisingly there has been very little empirical work on measurement itself. One recent experiment (Bryant & Kopytynska, 1976) did confirm Piaget's discovery that young children of five and six years are reluctant to use a stick as an intervening measure to compare two towers, but this same experiment also produced evidence that they do measure when it is absolutely clear that a direct comparison between the two quantities is out of the question. The children were given two blocks of wood, each with a hole whose complete depth was not visible sunk in the top, and they had to decide whether the two holes were equal in depth or not, and, if not, which was the deeper. Here they did use the stick to measure and to compare the two holes. It seems that young children have an idea of measurement, but do not always put this idea into effect at the right moment.

This raises the question of how it is that children eventually realize that direct comparisons are often a great deal less reliable than comparisons made with the help of an intervening measure. Piaget's answer to a question like this about the causes of intellectual change was usually couched in terms of conflict or more recently of 'perturbation' (Piaget, 1977). He argued that from time to time children find that they have two different and apparently conflicting ways of interpreting the same event, and that this puzzling state of

0007-1269/82/020243-09 $02.00/0 © 1982 The British Psychological Society

affairs throws them into intellectual disequilibrium. Eventually out of this inner turmoil emerges a new set of cognitive structures which copes with the events in the child's world more satisfactorily and more consistently.

The main trouble with this hypothesis, usually known as the equilibration hypothesis, is that although it gives a satisfactory account of the child's dissatisfaction with his existing intellectual structures, it does not explain exactly how he arrives at a better way of understanding his world. Piaget did change the causal side of his theory from time to time and particularly in his last years (Inhelder *et al.*, 1977). Nevertheless it is hard to find in it how it is that the child eventually produces the solution to his own dilemma. This is a gap which has been noted by others (Hamlyn, 1978).

There is an alternative hypothesis (Bryant, 1981*a*) which is the opposite of Piaget's. It is that a child realizes that a strategy works when he sees that it consistently produces the same solution as another strategy: it is agreement and not conflict between strategies which produces intellectual change.

The argument behind this hypothesis is simple. It is that checking one strategy against another will produce a much more convincing answer when the two strategies agree than when they disagree. If a child reaches the same solution with the help of two different strategies he can be reasonably sure that, barring some unlikely coincidence, both strategies are appropriate. But if they conflict he is in a quandary. He has nothing to tell him whether both strategies are wrong or whether one is wrong (and which one?), or even whether both are right but have produced an inconsistent answer through some careless error.

One way of distinguishing these two hypotheses is to turn to the measuring experiment, in which various types of comparison are possible which either agree or conflict with each other. If I am shown two towers placed at different levels and I make a direct visual comparison between them in addition to making an indirect one with the help of a measure, these two comparisons will from time to time produce conflicting answers because the first is less reliable than the second. But if the display is changed so that the towers are now side by side at the same level, a direct comparison and an indirect one will probably agree since both are reliable and both should produce the same correct answer.

So children who do not measure spontaneously in Piaget's task can be taught to measure either by methods which involve conflict between strategies or by methods which involve agreement between strategies. Conflict would involve, for example, demonstrating to the child that indirect measuring comparisons frequently produce different answers than do direct comparisons from different levels. Agreement would involve showing the child that indirect comparisons usually produce the same answer as direct comparisons from the same level. So we can see which type of experience – agreement or conflict – is more likely to lead to an increase in measuring.

Experiment 1. Agreement between strategies (IM + DS)

The aim of this experiment was to see whether children would begin to measure more after having seen that the results of their measurements agreed with the results of direct side-by-side comparisons. Thus the experiment tested whether agreement alone was sufficient to change children's behaviour.

Method

Children. There were 20 children divided into two groups of 10. The mean age of the first group, the *experimental group*, was six years five months (range 6·00–6·11) and of the *control group* six years five months (range 6·1–6·11). There was the same number of boys and girls in each group.

Material. There were blocks of wood in six different heights, which were 9, 8·75, 8·5, 8·25, 8·0 and 7·75 inches. All the blocks had the same width (2·5 in) and the same depth from front to back (1·5 in). There were five blocks in each size, each painted in a different colour, the colours being red, blue, yellow, green and white. There were also six black rods whose lengths were the same as the heights of the blocks.

Procedure

Pre-test. The children in both groups were given 10 trials; in each of these they had to compare two blocks of wood, one standing vertically on the floor and the other vertically on a table slightly to one side and 2 ft 5 in high. A black rod was always available, and on half the trials it was lying by the higher block and on the other half by the lower one. On half the trials the blocks were *different* in height, but the difference was always only ¼ in, so that the 8·75 in block was compared to the 8·5 in one, the 8·5 in to the 8·25 in one and so on. On the other five trials the two blocks were the *same* height as each other. In the five 'different' trials the rod was the same length as the height of one of the two blocks, and of course in the five 'same' trials it was the same as both blocks.

The two blocks were always a different colour, so the child was asked to find out whether for example the red brick was as tall as the blue one. Same and different trials were interleaved and their order was systematically varied between children. So were the colours and the heights of the blocks used on different trials.

The question was whether children would make direct comparisons or would use the rod to measure.

Training period

The experimental group. This followed immediately. It involved the same 10 problems with the same displays (though in a different order and with different colour combinations) as the pre-test did.

The crucial point about this group's training trials was that in every trial the child was made to make both an indirect measuring comparison (IM) and, as well, a direct side-by-side comparison (DS) of the two blocks, and had his attention drawn to the fact that the two judgements agreed.

The experimenter made the child make an IM comparison by showing the child how to use the rod as a measure and then persuading him to measure with it and make a judgement about the two blocks. The DS judgements were made when the experimenter lifted the lower block and put it beside the other one, and then asked for a comparison. On half the trials the IM judgement preceded DS, and vice versa on the other half. The IM judgements were always made from different levels, so that in those trials in which DS preceded IM the lower block was returned to its original level immediately after the first judgement was made.

The control group. These children made exactly the same comparisons as the children in the experimental group in exactly the same number. The only difference between the two groups was that the control children never had the experience of seeing two comparisons produce the same answer. The children in the control group made the same number of measurements and of direct comparisons but they made them on different trials, so that the two judgements never coincided.

They were given 20 trials. In half they were made to measure straightaway and discouraged from making a direct comparison: the blocks in these trials were always kept at different levels. In the other half the lower block was immediately lifted and put beside the higher one, and the child was asked to make a direct comparison. So these children both measured and made direct comparisons, but on different trials.

Post-test. This was identical to the pre-test, apart from some variation in the order of trials and in the colour combinations.

Results

Table 1 shows that direct comparisons from different levels were indeed unreliable. They were as likely to be wrong as to be right in this and in the other experiments. This fact will be taken for granted from now on and not mentioned again.

Table 2 shows that there was very little measurement by either group in the pre-test but that there was a considerable improvement on the part of the experimental group in the

Table 1. Success[a] in pre- and post-test trials in which direct comparisons were made from different levels (summed across pre- and post-tests)

Experiment	Experimental groups		Control groups	
	Mean no. of direct comparisons	Per cent correct of these comparisons	Mean no. of direct comparisons	Per cent correct of these comparisons
1	13·4	48·51	17·1	49·12
2	28·4	51·05	28·1	53·02
3	28·5	56·49	27·9	55·56
4	27·5	50·91	27·8	50·36

[a] Success is scored in terms of whether the blocks were correctly judged to be the same or different in height. Chance level is 50 per cent. None of these scores differs significantly from chance.

Table 2. Mean no. of trials (out of 10) on which the children measured

Experiment	Experimental group		Control group	
	Pre-test	Post-test	Pre-test	Post-test
1	0·9	5·7	0·8	2·1
2	0·4	1·2	0·5	1·4
3	0·7	0·8	0·9	1·2
4	0·6	1·9	0·9	1·3

post-test. The control group also improved but to a smaller extent. This result suggests that agreement between strategies on its own can lead to changes in behaviour. The evident superiority of the experimental group seems to establish that it was the agreement that caused the change and not the child's experience with measuring during the training trials since both groups had an equal amount of experience.

Experiment 2. Conflict between strategies I (IM vs. DDL)

The aim here was to see whether conflict on its own would lead to changes in behaviour.

Method

Children. There were 20 children divided into two groups. The mean age of the experimental group was six years four months (range 6·0–6·9) and of the control group six years five months (range 6·1–6·11), each with equal numbers of boys and girls.

Material. The same as Expt 1.

Procedure

Pre-test. The same as in Expt 1.

Training

Again the children in *the experimental group* had to make two comparisons about the same blocks in each trial, but this time the comparisons were likely to conflict on some trials. The two types of comparisons were measuring (IM) as in Expt 1 and direct comparisons from different levels (DDL). Since the latter are unreliable they should produce different answers from measuring judgements from time to time.

However, even when DDL judgements are at chance level they will, by chance, conflict with measuring judgements on only half the trials. So in order to equate the experience of conflict with the experience of agreement gained by the experimental group in the first experiment (10 trials), the training trials in this experiment continued until the children had produced 10 conflicting judgements: i.e. until on 10 trials they had said one thing about the blocks when they measured and a different thing when they made the direct comparison from different levels. This meant of course that the training session was longer for this experimental group than for the equivalent group in the first experiment. On half the trials the first judgement was an IM one, and on the other half it was the DDL comparison.

Each child in *the control group* was yoked to an individual child in the experimental group and was given double the number of trials, on half of which he measured, while on the other half he made a direct comparison from different levels. This meant that the control children made the same number of both types of judgement as the experimental group but on separate trials. They had the same overall experience, except for the fact that they did not experience conflict.

Post-test. The same as in Expt 1.

Results

The mean number of trials in the experimental group's training session was 25·2. Because the order of the two types of trial (IM before DDL and DDL before IM) was systematically varied in Gellermann series this meant that the children were given very nearly equal amounts of both trials. But when we looked at the trials in which these children did make conflicting judgements we found a contrast between the two types of trial. These conflicts occurred more when the child made a direct comparison first (DDL) and then measured (IM) (a mean of 6·5 conflicts in 12·4 trials) than when they measured (IM) first and made the direct comparison later (DDL) (a mean of 3·5 out of 12·8 trials). There was of course no chance of such conflicts in the control group.

But the conflicts experienced by the experimental group seemed to have no effect on the outcome, as Table 2 shows. Both groups hardly measured at all either before or after the training session. So knowledge that direct comparisons from different levels conflict with measurement did not help children solve the original problem. It did not prod them either into making these direct comparisons less or into measuring more.

Experiment 3. Conflict between strategies II (DDL vs. DS)

Perhaps the experimental group in the last experiment did not abandon direct comparisons from different levels because the conflict involved might have been the wrong sort of conflict. Another possible conflict is between direct comparison from different levels (DDL) and direct comparisons when the blocks are side by side (DS). We decided to try that too.

Method

Children. The 20 children were divided into an experimental group with a mean age of six years six months (range 6·00–6·11) and a control group with a mean age of six years five months (range 6·0–6·10).

Material. The same as before.

Pre-test. The same as before.

Training

As in the previous experiment trials continued for each child in the *experimental group* until he had produced 10 conflicting judgements. In each trial he was made to make a direct comparison from different levels and one side by side. There were two types of trial: DDL before DS and DS before DDL. Each child in the control group was yoked to a particular child in the experimental group and was given exactly twice his number of trials, or half the control group children made a DDL comparison, and half a DS one.

Post-test. As before.

Results

The mean number of trials in the experimental group's training session was 27·2. Again the conflicts occurred in one type of trial much more than in another. Where DDL preceded DS there was a mean of 7·2 conflicting judgements in 13·8 trials. When DS preceded DDL the mean number of conflicts was 2·8 in 13·4 trials. The control group made the same number of DDL and DS judgements but these never conflicted since they were about different displays.

Again the conflict had no effect. As Table 2 shows there was no difference between experimental and control groups.

Thus in three experiments the only improvement came in the first, in which children had the experience of two strategies coinciding. That produced change. Conflict, on the other hand, either between measuring and direct comparisons (Expt 1) or between two types of direct comparison (Expt 2), did not.

Experiment 4. IM + knowledge of results

It could be argued that this pattern of results might have nothing to do with agreement vs. conflict: it could simply be due to the fact that the children in the experimental group in Expt 1 were shown that measurement was right, while the children in the two following experiments were only shown what was wrong. Being shown the right thing tells you what to do next. Being told what is wrong does not. In a way this is half our case, since our argument against conflict is that it will tell a child that something is wrong, but not what to do about it. However it is certainly true that the success of the experimental group in the first experiment might not be due specifically to the children seeing that two strategies coincide.

In order to check this a final experiment was designed in which the experimental group was told that its measurements were right. They did not have the experience of seeing that measuring produces the same answer as another strategy.

Method

Children. The 20 children were divided into an experimental group and a control group both with a mean age of six years six months (range 6·0–6·11).

Material. Same as before.

Pre-test. Same as before.

Training

The same 10 displays as in the pre-test were presented to the *experimental group* but this time the child was told that if the blocks were the same height each would have Xs on its back, while if they were different heights the taller would have a circle on its back. In each trial the child was encouraged to measure and then after he had made his judgement the blocks were turned round, so that the child saw whether he had been correct. (In fact with the help of the experimenter the measuring judgements were all correct.) The signs were a way of telling the child that he was right and that measuring worked, and this point was hammered home to the children at the end of each trial.

The *control group* was told about the signs but not what they meant. The children were given 20 trials and in half they measured without being told whether they were right or not, while in the other half they simply had to guess whether the bricks had two crosses or one circle on their backs. Thus they had an equal experience of measuring and of dealing with the signs, but on separate trials.

Post-test. As before.

Results

Table 2 shows that there was some improvement in the experimental group but that they did not seem to measure as much as the children in the first experiment. Being told that measuring is right does not seem to be the reason for the experimental group's success in the first experiment. This means that the experience of seeing that two strategies coincide was probably the reason for their starting to measure.

The results from all four experiments were analysed in one analysis of variance in which the main terms were Expts (1, 2, 3, 4), groups (experimental, control) and tests (pre-, post-). This produced a significant second-order interaction (experiments × groups × tests, $F = 13.49$, d.f. $= 3, 72$, $P < 0.01$), and a subsequent Newman–Keuls test demonstrated that this was due to the post-test score for the experimental group in Expt 1 being significantly higher than their pre-test score and also higher than all other scores. In other words the interaction was caused by the fact that only these children measured more as a result of training experience.

Discussion

The main question behind these experiments was how a child establishes for himself when and where it is right to use particular intellectual strategies. The results support the idea that he does this by checking one strategy against another. If they agree his confidence in them increases: if they conflict he is no further forward.

Of course, the evidence is limited. The number of children was not large and only one age group was considered. Only one cognitive skill – measuring – was involved and only one type of measuring at that. Nor did we look to see how permanent the effects were. Nevertheless the controls were stringent – more stringent than is customary in training experiments with children – and the results were clear-cut. Agreement between strategies did improve measurement and conflict did not.

Moreover the *a priori* arguments for the hypothesis about agreement are strong. It is a system that could work. When a child reaches the same answer by different routes it's highly likely that both routes are good routes. Moreover many different types of problem can be solved in more than one way. The two rows of beads placed alongside each other can be compared in number either by one-to-one correspondence or by counting. Both methods will say which row is more numerous and both should say the same row. Or if a child has to work out how many oranges there are in five boxes each of which contains eight oranges he can do so either by counting or by adding fives or by multiplying. It is so easy to think of examples that one's difficulty is in finding a cognitive problem that cannot in principle be solved in more than one way. So the theory about the effects of agreement could be applied to a wide range of cognitive tasks.

The alternatives are not convincing. We have already noted the main problem about the conflict hypothesis: it could tell the child that something is wrong, but it will not tell him what is wrong and/or certainly will not tell him what is right. Moreover the evidence for the effects of conflict is particularly weak. Piaget (1977) consistently appealed to the training experiments of Inhelder *et al.* (1974), and some of his colleagues (Bovet, 1981) quoted the causal experiment of Lefebvre & Pinard (1972) as good evidence that conflict does lie at the heart of intellectual development. But the conflicts studied were between what the child expected to happen and what actually transpired: the experiments did not deal with the possibility that a child might possess two different strategies which produce two opposing interpretations of what is going on around him. Worse still these were very badly designed experiments (Bryant, 1981*b*). Any training experiment whose aim is to isolate a cause of development should include a control group in which the children receive exactly the same experiences as those in the experimental group apart from the crucial factor which is thought to cause development changes – in this case, conflict. None of these experiments had anything like adequate controls and this means that their results could simply have been due to children becoming more familiar with the experimental material (a mundane alternative which was rigidly excluded in our experiments).

Is there perhaps a third way? Recently several people have stressed the effects of social communication (Hamlyn, 1978; Perret-Clermont, 1980; Russell, 1981). In fact the one attempt in our experiments simply to tell the children that measuring was correct did not have any effect, but this is not reason enough to reject this hypothesis. Its main conceptual problem is that it does not explain its own limitations, for, if communication were all, it is difficult to see why intellectual development could not be polished off in one concentrated one-hour tutorial. Children may benefit from being told what is correct, but these benefits plainly cannot account for all the constraints on their development.

This weakness in theories about language and communication was always one of Piaget's main points. Our hypothesis and his have that much in common. So perhaps we should ask again how alien to Piaget's ideas is our notion about agreement between strategies. It seems in fact to be the opposite of his main ideas about the causes of development which were dialectical (and therefore argumentative) in nature. The Hegelian *Sturm und Drang* of the thesis, antithesis and eventual synthesis played an important part in Piaget's causal ideas and led inexorably to the idea that the inner battle between two opposing views is resolved in the end by the creation of a new view. Nothing could be further from our hypothesis about agreement between strategies. But in his later writing Piaget (1977) did extend his model of equilibrium and disequilibrium, and talked as well of the coordination of strategies or schemata leading to qualitative changes. These ideas were never set out precisely and they were certainly never tested. Perhaps our experiments could be looked on as an investigation of some of Piaget's later ideas.

Acknowledgements

Editorial responsibility for this paper was assumed by Professor M. Coltheart.

References

Bovet, M. (1981). Cognitive mechanisms and training. In M. P. Friedman, J. P. Das & N. O'Connor (eds), *Intelligence and Learning*. New York: Plenum.

Breslow, L. (1981). Re-evaluation of the literature on the development of transitive inferences. *Psychological Bulletin*, **89**, 325–351.

Bryant, P. E. (1981*a*). Piaget and his struggles. Paper given to the British Memorial to Piaget Conference, Eastbourne.

Bryant, P. E. (1981*b*). Training and logic. In M. P. Friedman, J. P. Das & N. O'Connor (eds), *Intelligence and Learning*. New York: Plenum.

Bryant, P. E. & Kopytnyska, H. (1976). Spontaneous measurement by young children. *Nature, London*, **260**, 773.

Bryant, P. E. & Trabasso, T. (1971). Transitive inferences and memory in young children. *Nature, London*, **232**, 456–458.

Hamlyn, D. W. (1978). *Experience and the Growth of Understanding*. London: Routledge & Kegan Paul.

Inhelder, B., Garcia, R. & Vonèche, J. (1977). *Epistémologie Génétique et Equilibration*. Neuchâtel: Delachaux & Niestlé.

Inhelder, B., Sinclair, H. & Bovet, M. (1974). *Learning and the Development of Cognition*. London: Routledge & Kegan Paul.

Lefebvre, M. & Pinard, A. (1972). Apprentissage de la conservation des quantités par une méthode de conflit cognitif. *Canadian Journal of Behavioural Science*, **4**, 1–12.

Perret-Clermont, A.-N. (1980). *Social Interaction and Cognitive Development in Children.* London: Academic Press.

Piaget, J. (1977). *The Development of Thought: Equilibration of Cognitive Structures.* Oxford: Blackwell.

Piaget, J., Inhelder, B. & Szeminska, A. (1960). *The Child's Conception of Geometry.* London: Routledge & Kegan Paul.

Russell, J. (1981). Cognitive structures and verbalised beliefs. Paper given to the British Memorial to Piaget Conference, Eastbourne.

Shultz, T. R., Pardo, S. & Altmann, E. (1982). Young children's use of transitive inference in causal chains. *British Journal of Psychology,* **73**, 235–241.

Thayer, E. & Collyer, C. (1978). The development of transitive inference: A review of recent approaches. *Psychological Bulletin,* **85**, 1327–1343.

Trabasso, T. (1977). The role of memory as a system in making transitive inferences. In R. V. Kail & J. W. Hagen (eds), *Perspecting or the Development of Memory and Cognition.* Hillsdale, NJ: Erlbaum.

Requests for reprints should be addressed to P. E. Bryant, Department of Experimental Psychology, University of Oxford, South Parks Road, Oxford OX1 3UD, UK.

British Journal of Psychology (1982), **73**, 253–266   *Printed in Great Britain*

The child's appreciation of the necessary truth and the necessary falseness of propositions

James Russell

Two experiments were performed in order to determine the extent to which children in the age range of five to 10 years can discriminate between (*a*) necessarily true vs. contingent propositions and (*b*) necessarily false vs. contingent propositions. In each study five types of sentence pairs (30 examples of each) were presented and success was assessed by the number of errors made. Children were either taught the basis of the discrimination by the experimenter trial-by-trial *post hoc* or received no such instruction. Children in the five to six age range appreciated the necessarily true/contingent distinction with teaching, and the necessarily false/contingent distinction without teaching, although ease of discrimination varied strongly with sentence type. The data were interpreted as being contradictory to the Piagetian account of the development of necessity, and as suggesting that linguistic experience may play a more central role in the acquisition of logical reasoning than Piaget proposed.

Perhaps the most distinctive claim made within Piaget's theory of cognitive development is that our notion of logical necessity develops out of the mental manipulation of interiorized actions. The crucible of necessity is the systematization of the infant's actions, which gradually become interiorized and structured into a conceptual appreciation of logic.

It is a central tenet of Piagetian theory that a child who regards a logical principle such as transitivity (e.g. A > B, B > C, therefore A > C) as necessary does so by virtue of having first established it as 'possible or probable' by the 'empirical groping' (Piaget, 1971, p. 316) of action on seriated elements, then by mentally relating these actions within a whole or closed structure. Only then does 'transitivity appear "necessary", and this logical "necessity" [become] recognised not only by some inner feeling...but by the intellectual behaviour of the subject, who uses the newly mastered deductive instrument with confidence and discipline' (Piaget, 1971, p. 316). Knowledge of the fact of deductive necessity arises, therefore, out of the mental coordination of interiorized actions in a closed system rather than some intuition of necessity governing how the child regards concrete situations.

It is not until adolescence that the appreciation of necessity can govern the child's intellectual behaviour, as opposed to being regarded as a consequence of a concrete principle. The ability to combine possibility and deduction within hypotheses, which characterizes 'formal operational' thought, is impossible without the appreciation of necessity, argues Piaget, because hypotheses would not be constructed unless 'formal level subjects look[ed] for necessity immediately' (Inhelder & Piaget, 1958, p. 17).

The evidence for Piaget's claim that children appreciate concrete operational principles as logically necessary is somewhat equivocal. Some studies have supported this claim by showing how conservers have greater confidence in their judgements than non-conservers, irrespective of age, time of acquisition and social dominance (Miller & Brownell, 1975; Miller *et al.*, 1977; Russell, in press). But there is also a body of evidence sometimes interpreted as showing no such difference; indeed as showing that even adults do not appreciate conservation as a necessary truth (see review by Hall & Kaye, 1978). Moreover, Markman (1978) has provided data appearing to suggest that class-includers do not appreciate the necessity of their conclusion until some three or four years after becoming able to draw it.

0007-1269/82/020253-14 $02.00/0 © 1982 The British Psychological Society

There are two areas in which data should be collected if we are to acquire any further insight into the development of necessity. The first is the child's knowledge of necessary truth and falsity (tautology and contradiction) as properties of linguistic *propositions* irrespective of any context. Piaget (1970, p. 8) dismisses the thesis that the child's knowledge of necessity may originate in his acquaintance with linguistic forms as a species of Logical Positivism. However, the suggestion that the development of notions of necessity is at least aided by the child's reflective awareness of the linguistic–conceptual system does not entail Logical Positivism. Be that as it may, the present study gauged the child's understanding of necessity within propositions through a discrimination task in which five- to 10-year-old children had to understand the difference between necessarily true or necessarily false sentences on the one hand and contingent sentences on the other.

Second, we know very little about the child's *comprehension* of the principle of necessity as expressed in language because studies have typically been concerned with either the child's characterization of his own answers to concrete operational problems or his answers to logical puzzles. It is possible that such studies have been masking a basic competence in understanding necessity. For example the child may be able to appreciate the force of an argument based on an appeal to necessity before he can mount such an argument for himself. Our study addressed this question by comparing children's ability to extract the principle of necessity vs. contingency spontaneously with a situation in which they were taught the basis of the discrimination. If children can benefit from such teaching then they must have some 'receptive' understanding of necessity. This distinction between receptive and spontaneous understanding is analogous to that between 'comprehension' and 'production' in language development (see Ingram, 1974).

Experiment 1
Method

In the first study children were presented with 30 pairs of contrasting sentences, necessarily true vs. contingent. One of the sentences of each pair was repeated after each presentation in order that the child could make a non-verbal response to its necessity or contingency. Sentences were presented in pairs in order to heighten the necessary/contingent contrast.

Half of the children had the basis of the distinction explained to them by the experimenter (the 'teaching' condition) and half had to extract the basis of the distinction for themselves (the 'no teaching' condition). This was done primarily to compare the child's comprehension of necessity as expressed through another's language with the child's spontaneous application of the principle of necessity in the solution of a problem. An additional reason for comparing these groups was that as the dimension on which the procedures differed was in respect of verbal characterizations of the distinction in one there was thereby provided a means of determining whether success on the teaching condition could have been achieved solely by the extraction of some incidental, non-logical clue about the distinction. To illustrate: if a substantial superiority were found in the teaching condition together with chance level responding in the no teaching condition, then the success of the children who had received teaching must have been achieved by virtue of what had been said by the experimenter rather than by virtue of syntactic differences between sentences, differences in word frequency of crucial terms, differences in reader's tone of voice, and so on: a 'clever Hans' explanation would be rendered untenable. Nevertheless every effort was made to employ sentence pairs as similar as possible.

Children. These were 240 children who were attending schools in Liverpool and Cheshire with upper working-class to lower middle-class intakes. They were divided into three age groupings of 80 children as follows: mean age 5·8 years (range 5·2 to 6·7 years); mean age 8·1 years (range 7·4 to 8·8 years); mean age 9·6 (range 9·1 to 10·4 years). Each of these three groups was divided into two groups of 40 children, one of which constituted a teaching group and the other a no teaching group. The mean ages of the children in the teaching and no teaching groups at each age level were as follows (with the teaching group means presented first): (youngest children) 5·8 years and 6·2 years;

(intermediate age children) 7·8 years and 8·3 years; (oldest children) 9·5 years and 9·9 years. Each of these six subgroups was divided further into five subgroups which each received a different kind of necessary/contingent discrimination.

Assignment to groups was random apart from the constraint that for teaching vs. no teaching comparisons at each age level the two groups of children tested on each of the five types of discrimination were age-matched on the criterion of a child having an equivalent in the other group within at least six months of his or her own age. Frequently age differences were less. Sex differences were balanced across groups.

Material. There were 30 examples of each of the five kinds of necessary/contingent distinction employed here. Some examples of each of these five sentence types are presented in Table 1. A basic syntactic equivalence was maintained between the sentences of each pair as well as an equal number of words in almost every case. The five sentence types will now be described.

Definitional sentences were those in which one of the sentences in the pair was true by definition (e.g. 'John's dad is a man' vs. 'John's dad is a farmer').

Situational sentences were those whose description of a situation had to be true (e.g. 'There are people in the crowd' vs. 'There are children in the crowd').

Relational sentences contained two terms which necessarily had to be related in the way expressed (e.g. 'My green shirt is the same colour as my green tie' vs. 'My green shirt is the same material as my green tie').

Empty sentences were similar to the definitional ones except that the necessity was less strong because it was logically possible, though unlikely, for the negation to hold (e.g. 'That zebra has stripes' vs. 'That zebra has babies').

Negated sentences were those where the predicate was the equivalent in negative form of the adjective qualifying the subject (e.g. 'The fat man is not thin' vs. 'The fat man is not well').

The apparatus for the presentation of the sentences consisted of a large toy bear with an extension loudspeaker from a tape deck in its head. This was used in order to make what could prove a tedious task more interesting to children. The tape could be turned on and off by the experimenter via a remote-control switch. Four presentation orders for each sentence type were recorded on cassettes with order within pairs and repeated sentence (i.e. necessary or contingent) being varied independently. The sentences had been recorded by a male speaking in a slow 'bear-like' voice, with a pause of one second between each sentence and its comparison in a pair, and of four seconds between the presentation of a pair and the repetition of one of the members of the pair.

The apparatus on which the child's responses to the sentences were made consisted of a small metal box with a domed top of red glass and a rubber lever on its left- and right-hand sides (the 'response box'). Inside the box there was a bell and a light bulb located behind the glass. A remote-control switch determined whether pressing the right-hand or the left-hand lever activated (simultaneously) the bell and light.

Procedure. The following features were common to the procedures of both the teaching and the no teaching groups. Thirty necessary/contingent sentence pairs were presented to children individually in order to assess whether they could learn to press one lever of the response box for necessary sentences and the other lever for contingent sentences. Which lever (left-hand or right-hand) was correct for which kind of proposition (necessary or contingent) was varied across subjects. The child heard each pair and then had to respond when one of the pair was repeated. The child received immediate feedback as to correctness: the bell and light were activated when the child had depressed the correct lever. A session was terminated either when the child had made a run of 10 trials with no errors or with only one error, or when all 30 sentence pairs had been presented.

The toy bear and the child sat across from each other at a low table and the (female) experimenter sat to one side of the table. The response box was on the table in front of the child. The experimenter held the remote-control switches of the response box and the tape-recorder. Pilot studies had highlighted words which might have presented vocabulary difficulties for the younger children, so these were explained by the experimenter during testing. The procedures peculiar to the teaching and the no teaching conditions will now be described.

Teaching. This essentially involved the explanation of the distinction as it was represented in the sentence pair on which the child had *just* responded: all instruction was *post hoc*. Children from the teaching group were told that they were going to play a game in which they had to work out 'when

Table 1. A selection of six sentence pairs from the set of 30 used for each of the five sentence types on the necessarily true vs. contingent discrimination

Definitional

The giant is tall. / The giant is angry.	That rose is a flower. / That rose is a present.
John's sister is a girl. / John's sister is a Brownie.	The red hat is coloured. / The red hat is small.
The circle is round. / The circle is big.	
Our dinner is food. / Our dinner is cold.	

Situational

The walking man is on his feet. / The walking man is on his own.	Those mums and dads have children. / Those mums and dads have arrived.
John knows who his friend is. / John knows where his friend is.	The beach is near the sea. / The beach is near the shops.
The man wearing a hat has something on his head. / The man wearing a hat has something under his arm.	The winner of the race finished first. / The winner of the race finished tired.

Relational

The man who came yesterday came before the man who came today. / The man who came yesterday was taller than the man who came today.	We were in front of the man who was behind us. / We were in front of the man who was behind them.
The expensive watch cost more than the cheap watch. / The expensive watch is newer than the cheap watch.	The mark on the ceiling is higher than the mark on the floor. / The mark on the ceiling is lighter than the mark on the floor.
The boy who sat between the girls had a girl on each side. / The boy who sat between the girls had a girl on his lap.	The fast train takes less time than the slow train. / The fast train takes less people than the slow train.

Empty

The coat is to wear. / The coat is for sale.	The aeroplane flies through the sky. / The aeroplane flies through the night.
That wood comes from trees. / That wood comes from abroad.	That cat has whiskers. / That cat has fish.
That car has some wheels. / That car has some rust.	The ship sails on water. / The ship sails on Tuesdays.

Negated

The happy children are not sad. / The happy children are not hungry.	The old lady is not young. / The old lady is not hurt.
The loud music is not quiet. / The loud music is not nice.	The wide road is not narrow. / The wide road is not dangerous.
The clean bottle is not dirty. / The clean bottle is not useful.	The heavy bag is not light. / The heavy bag is not full.

Teddy has said something that must be true/is always true [the actual wording was flexible] and when he has said something that may or may not be true'. The child was then told the modes of presentation and of responding. The session did not begin until the child could repeat the instructions sufficiently well to satisfy the experimenter that he or she had understood them.

The child was next instructed to press the left-hand lever (for example) for the necessarily true sentences ('which have got to be true...') and the right-hand lever for the contingent sentences ('which may or may not be true'). When the bear produced the first pair the experimenter repeated each sentence in turn and asked the child whether he or she thought it was necessarily true or contingent, employing the same form of wording as before. She then said something like: 'Well let's see which one the Teddy says again'. After the bear had repeated one of the sentences the child was told to press which lever he or she thought was correct. If the response was incorrect the experimenter depressed the other lever to show the child that it activated the light and bell.

Then, whether or not the response had been correct, the experimenter explained why one of the sentences was necessarily true and the other contingent. For example, if the pair had been 'This water is wet' vs. 'This water is dirty' she might say that the first one has got to be true because '...all water is wet, isn't it? Can you imagine what dry water would be like! So to say that water is wet is not to tell us something new, because water can't be dry. But of course water does not have to be dirty does it? Quite a lot of water is clean. So to say that this water is dirty is to tell us something that's not obvious. So 'This water is wet' has got to be true but 'This water is dirty' may or may not be true – we would have to look at the water to find out...'

Or if the pair had been 'The winner of the race finished first' vs. 'The winner of the race finished tired', the child was sensitized to the impossibility of somebody being called the winner of the race but *not* finishing first, that this is what we mean by a 'winner' – but that it may or may not be the case that a person who wins a race is tired afterwards, and so on.

The experimenter did not work from a script, but she had previously rehearsed the kind of reasoning and illustrations she would produce for each sentence pair. When the teaching was complete the experimenter reminded the child which side was for which kind of sentence and then went on to the next pair.

No teaching. For children allocated to the no teaching group the procedure was explained as in the teaching group but this time the child was told that he or she had to find out the kinds of sentences that 'worked' the different levers. It was reiterated that the point of the game was to puzzle out the 'clue' about the difference between the two kinds of sentence that the bear would say.

After the pair had been produced the experimenter repeated the sentences and asked the child if he or she could tell how they were different, apart from the fact that they had different words in them. He was then told to repeat them himself and (after the first trial) asked which he thought was a 'left-hand' and which he thought was a 'right-hand' kind of sentence. When the bear had repeated one of the sentences the experimenter told the child to decide which lever that kind of sentence worked and then press it. If the child was correct the experimenter said something like: 'You see, that is the kind of sentence which you need to press *this* lever for, the one nearer to me on the left'. She then repeated the sentence. For example: 'Ones like "The red hat is coloured" work this left-hand lever on my side of the table. But if the Teddy had said "The red hat is small" then the *other* lever would have worked the box.' If the response had been incorrect the experimenter said something of the following kind: 'No, that isn't the kind of sentence that you press the right-hand lever for. For ones like "The red hat is coloured" you have to press this left-hand lever on my side of the table. Watch...[She presses the lever to show the bell and light being activated]. But if Teddy had said "The red hat is small" then you would have been correct.' She then reiterated that sentences like 'The red hat is coloured' work the left-hand lever and that sentences such as 'The red hat is small' work the right-hand lever. All those children from the no teaching group who were able to attain criterion before all 30 pairs had been presented were asked how they knew which side to press.

Results

The most prominent result was the very marked superiority in the performance of the teaching group over the no teaching group. This can be seen from the mean numbers of errors for each testing condition at each age level shown in Table 2. The numbers of

Table 2. The mean error scores on the necessarily true vs. contingent discrimination with sentence types collapsed (standard deviations in parentheses and numbers of children attaining criterion in brackets)

Testing conditions: Mean ages of groups	Teaching	No teaching
5·8 years	7·10 (SD = 6·04) [24]	14·07 (SD = 4·63) [6]
8·1 years	3·05 (SD = 3·93) [35]	13·62 (SD = 5·09) [8]
9·6 years	3·27 (SD = 4·33) [35]	10·95 (SD = 5·93) [12]

$n = 240$.

children attaining criterion performance, which are also shown in the table, further illustrate this superiority.

The analysis consisted of an ages (3) × testing conditions (2) × sentence types (5) ANOVA on the error scores. This produced the expected main effect of conditions (teaching/no teaching), with $F = 183·33$, d.f. = 1, 210, $P < 0·0005$.

It is possible to extract some information about the youngest children's apprehension of the distinctions by considering the teaching data alone. Table 2 shows that 24 of these children (60 per cent of them) attained criterion (i.e. made a run of 10 trials with no errors or with only one error). This does not give a measure of the extent to which five- to six-year-old children were benefiting from teaching *per se* but it does illustrate such children's high level of ability in cognizing the distinction. Moreover, in view of the fact that some of these children were probably forgetting the association between necessary/contingent sentences and the left-/right-hand levers, it is likely that these scores represent an underestimation of competence. In fact, because success was dependent upon position memory as well as on discriminative ability, scores for both teaching and no teaching groups will be, if anything, an underestimate of discriminative capacity.

In addition to a significant effect of age ($F = 11·28$, d.f. = 2, 210, $P < 0·01$), the ANOVA also produced a significant interaction between ages and testing conditions with $F = 3·34$, d.f. = 2, 210, $P < 0·05$. This is illustrated in Fig. 1*a*. The figure shows that between the age levels of 5–6 and 7–8 years there was a sharp drop in mean errors in the teaching group, which levelled out in the older children. (This levelling out can be interpreted as a ceiling effect given that there is little room for improvement beyond a mean of 3·05 errors on such a task.) Against this we see little evidence of improvement across the three age levels in the no teaching group.

A simple effects analysis showed, in fact, no significant difference in performance between the age groups under the no teaching condition ($F = 2·32$, d.f. = 2, 210, $P > 0·05$), whilst there was such a significant difference under the teaching conditions ($F = 7·07$, d.f. = 2, 210, $P < 0·01$). Therefore, what had improved with age was the ability to benefit from verbal instruction rather than the ability to extract the principle spontaneously.

There was found to have been a significant main effect of sentence types with $F = 6·59$, d.f. = 4, 210, $P < 0·01$; but the interaction between sentence types and testing conditions fell well short of significance, with $F = 1·03$, d.f. = 4, 210, $P > 0·1$. Thus, although some sentence types were more difficult than others, this differential difficulty was not significantly greater under the teaching condition, as Fig. 1*b* seems to suggest was possible. Therefore differential difficulty inhered in the sentence types themselves rather than in the

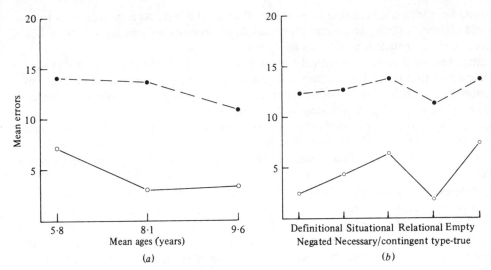

Figure 1. Graphs of (*a*) the relation between age level and whether the child received teaching or did not, and (*b*) the relation between sentence type and receipt of teaching, in the necessarily true vs. contingent experiment. ○—○, teaching; ●– – –●, no teaching.

relative difficulty of teaching them. The negated sentence type proved the most difficult discrimination; indeed only one of the youngest group of children under the teaching condition was able to attain criterion on it.

No cases were discovered of children from the no teaching group who had attained criterion within the 30 trials being able to verbalize the basis of their success in anything like the terms that the experimenter was using to characterize the distinction to the teaching groups ('must be true', 'always true', etc.). Of the 27 children who attained criterion in this way in the no teaching group, 10 just said they knew that one of the sentences was 'right', and the remainder said that they did not know how they knew which lever to press.

In order to determine whether there were systematic differences in difficulty between the 30 stimulus sentences of each type a one-way, repeated measures ANOVA was performed for each of the five sentence types encountered by each subgroup of 48 children. To make this possible a correct response was counted as '2' and an incorrect response as '1'. None of these analyses resulted in an effects term significant at the 0·05 level. However, children's 'protests' in the teaching condition when a pair had been explained after an incorrect response suggested that some examples of necessity may have been ambiguous. Specifically, those verbalizations centred around the fact that in ordinary usage a sentence necessary in form may not be interpreted as self-evidently true. The principal examples of this ambiguity were as follows: 'The sun is hot' (often said in conversation about hot weather); 'John knows who his friend is' (in the sense of knowing whom to trust); 'The left-handed boy is not right-handed' (that is, not even slightly so); 'The dwarf is short' (even for a dwarf).

Discussion

These results show that children who are within, what Piagetians would term, the 'late preoperational' age range (five to six years) are capable of appreciating an adult's description of how necessary truth can be a characteristic of linguistic propositions. Moreover this receptive understanding of necessity considerably improves into the 'early concrete operational' period (seven to eight years); although the present data cannot demonstrate later improvement due to a ceiling effect on the task. Against this, five- to 10-year-old children's ability to extract the principle of necessity vs. contingency for themselves, without instruction, is uniformly poor.

This latter finding is consistent with the Piagetian claim, discussed above, that it is not until adolescence that the individual can spontaneously utilize the principle of necessity in the solution of a problem. On the other hand, the former finding of receptive competence in cognizing propositional necessity does not support Piagetian theory. It would be inaccurate to say that any of Piaget's claims have been directly contradicted by these data because Piaget, to the author's knowledge at least, never predicted how children would perform on such a task. Nevertheless here are two respects in which Piagetian theory is not supported.

First, children of five and six are likely to have little competence on concrete operational tasks, and yet they have been shown here to have at least a receptive understanding of necessity. This does not accord well with the Piagetian claim that children's appreciation of necessity is the outgrowth of reflection on concrete operational principles. It may, however, be objected that Piaget was concerned with the child's mental orientation to his or her answers to problems: he did not address the issue of receptive understanding of necessity. Admittedly, but this 'objection' can be reinterpreted to provide the second reason why Piaget is not supported by the data. Indeed Piaget did *not* address himself to the possibility of receptive understanding of necessity; he did not acknowledge it and could therefore give it no developmental role to play. What can be regarded, then, as a demonstration of such a competence fits uncomfortably with Piagetian theory.

The differential ease of the sentence types appears principally to have been a function of linguistic complexity, as would be expected. However, the finding that the negated sentence type presented the most difficult discrimination is not quite so predictable. This can be interpreted in terms of the hypothesis that the function of the negative form is to negate a previously assumed positive proposition and that when a sentence does not have this function (as here) it is more difficult to process (Greene, 1970). Donaldson (1970) and de Villiers & Flusberg (1975) have produced evidence that young children find descriptions with negative referents very difficult to complete; though more recent data from Watson (1979) suggest that the effect can be mitigated.

These data only bear on the child's understanding of necessary *truth*, or tautology. However tautology is only one face of necessity, the other being contradiction, or necessary falsity. Thus, the next study concerned the child's ability to distinguish between necessary falsity and contingency.

Experiment 2

The methods, materials and procedures employed in the second experiment were virtually identical to those of the first experiment. The essential difference consisted in the use of necessary *false* vs. contingent sentences (see Table 3). This meant that children in the teaching group had to be told that their task was to discriminate sentences which 'have to be untrue' from sentences which 'may or may not be untrue':

Definitional-false (e.g. 'John's sister is a boy' vs. 'John's sister is a Brownie'); *situational-false* (e.g. 'The swimming man is out of the water' vs. 'The swimming man is out of the race'); *relational-false* (e.g. 'The man is younger than the boys' vs. 'The boys are noisier than the man'); *empty-false* (e.g. 'The car has some wings' vs. 'That car has some rust'); *negative-false* (e.g. 'The red hat is not coloured' vs. 'The red hat is not small').

Children. As a pilot study had shown this task to be considerably easier than the previous (necessary *true* vs. contingent) discrimination, only the two younger groups of children were tested. All children

Table 3. A selection of six sentence pairs from the set of 30 used for each of the five sentence types on the necessarily false vs. contingent discrimination

Definitional-false

The headmistress is a man.
The headmistress is a singer.

John's dad is a child.
John's dad is a farmer.

The coin is paper.
The coin is 10p.

The ruler should be made jagged.
The ruler should be made of plastic.

That cabbage is a flower.
That cabbage is a beauty.

The dwarf is tall.
The dwarf is friendly.

Situational-false

When John sings he is silent.
When John sings he is happy.

The man watching us has his eyes closed.
The man beside us has his eyes closed.

The swimming man is out of the water.
The swimming man is out of the race.

The dreaming man was awake.
The dreaming man was snoring.

The man who saw the car for the first time had seen it before.
The man who drove the car for the first time had seen it before.

The boy with three pencils has only two things.
The boy with three pencils has only two brothers.

Relational-false

The boy who went home last left before the rest.
The boy who went home last left for a rest.

The man is younger than the boys.
The boys are noisier than the man.

The man we followed was behind us.
The man we followed was looking for us.

The winner of the race had taken most time.
The winner of the race had taken most care.

The white cat has darker fur than the grey cat.
The white cat has lighter fur than the white mouse.

John is taller than the boy who is taller than him.
John is thinner than the boy who is shorter than him.

Empty-false

The football is square.
The football is white.

The snow is red.
The snow is melting.

The house has a paper roof.
The house has a large garage.

The clouds are on the ground.
The balloon is in the sky.

The nurse looks after people who are well.
The nurse looks after people who cannot walk.

The zebra has spots.
The zebra has babies.

Negated-false

Ten is not a number.
Ten is not a lot.

That cat is not an animal.
That cat is not a mother.

The sea is not watery.
The sea is not calm.

The apple is not a fruit.
The apple is not a present.

The shoes are not footwear.
The shoes are not jumble.

The train-set is not a toy.
The train-set is not a surprise.

were attending schools in Cheshire. There were 80 children in the younger group, which had a mean age of 5·9 years (range: 5·3–6·9 years), and 80 children in the older group, with a mean age of 7·9 years (range: 7·2–8·6). None of the children had acted as subjects in Expt 1.

Table 4. The mean error scores on the necessarily false vs. contingent discrimination with sentence types collapsed (standard deviations in parentheses and numbers of children attaining criterion in brackets)

Testing conditions: Mean ages of groups	Teaching	No teaching
5·9 years	3·92 (SD = 4·71) [33]	10·32 (SD = 5·67) [13]
7·9 years	1·62 (SD = 2·24) [40]	4·27 (SD = 4·20) [32]

$n = 160$.

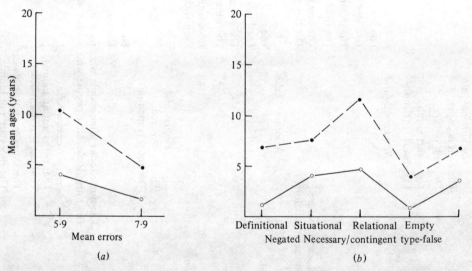

(a)   (b)

Figure 2. Graphs of (a) the relation between age level and whether the child received teaching or did not, and (b) the relation between sentence type and the receipt of teaching, in the necessarily false vs. contingent experiment. ○—○, teaching; ●– – –●, no teaching.

Results

As is evident from Table 4, a marked superiority in the performance of the teaching group over the no teaching group was re-encountered. However these mean errors also show that this discrimination was a very easy one compared to the discrimination in Expt 1. For example, only the no teaching subgroup of younger children tested on the relational sentence type contained no subjects who had attained criterion. At the higher age level, although the teaching group remained more successful, performance in the no teaching group was uniformly impressive, with even the relational subgroup of no teaching children attaining criterion in 50 per cent of cases.

A three-way ANOVA was again applied to the data: ages (2) × testing conditions (2) × sentence types (5). The familiar main effects of age ($F = 43·08$, d.f. = 1, 140,

$P < 0.005$), sentence type ($F = 8.63$, d.f. $= 4$, 140, $P < 0.01$), and testing condition ($F = 47.78$, d.f. $= 1$, 140, $P < 0.005$) were encountered. The only significant interaction (see Fig. 2*a*) was between age and testing condition, with $F = 7.88$, d.f. $= 1$, 140, $P < 0.01$. In the previous experiment such an interaction had resulted by virtue of the marked improvement of the teaching group relative to the no teaching group. Here the opposite was the case: the decrement in errors was steep in the no teaching group relative to that in the teaching group. This was because under the teaching condition the younger subgroup had a mean of only 3.92 errors, so even if the older subgroup made a mean of zero errors, the no teaching group's degree of improvement could not be matched: there was insufficient 'room' for improvement. However, *post hoc* analysis of the teaching group data did reveal that the older children's error scores were significantly lower ($P < 0.01$) than those of the younger children.

As Fig. 2*b* demonstrates, the differential difficulty between sentence types was very similar to that for necessarily true vs. contingent sentences. Also repeated was the lack of interaction between sentence type and teaching/no teaching ($F = 1.47$, d.f. $= 4$, 140, $P > 0.1$): the profile of difficulty was much the same for both conditions. This reinforces the conclusion from Expt 1 that differential difficulty was an inherent function of the sentences not of teaching them.

There were again found to be no significant differences in difficulty between the 30 sentences of each type when one-way ANOVAs were applied to the data of the kind used in Expt 1. This time all spontaneous comments were recorded as they had been quite revealing in the previous study. Most frequently the spontaneous comments concerned the fact of contradiction on first hearing a sentence (e.g. 'You *never* have square footballs'). Rarely did children reject the contradiction, as in the following example: 'When daddies are just born they're young!'. There were more comments about the oddity of the empty sentences (45 per cent of total) than about that of any other sentence type. This is consistent with the ease of this discrimination evident from the learning data, which is in turn consistent with the results of Expt 1.

Of the 58 children who attained criterion under the no teaching condition 50 gave an intelligible response to the question of how they knew which lever to press. Thirty-six said some were always 'wrong', 'funny', 'odd', etc.; 12 said that one set of sentences was always 'right' and the other 'wrong'; and two said that one set was wrong and the other 'could be wrong'. Therefore the large majority could conceptualize the basis of their discrimination.

One incidental pattern which emerged in the course of testing was for children from no teaching groups to laugh, snigger or look at the experimenter with puzzlement when the contradictory sentences were played, *even when they continued to respond at a chance level.* It is unlikely that this was due to understanding the distinction but forgetting which lever to press, because similar memory difficulties were present under the teaching condition and there was little evidence of forgetting here. More likely they were responding to the strangeness of a statement without extracting this strangeness as the 'clue' to the solution of the problem. Thus the child's perception of contradiction may be more basic than the learning data suggest.

Discussion

The most noticeable feature of these data is the ease of the necessary false vs. contingent discrimination, both absolutely and relative to the necessary true vs. contingent discrimination in Expt 1. Even the no teaching groups were very successful, with 32.5 per cent of the younger group attaining criterion performance.

If we conclude that the children in this study were 'understanding the principle of contradiction' then our results clearly run counter to Piaget's proposals. Within Piaget's theory the younger children in the group should have little, if any, understanding of concrete operational principles and even the older children's understanding should be tied to concrete situations. In fact in one of his last volumes Piaget (1980) reported a series of experiments partly in order to illustrate how understanding contradiction (e.g. $A = B$, $B = C$, but $A > C$) can only occur as a consequence of constructing reversible mental operations. More crucially because children from the no teaching group were applying the principle of necessary falsity, or contradiction, spontaneously it could plausibly be argued that they were evincing something that Piaget would have regarded as a *formal* operational capacity.

But it is possible to object that the children here were not distinguishing necessary falsity from contingency at all, but merely discriminating sentences that sounded silly from sentences that sounded sensible. Indeed, the comments and occasional laughter of the children would support such an interpretation.

It must be admitted that for the empty sentences this objection has some force. Consider, for example, 'The book is a brick one' and 'The cheese is to drink'. But the vast majority of the sentences were not of this nature and must have required more than just a 'sense of the ridiculous' in their discrimination: 'To see the man above us we had to look down' (relational), 'The boy with an egg in each hand is carrying three things' (situational), for example. Moreover such an objection would be based on the assumption that the perception of incongruity sufficient to judge something to be ridiculous bears no developmentally important relationship to the perception of incongruity sufficient to judge logical contradiction. Although we cannot treat the ridiculous as merely the contradictory with a human face, when we accept that there is at least a continuum from 'implausible' to 'ridiculous' to 'logically contradictory' we thereby admit the problems inherent in treating the understanding of contradiction as a formal, abstract capacity quite distinct from the appreciation of its more concrete, empirical relatives.

Finally, what explanation can be given for the ease of this task relative to the necessary truth vs. contingency discrimination? One explanation might be based on the suggestion that a necessarily true proposition is normally or frequently perceived as such by the process of cognitively constructing its opposite and appreciating the resultant contradiction. This *is* a mere speculation, but a plausible speculation given the manifest difficulty (experienced by the experimenters here) of explaining why some statement is self-evident without referring to the impossibility of its contradiction. For example the status of 'This water is wet' is best brought into relief by its opposite 'This water is dry'. On this model the necessary false vs. contingent discrimination was easier because it involved one cognitive 'operation' rather than two.

General discussion

There are two main respects in which these data suggest a divergent approach from the Piagetian to the development of necessity. The first involves the role of receptive understanding of necessity, relative to its spontaneous application. The second concerns the developmental significance of cognizing necessary truth and falsity as properties of linguistic expressions.

To deal with the question of receptive understanding, we found in Expt 1 that although children between five and 10 years have great difficulty in applying the principle of necessary truth in the discrimination they are well able – relative to sentence type – to comprehend the explanation of the principle; thereby suggesting a receptive understanding of necessity. Piaget's method of data collection (questioning plus 'clinical' probing) as well as his construal of the child as essentially 'active' made it inevitable that this receptive form of understanding would be given little due.

It would be grossly inaccurate to claim, of course, that Piaget could not locate such a form of understanding in his theory. He had employed the concept of 'assimilation' (*passim*), and thus we can consider an assimilatory capacity as being equivalent to the child's capacity for benefiting from experience. But to say that the children in the experiments benefited from the teaching because they had the assimilatory capacity to do so is circular. Analogous problems arise in the interpretation of Piagetian training studies (see Beilin, 1976).

What we are calling here 'receptive understanding' is very similar to Vygotsky's concept of a 'Zone of Proximal Development' which Vygotsky defined as 'the distance between the actual developmental level as determined by independent problem solving and the level of potential development as determined through problem solving under adult guidance or in collaboration with more capable peers' (Vygotsky, 1978, p. 86). But, of course, to posit such a notion is only to *face* a fundamental problem in developmental psychology, not to solve one. We have to say, among other things, how this form of receptive understanding comes about.

Turning now to the role of linguistic processes in the growth of necessity, we must ask what kind of alternatives there might be to the Piagetian theory of necessity, alternatives which give the appreciation of the necessary truth and falsity of propositions a central role in development. There is, for example, the social transmission alternative, elements of which are to be found in Vygotsky (1962) and in modern social behaviourism (see Rosenthal & Zimmerman, 1978). This approach regards the laws of logic as a set of cultural conventions which are passed on to the child via the linguistic system as part of the process of enculturization. The main difficulty with this approach is that it has few conceptual resources for explaining why the child comes to regard certain conventions *as* necessary *vis-à-vis* non-logical conventions such as those of a legal system or of phatic speech.

What we require is a theory which focuses on the linguistic system, not as a mere vehicle for the transmission of logical laws, but as an object of reflection. Such a theory was attempted by the early genetic epistemologist J. Mark Baldwin. Although Baldwin stressed the social origins of knowledge he realized that logical necessity was something beyond a social convention. He saw the child as developing a conception of necessary truth and implication by a negative process which Baldwin called 'limitation' (see Baldwin, 1908, chapter 8, and Russell, 1978, pp. 68–70). In the verbal context limitation means the child's awareness of being prevented from attaching certain predicates to certain subjects. His awareness of what *cannot* be said then moulds his conception of what cannot be denied or negated. (Baldwin rooted the mental act of limitation in the literal act of denial or exclusion from attention in the sensori-motor period.) Essentially, necessity, for Baldwin, was the product of understanding what the linguistic system cannot allow. Our finding that the appreciation of necessary falsity is far easier than that of necessary truth appears to support this suggestion, and also accords with the interpretation of the finding given above in terms of the appreciation of a tautology requiring two mental operations rather than the one required for contradiction.

In an interview shortly before his death Piaget (reported in Broughton & Freeman-Moir, in press) said that he only ever read the *first* volume of Baldwin's great work *Thought and Things*. Whether Piaget's theory of necessity might have been modified had he gone on to the second volume, in which Baldwin presents a theory of logical development in terms of such processes as limitation, we can only speculate.

Acknowledgements

This research was supported by Social Science Research Council project grant HR 5239. I am most grateful to Mary McMurran and Pamela Lyon for assistance. The cooperation of head teachers, staffs and pupils of the following Liverpool and Cheshire primary schools is warmly acknowledged: Booker Avenue, Childwall, Crosby Road North, Forefield, Hunts Cross, Meadow Bank, Moss Pitts, Wallerscote.

References

Baldwin, J. M. (1908). *The Cognitive–developmental Psychology of James Mark Baldwin*, vol. 2. London: Swan & Sonnenschein.
Beilin, H. (1976). Constructing cognitive operations linguistically. In H. W. Reese (ed.), *Advances in Child Development and Behaviour*, vol. II. London: Academic Press.
Broughton, J. & Freeman-Moir, D. J. (eds) (in press). *The Foundations of Cognitive–Developmental Psychology: The Theory of James Mark Baldwin*. New York: Ablex.
de Villiers, J. G. & Flusberg, H. B. T. (1975). Some facts one simply cannot deny. *Journal of Child Language*, 2, 279–286.
Donaldson, M. (1970). Developmental aspects of performance with negatives. In G. B. Flores d'Areais & W. J. M. Levelt (eds), *Advances in Psycholinguistics: Research Papers*. Amsterdam: North Holland.
Greene, J. M. (1970). The semantic function of negatives. *British Journal of Psychology*, 61, 17–22.
Hall, V. C. & Kaye, D. B. (1978). The necessity of logical necessity in Piaget's theory. In L. S. Siegel & C. J. Brainerd (eds), *Alternatives to Piaget*. London: Academic Press.
Ingram, D. (1974). The relationship between comprehension and production. In R. L. Schiefelbusch & L. L. Lloyd (eds), *Language Perspectives: Cognition, Retardation and Intervention*. London: Macmillan.
Inhelder, B. & Piaget, J. (1958). *The Growth of Logical Thinking from Childhood to Adolescence*. London: Routledge & Kegan Paul.
Markman, E. M. (1978). Empirical versus logical solutions to part–whole comparison problems concerning classes and collections. *Child Development*, 49, 168–177.
Miller, S. A. & Brownwell, C. A. (1975). Peers, persuasion and Piaget: Dyadic interaction between conservers and non-conservers. *Child Development*, 46, 992–997.
Miller, S. A., Brownwell, C. A. & Zukier, H. (1977). Cognitive certainty in children: Effects of concept, developmental level and method of assessment. *Developmental Psychology*, 13, 236–245.
Piaget, J. (1970). *Genetic Epistemology*. New York: Columbia University Press.
Piaget, J. (1971). *Biology and Knowledge*. Edinburgh: Edinburgh University Press.
Piaget, J. (1980). *Experiments in Contradiction*. Chicago: Chicago University Press.
Rosenthal, T. L. & Zimmerman, B. J. (1978). *Social Learning and Cognition*. New York: Academic Press.
Russell, J. (1978). *The Acquisition of Knowledge*. London: Macmillan.
Russell, J. (in press). Cognitive conflict, transmission and justification: Dyadic interaction in conservation attainment. *Journal of Genetic Psychology*.
Vygotsky, L. S. (1962). *Thought and Language*. Cambridge, MA: MIT Press.
Vygotsky, L. S. (1978). *Mind and Society*. Cambridge, MA: Harvard University Press.
Watson, J. M. (1979). Referential description by children in negative form. *British Journal of Psychology*, 70, 199–204.

Requests for reprints should be addressed to James Russell, Department of Psychology, University of Liverpool, PO Box 147, Eleanor Rathbone Building, Myrtle Street, Liverpool L69 3BX.

British Journal of Psychology (1982), **73**, 267–276   *Printed in Great Britain*

Class inclusion and conclusions about Piaget's theory

Leslie Smith

An interpretation of Piaget's account of how a child understands class relationships that is compatible with the account put forward by recent critics is proposed. It is claimed that Piaget's account is distinctive because it is an investigation of logical competence and so seeks to explain a child's understanding of the necessity of certain class relationships and not just their correctness. Central to Piaget's account is his claim that a child who understands inclusion must be able to characterize and systematically interrelate the positive, observational properties of a subclass with its negative, inferential properties. By contrast, recent experimentally based accounts allow inclusion to be understood by means of the positive, observational properties of a subclass alone and so allow the correctness of that relation, but not its necessity, to be comprehended. It is claimed that the understanding of correctness may be developmentally prior to the understanding of necessity and in consequence that Piaget's account is compatible with the accounts of his critics. Compatibility is also guaranteed by the fact that the former states necessary, unlike the latter who state sufficient, conditions of understanding.

It is to Jean Piaget that is owed the major psychological investigation of class relationships. In one of his first papers Piaget realized that the words 'some' and 'all' remain opaque to a child's understanding, as is shown by the inability of young children to deduce whether all, some or none of a collection of flowers are yellow if a portion of them are (Piaget, 1921, p. 450). His mature treatment of the topic is contained in three studies (Piaget, 1952, 1977*a*; Inhelder & Piaget, 1964) which support the conclusion of the early study but considerably extend its explanation. Recent experimental studies have not always supported Piaget's conclusion and have tended to suggest that children (might) attain an understanding of class relationships at an age earlier than that allowed by Piaget. The main aim of the present paper is to clarify one central feature in Piaget's account which seems to have been overlooked by others, namely the importance that the account accords to the presence of necessity in a child's understanding. In what follows, the discussion will (1) review Piaget's account of a child's understanding of class relationships, (2) identify and contrast some of the findings of recent experimental studies of this problem and (3) attempt to evaluate the dispute by showing how Piaget's account is importantly different from that of his critics and so compatible with, since distinct from, their accounts.

(1) Piaget's account

Piaget's account of a child's understanding of class relationships may be reviewed under three headings since that account is stated to be (*a*) an account of a child's logical competence with respect to his understanding of class relationships, (*b*) the members of which are to be identified by their negative, inferential – and not merely positive, observational – properties, (*c*) which condition is a necessary condition of understanding the necessity of certain class relationships.

(*a*) Piaget has clearly stated his interest in a child's deductive capacities both in early and in recent writings, for example:

> one can think what one wants of formal logic...But what nobody must dispute is that formal thought can be studied as a psychological fact...I call formal reasoning that reasoning which, from one or several propositions, draws a conclusion to which *the mind assents with certainty*, *without thereby having recourse to observation*. What is beyond dispute is that such reasoning exists (Piaget, 1922, p. 222 – translation and emphasis mine).

0007-1269/82/020267-10 $02.00/0 © 1982 The British Psychological Society

Two points should be noticed here. Firstly, a distinction is drawn between a child who understands that a conclusion *has to follow* from certain premises and a child who understands that a conclusion is true (correct) on the basis of observational evidence. This distinction is a well-founded one since someone who finds out by careful measurement that the interior angles of a Euclidean triangle are equal to 180 degrees does not thereby understand that this same conclusion is a deductive consequence of certain geometrical propositions; again, a young child who sees that his square jigsaw has four corner pieces might fail to see that his jigsaw has to have four such pieces if it is to be a square one. It is, therefore, one thing to make a correct claim about the observed properties of an object; it is quite another to realize that a certain claim is a necessarily true one. Piaget's interest resides primarily in the latter of these and any interest in the former is dependent upon this interest. Secondly, Piaget in early investigations tried to find instances of a child's understanding of necessity in his conscious thought and the verbal reports based upon that thought. In later works, he rejected such an approach on the grounds that a child's logical competence is not restricted to his ability to make formal, deductive inferences. It is beyond the scope of the present paper to discuss Piaget's structuralist theory in detail. It is sufficient to note that his structuralist theory requires the use of different logical systems at different developmental points, corresponding to a child's possession of cognitive structures such as schemes or groupings, and that the point behind this use of logical models of development is to chart the progress in a child's understanding of the necessity of some claim as the outcome of his previous understanding of the correctness of that claim.

The continuity of Piaget's interest in a child's logical competence, or capacity to understand deductive necessity, may now be documented because of its importance to the ensuing discussion. Piaget makes substantially the same point as the claim made, in the quotation just given, in his paper on the reasoning ability of formal operational children (Piaget, 1972, p. 159), since such children are taken by him to be capable of deducing the logical consequences of the hypotheses they form, whatever the truth-value of those hypotheses. In his account of infant development, Piaget points out that his commitment to there being a functional *a priori* does not require his commitment to there being a structural *a priori* at the outset of development (Piaget, 1953, p. 3). In his first, mature report on class-inclusion studies, Piaget stated that his aim was to show how a child becomes aware of the necessity that is displayed in his own operations (Piaget, 1952, p. 161). A child eventually understands not just that a whole has more members than one of its parts but that this is necessarily so:

> an 'intensive' quantification necessarily intervenes in the relations of inclusion that are inherent in every additive composition. Indeed, from the additive point of view, there are *necessarily* 'more' elements in a whole than in one of its parts (Piaget & Szeminska, 1941, p. 199—my translation and emphasis).

It is unfortunate that the term 'necessarily' is omitted in the standard translation (Piaget, 1952, p. 162) of this claim with a consequential failure to make explicit in English what the precise modal status of the claim is. In general, a child possesses an operational structure when that structure is closed and the criterion of closure cited by Piaget is the presence of necessity in a child's understanding (Piaget, 1978, p. 124).

(*b*) Piaget's account of a child's understanding of class relationships makes particular use of the general distinction noted in (*a*). A child who uses an operational structure, namely a grouping* (Piaget, 1952, p. 181), is one who does understand the necessity of certain

---

* The third sentence of the last paragraph of the Introduction (Piaget, 1952, p. 162) might be better translated as: 'in other words, is not the additive composition of classes, which is the sole way to unite the latter in a coherent "grouping" of hierarchical inclusions and so to assign them a precise structure, the psychological counter-part of the additive composition of numbers...' (Piaget & Szeminska, 1941, p. 200).

class relationships, unlike a pre-operational child who may merely understand the correctness of those relationships. The latter may correctly and consistently allocate individuals to classes or draw pictures of the classes so formed and he may have some conception of the difference between a whole and a part on the basis of an object's graphic or perceptual properties (Piaget, 1952, p. 171; Inhelder & Piaget, 1964, pp. 8, 98). A child who possesses an operational structure has a greater logical competence than his pre-operational counterpart. In his most recent statement of position, Piaget takes there to be two conditions whose presence is required for a child to possess an operational structure that permits an understanding of inclusion-relations:

> inclusion is correctly understood, and so quantifiable in the form $nA < nB$ only if two conditions are met... (1) it is necessary that subclass A (for example daisies) forms a part of a total class B which is resistant and permanent enough to conserve its extension when the subject centres his attention on its subdivisions...(2) it is further necessary to subdivide the whole B into subclasses A and A' which are explicitly characterized by partial negations: $A' = $ *the B which are not A and* $A = $ *the B which are not A'* (Piaget, 1977a, p. 88 – translation and emphasis mine; see also Inhelder & Piaget, 1964, p. 106).

The first of these conditions states that a child should be able to compare a subclass with its total class such that decomposition of the latter does not preclude its reformation. The second condition is more complex and states that a child should be able to understand both that $A = B - A'$ and that $A' = B - A$.

To see the complexity of this condition, consider a case where a child is presented with nine flowers (class B), seven of which are daisies (class A) and two of which are roses (class A'). Here the classes are characterized by their positive, observational properties. But these classes may be differently characterized since either of the subclasses may be identified by subtraction of the other subclass from their total class. Thus the class of daisies (A) is the class of flowers (B) minus the class of roses (A') and so $A = B - A'$; and the class of roses (A') is the class of flowers (B) minus the class of daisies (A) and so $A' = B - A$. Thus both class A and class A' can be characterized negatively and inferentially – negatively because members of class A are the members of class B which are *not* members of class A' and inferentially because the formation of class A is inferred on the basis of the subtraction of class A' from class B. Now it is this latter type of characterization, in terms of the negative and inferential properties of a class, that is appealed to by Piaget as the second condition cited. Subclasses A and A' may be characterized in two alternative ways which are extensionally equivalent, since they pick out the same objects, but which are not psychologically interchangeable, since they are intensionally distinct. Only a child who can systematically relate the extensions of these subclasses with their intensions,* both positive and observational as well as negative and inferential, will understand inclusion-relations.

It is evident that Piaget is attributing to an operational child some understanding of complementation. Piaget is not claiming that the possessor of a grouping will, when he understands that class A is included in class B, take class A' to be the class of any object whatsoever that is not a member of class A; if that were Piaget's claim, then he would be attributing to such a child an understanding that class A together with class A', which is strictly the logical complement of A, exhaust the universe. Certainly, Piaget does use the standard notation of the theory of classes, for example when he claims that subclass A and its complement A' are disjoint and so that $A \times A' = 0$ (Inhelder & Piaget, 1964, p. 7). But what Piaget does claim is that the user of a grouping will have a partial understanding of complementation: given three classes, where A and A' are subclasses of B, a child will understand that these classes are interderivable since, relative to a universe consisting of class B, class A remains when class A' is subtracted from class B and class A'

* The last two occurrences of 'comprehension' (Piaget, 1952, p. 161) should read 'intension'.

remains when class A is subtracted from class B. Piaget does not deny that the user of a grouping understands that there are classes other than classes A, A' and B, for example the class of tulips, the class of animals, the class of birds, and so on. What he does deny is that such a child must use his understanding of those other classes for him to characterize classes A and A' by their negative and inferential properties. Indeed, children who do understand that a class B has more members than one of its subclasses, A, will not typically understand that the membership of class B', which is the complement of class B, is smaller than the membership of class A', which is the complement of class A (Inhelder & Piaget, 1964, p. 291; Piaget, 1977a, p. 82).

It may now be apparent why Piaget's claim that his two conditions are conditions for the correctness of a child's understanding of inclusion relations is also a claim that such an understanding will embody an understanding of necessity: it is necessarily the case that class A is formed by the subtraction of class A' from class B, given a universe consisting of class B, and so a child who correctly understands that this is so is also one who understands the necessity of this link. This claim is distinct from the false claim that such a child necessarily understands the link. It is for this reason that Piaget contrasts the position of a child who has an intuitive but non-deductive understanding (Piaget & Szeminska, 1941, p. 215, 'non-deductive' is omitted from the translation; Piaget, 1952, p. 175) with that of the possessor of a grouping.

What is the criterion for attributing to a child an understanding of necessity? Piaget denies that a verbal criterion is reliable and so does not look for a child's use of words such as 'necessary'. Nor does he require that a child should be capable of reflecting on associated concepts. What is decisive is the inclusion-question itself. In its most general form, the question to ask is: are there more members of A or more members of B? (Piaget & Inhelder, 1969, p. 169). To give a correct answer to some instance of this question a child is required to count the members of A; to count the members of B; and to subtract the former result from the latter. A child who correctly concludes that B has more members than A (when this is in fact the case) is one who must be able to identify the members of class A' by their possession of a negative, inferential property and so must be able to characterize members of class A' both by their being roses and by their being that which remains when the daisies are subtracted from the flowers ($A' = B - A$). Similarly, that child must also be able to see that class B has more members than its other subclass, A', and in consequence must be able to characterize class A by either mode of characterization ($A = B - A'$). A child's use of words such as 'as well' (Piaget, 1952, p. 176; Inhelder & Piaget, 1964, p. 108) is a confirmation that this is so. The criterion used by Piaget is, then, the selection of a question the correct answer to which requires a child to make the stipulated deductions as a condition of that answer's being the correct answer that it is.

(c) It is clear that the conditions stated by Piaget are necessary conditions. Since this is explicit in the quotation given in (b), no further comment is needed. A necessary condition is not, of course, a sufficient condition.

In sum, Piaget's account is an account of a child's logical competence and the two conditions that he cites, namely the ability to form stable classes and the ability to inter-relate a pair of subclasses and a total class in a deductive manner, are necessary conditions of a child's being able to understand the necessity of certain class relationships.

(2) Experimental studies

Discussion in the present section will be limited in aim and will review recent experimental studies of a child's understanding of class relationships. The main aim of the review will be that of showing the distinctiveness of Piaget's account of the understanding of class relationships.

McGarrigle *et al.* (1978), whose study has been reviewed by Donaldson (1978), have an interest in performance factors relevant to the understanding of class relationships and are concerned with the perceptual salience of the classes under investigation. Their concern is with a child's ability to interrelate classes on the basis of positive, observational properties alone since a child is presented with an array consisting of four cows such that: class A = the three *black* (cows), class A' = the one *white* (cow), class B = the four *cows*, and class C = the four *sleeping* (cows). Evidently, class C has the same members as class B and so children can more easily answer a test-question 'Are there more black cows or more sleeping cows?' than a test-question 'Are there more black cows or more cows?'. To see why the former is an easier question, it may be noted that a child can correctly answer the former test-question by quantifying the membership of class A, by quantifying the membership of class C and by subtracting the result of the former count from that of the latter. Thus a correct answer is available to a child who does not understand that some members of class B are not members of class A and so does not understand that some $A' = B - A$. But if this is so, then such a child may have a correct understanding of the class-relationships in the array without an understanding of the necessity of certain of those relationships. By contrast, the latter test-question is one that is favoured by Piaget. To answer that question correctly, a child must quantify the membership of class A, quantify that of class B and then subtract the result of the former from that of the latter. It is a condition of his being able to do this successfully that he should be able to understand that $A' = B - A$ and so any correct understanding possessed by such a child will be one that displays necessity. McGarrigle *et al.* (1978) do not specify the status of the conditions that they wish to establish but it is clear that their concern is different from that of Piaget.

An essentially similar study is reported by Meadows (1977), who states that her interest is in both competence and performance and who wishes to replace Piaget's account with one that stresses performance factors. Children are presented with an array consisting of coloured spots such that: class A = the five *pink* (spots), class A' = the three *blue* (spots), class B = the eight *spots*, and class C = the eight *round* (spots). Classes B and C have the same membership and so children can answer the test-question 'If I took away the blue ones, what would be left, the pink ones or the blue ones or the round ones?' without having to understand that some members of class B are not members of class A. Once again, the use of class C, over and above classes A, A' and B, which has the same members as class B allows a child to have a correct understanding of the relationships but not one that displays necessity. Meadows (personal communication) claims that her test-question is taken from Piaget; yet the question cited has no equivalent in the list offered in Piaget's main account (Inhelder & Piaget, 1964, p. 101), although it does have an equivalent in a later review (Piaget & Inhelder, 1969, p. 169). (See also Section 3 below.) Meadows also claims that the conditions that she discusses are both necessary and sufficient for the understanding of inclusion and so her account is different from Piaget's account in this respect as well.

Markman & Seibert (1976) and Markman (1979) are interested in performance factors relevant to the understanding of inclusion and propose that a child's understanding of the inclusion-relation is facilitated by his understanding of certain types of part–whole relations. On this view, collections are distinguished from classes by possession of a natural organization, by being wholes in more than an abstract sense and by being referred to by singular nouns (Markman & Seibert, 1976). It is claimed that children can more easily give a correct answer to a collection-question, 'Who would have more pets, someone who owned the baby frogs or someone who owned the family?', than to a class-question, 'Are there more frogs or more baby frogs?' (Markman & Seibert, 1976) and so that an understanding of the former facilitates that of the latter (Markman, 1979). It is not stated whether this condition is to be taken as a necessary or as a sufficient condition. It seems clear, however, that a child may correctly answer the former question without understanding necessity. Let class A = the four *baby* (frogs), class A' = the two *big* (frogs), class B = the six *frogs* and collection/class C = the six members of the family. Since the membership of class B and collection/class C is the same, a child who correctly quantifies the membership of A and C and who performs the requisite subtraction may correctly answer the collection-question. Yet such an answer does not require a child to understand that some members of class B are not members of class A and so such a child is not required to comprehend the necessity of the link. Thus this account is distinct from that of Piaget.

Trabasso *et al.* (1978) cite evidence that might constitute a different type of challenge to Piaget's account and confirmation of their case is provided by a different set of experiments carried out by McGarrigle *et al.* (1978). The previous studies cited in this section attempt to show that Piaget's account is too restrictive on the grounds that some types of class-inclusion question are more easily comprehended than others. The challenge now to be considered rests on the claim that Piaget's account is too restricted on the grounds that children find class relationships that do not involve inclusion to be just as difficult to comprehend as those that do involve inclusion. Trabasso *et al.* (1978, pp. 157–160) present children with two systems of classes as follows: class A = the eight *animals*, class A_1 = the six *dogs*, and class A_2 = the two *cats*, whilst class B = the eight *fruits*, class B_1 = the four *apples*, and class B_2 = the four *oranges*. Children are invited to answer a standard inclusion-question, 'Are there more dogs or more animals?', and so make an A_1/A comparison and also to answer a between-class question, 'Are there more dogs or more fruits?', and so make an A_1/B comparison. Only the former of these, claim Trabasso *et al.* (1978, p. 159), has an inclusion-relation; yet the results show that children find these questions to be *equally* difficult. What is suspect about their case is the claim that Piaget's theory would predict that children should find an A_1/B comparison to be easier than an A_1/A comparison. Firstly, exception can be taken to their contention that to count the membership of class A_1, a child will count the membership of A_1 and of class A_2; add the results of the two counts to quantify the membership of class A; and then subtract the result of the count of class A_2 from the previous addition (Trabasso *et al.*, 1978, p. 159). The interpretation of Piaget's account presented in Section 1(*b*) above diverges from this by allowing that a child will count the membership of class A_1; count the membership of class A_2; and, as a condition of his adding together the results of these counts, understand that A_1 is the subtraction of A_2 from A. It is a condition of a child's being able to add together two subclasses to form a superordinate class that he should be able to subtract one of the subclasses from the superordinate class to yield the other subclass. Disagreement occurs, therefore, as to the interpretation of Piaget's account.

Secondly, even if the interpretation of Trabasso *et al.* is accepted in preference to that presented in Section 1(*b*) above, it does not follow that Piaget's account predicts that an A_1/B comparison should be easier than an A_1/A comparison. To count the membership of class B, when making an A_1/B comparison, a child must count the membership of class B_1, count that of B_2 and add the two results together. But it is clear that only a child who understands that class B is an including class, and so that class B_1 and class B_2 are included classes in that class B, can add the two results together. So an inclusion-relation is, *pace* Trabasso *et al.*, involved in the quantification of class B, for a child who cannot understand inclusion cannot quantify class B. Moreover, on this same interpretation, a child who wishes to quantify class A_1 is required to subtract class A_2 from class A and so a child is, once again, required to understand that class A includes classes A_1 and A_2. It follows that the analysis of Piaget's account provided by Trabasso *et al.* does require that a child who makes an A_1/B comparison should be able to understand inclusion-relations as a condition of his being able correctly to quantify both class A_1 and class B.

Thirdly, an inclusion-relation is still involved in an A_1/B comparison if the interpretation of Piaget's account that is presented in Section 1(b) is accepted. An ability to understand inclusion would not be required for the quantification of class A_1; but it would be required for the quantification of class B, which is admitted to be a superordinate class in relation to B_1 and B_2 and which could not be correctly quantified by a child who did not understand that this is so. Thus, on either interpretation of Piaget's account, an inclusion-relation is involved in an A_1/B comparison, as well as in an A_1/A comparison, and it is presumably for this reason that children find both types of comparison to be equally difficult. For both require an understanding of necessity, the absence of which excludes success in either case.

A similar conclusion applies to the study carried out by McGarrigle *et al.* (1978). Children are presented with an array consisting of four cows, two of which are black and two of which are white, and four horses, two of which are black and two of which are white. To give a correct answer to a between-class question, such as 'Are there more white cows or more horses?', a child must understand that the class of horses is an including class in relation to its two subclasses. Thus although the invited comparison does not embody an inclusion-relation, it is a condition of a child's being able to quantify the membership of one of the classes in the comparison that he should be able to understand inclusion. Once again, the absence of necessity in a child's understanding results in a failure correctly to answer the question asked.

Judd & Mervis (1979) have an interest in factors that influence a child's performance on class-inclusion problems and attempt to state necessary conditions that facilitate successful performance, namely counting the membership of the classes and awareness of contradiction between incorrect answers to an inclusion-question and correct counting of the classes. It is claimed that the second of these conditions is the important one, when a child is asked a standard inclusion-question. Judd & Mervis note that their evidence is consistent with Piaget's account and it is apparent why this is so. The interpretation of Piaget's account suggested here is that it requires a child to perform a deductive inference and so requires him to understand necessity. Let class $B =$ the class of *toys*, class $A =$ the class of *balls* and class $A' =$ the class of *teddy bears*. A child who does understand inclusion is one who understands that $B = A + A'$; and that $A = B - A'$; and that $A' = B - A$. Further, a child's understanding of the latter pair in this trio is a deductive consequence of his understanding the first member of the trio. Thus a child who can correctly count the members of class B is committed to the first member of the trio, $B = A + A'$; but if that child then claims that the membership of class A exceeds that of class B, he is committed to a denial of $A = B - A'$. Thus that child's total response is contradictory since his commitment to $B = A + A'$ requires his commitment to $A = B - A'$, yet the child's responses show that he accepts only the former of these and not the latter. It is clear that the elimination of contradictions is an essential task that faces any child who misunderstands inclusion-relations in this way. Thus the account suggested by Judd & Mervis is compatible with Piaget's account.

In conclusion, it is clear that Piaget's account is untouched by his critics. His account, unlike their accounts, is primarily concerned with the investigation of logical competence; his account, unlike their accounts, investigates a child's ability to interrelate the negative, inferential properties of a subclass with its positive, observational properties; his account, unlike their accounts, attempts to state necessary conditions alone for the understanding of inclusion-relations. The most important difference arises from the fact that whilst his critics seek to investigate the correctness of a child's understanding of class relationships, Piaget seeks to investigate the extent to which a child understands the necessity (if any) of those relationships.

(3) **Evaluation**

The aim of the present section is to show that Piaget's account is compatible with, even though distinct from, that of his critics; to identify possible sources of confusion in Piaget's account; and, finally, to indicate why the inclusion-relation is centrally important to Piaget's theory of genetic epistemology.

There are two reasons why Piaget's account is compatible with that of his critics. Firstly, even though the latter investigate the correctness of a child's understanding of inclusion, in contrast to the former who investigates the necessity displayed in such understanding, it is clear that the type of investigation carried out by Piaget presupposes the type of investigation carried out by his critics. For a child who understands that an including class is one that, necessarily, has more members than a class that it includes is a child who understands the correctness of this claim. Thus correctness of understanding is presupposed for a child to have an understanding of necessity. Now this claim is unexceptional. Yet it hides an empirical question, for only empirical research can determine whether a child who understands necessity is one who gains that understanding *concurrently* with his understanding of correctness or *consecutive* to his understanding of correctness. It is apparent, from the research cited in Section 2, that a child may understand correctness even though he does not understand necessity and thus it may be argued that a child's understanding is consecutive rather than concurrent. Thus the distinction between correctness and necessity is crucial to this empirical question. The critics seem not to draw this distinction and so criticize Piaget on the grounds that a child can correctly understand inclusion-relations at an age earlier than that allowed by his account. In consequence they overlook the difference between themselves and Piaget. Yet Piaget seems to suppose that an understanding of necessity is concurrent with that of correctness and so fails to see that one is a developmental antecedent of the other. If the argument presented here is accepted, it can be claimed that Piaget's account is compatible with that of his critics.

Secondly, Piaget's account is one that presents necessary conditions of understanding, unlike his critics who (tend to) state sufficient conditions. But there is an interesting asymmetry here. That X_1 is a sufficient condition of Y does not exclude there being some other factor, X_2, from also being sufficient for Y and thus Y will be present when either X_1 or X_2 is present. Thus Y may be present, given X_1 is present, even though X_2 is absent and Y may be present, given X_2 is present, even though X_1 is absent. By contrast, if Z_1 and Z_2 are necessary conditions of Y, then the absence of either Z_1 or Z_2 results in the absence of Y. Thus Y will be absent, given the absence of Z_1, even though Z_2 is present and Y will be absent, given the absence of Z_2, even though Z_1 is present. It follows from this that *if* Piaget's account does state necessary conditions for the understanding of inclusion, his account must be accepted as being more basic than any account that presents conditions that are (severally) sufficient for the understanding of inclusion. Thus an account that states necessary conditions must be compatible with any account stating sufficient conditions. So even if, contrary to the argument of the previous sections, Piaget's account was not distinct from that of his critics, there would still be good reason to retain his account just if it states necessary conditions of understanding rather than sufficient conditions.

Two possible sources of confusion in Piaget's account may be mentioned. Firstly, Piaget sometimes uses 'easy' versions of his class-inclusion question, 'Are there more wooden beads or more brown beads?' (Piaget, 1952, p. 164); sometimes includes such questions in reviews of his own work (Piaget & Inhelder, 1969, p. 169); sometimes uses collection questions, 'Are there more flowers or more daisies in this bunch?' (Piaget, 1977a, p. 84; see also Inhelder & Piaget, 1964, p. 101); and so makes it difficult for his reader to appreciate the importance of the 'hard' version such as 'Are there more primulas or more flowers?' (Inhelder & Piaget, 1964, p. 101). Secondly, Piaget does not, perhaps, signal clearly enough his use, with modification, of the notation taken from the theory of classes. Thus A' is to be taken *both* as a subclass that is observationally characterizable *and* as a complementary class that is inferentially characterizable (Piaget, 1952, pp. 163 and 172 respectively; Inhelder & Piaget, 1964, pp. 100 and 103 respectively). In this respect, however, the English reader is not helped by mistranslation of logical and structuralist concepts. Taken together, these two deficiencies suggest that the interpretation presented in Section 1 above is one to be extracted from the work of Piaget rather than one that is explicitly stated in that work.

Finally, brief reference may be made to the place of the inclusion-relation in Piaget's genetic epistemology. On this view, any biological system will display a functioning that is logical in nature. Thus instances of inclusion are cited by Piaget where one characteristic (and not just one class) is embedded in some other, as the characteristic of being a domestic cat is embedded in that of being a cat (Piaget, 1971, p. 159), or where one action-scheme is included in that of another (Piaget, 1953, p. 239). A child's understanding of the (correctness and necessity of) inclusion-relation arises out of what Piaget takes to be these more primitive biological counterparts and further claims that the equilibratory process that links them is one that requires a child systematically to interrelate an object's negative and affirmative characteristics (Piaget, 1978, pp. 10–11). Since processes of abstraction and generalization are allied to the process of equilibration, it is clear that a child's understanding of inclusion-relations is a striking instance of the claim that:

> any generalization tied to empirical abstraction is only extensional and consists in refinding in new objects a property that already existed there... by contrast, reflective abstraction consists in the introduction into new objects of properties that they did not possess (Piaget 1977b, p. 318 – my translation).

What the child who understands the necessity of an inclusion-relation can do is to introduce the property of necessity by applying it to instances of inclusion the understanding of which is necessary for his cognitive development to be completed.

In sum, Piaget's account is both distinctive and important. It has been the object of the present paper to discuss its distinctiveness and so support the conclusion suggested by Winer (1980, p. 325) that 'class inclusion at different ages represents different skills or processes'. It has been beyond the scope of the paper to discuss the wider implications of Piaget's account in the context of his theory. It may be noted, however, that the account of the understanding of inclusion is not independent of the theory of genetic epistemology which is an attempt to trace the developmental route whereby a child has the capacity to make deductive, and so logically necessary, inferences.

Acknowledgements

I wish to thank Derek Wright and (anonymous) referees of this journal for their comments as a result of which this paper has been substantially improved. Any defects that remain are, of course, mine. Support for this study was provided by a SSRC postgraduate research award.

References

Donaldson, M. (1978). *Children's Minds*. Glasgow: Fontana.
Inhelder, B. & Piaget, J. (1964). *The Early Growth of Logic in the Child*. London: Routledge & Kegan Paul.
Judd, S. S. & Mervis, C. B. (1979). Learning to solve class-inclusion problems: The roles of quantification and recognition of contradiction. *Child Development*, **50**, 163–169.

Markman, E. M. (1979). Classes and collections: Conceptual organisation and numerical abilities. *Cognitive Psychology*, **11**, 395–411.

Markman, E. M. & Seibert, J. (1976). Classes and collections: Internal organisation and resulting holistic properties. *Cognitive Psychology*, **8**, 561–577.

McGarrigle, J., Grieve, R. & Hughes, M. (1978). Interpreting inclusion: A contribution to the study of the child's cognitive and linguistic development. *Journal of Experimental Child Psychology*, **26**, 528–550.

Meadows, W. S. (1977). An experimental investigation of Piaget's analysis of class inclusion. *British Journal of Psychology*, **68**, 229–235.

Piaget, J. (1921). Essai sur quelques aspects du développement de la notion de partie chez l'enfant. *Journal de Psychologie Normale et Pathélogique*, 449–481.

Piaget, J. (1922). Essai sur la multiplication logique et les débuts de la pensée formelle chez l'enfant. *Journal de Psychologie Normale et Pathélogique*, 222–261.

Piaget, J. (1952). *The Child's Conception of Number*. London: Routledge & Kegan Paul.

Piaget, J. (1953). *The Origins of Intelligence in the Child*. London: Routledge & Kegan Paul.

Piaget, J. (1971). *Biology and Knowledge*. Edinburgh: Edinburgh University Press.

Piaget, J. (1972). Intellectual evolution from adolescence to adulthood. *Human Development*, **15**, 1–12. Reprinted in P. N. Johnson-Laird & P. C. Wason (eds), *Thinking: Readings in Cognitive Sciences*. Cambridge: Cambridge. University Press, 1977.

Piaget, J. (1977*a*). *Recherches sur l'Abstraction Réfléchissante*, I. Paris: Presses Universitaires de France.

Piaget, J. (1977*b*). *Recherches sur l'Abstraction Réfléchissante*, II. Paris: Presses Universitaires de France.

Piaget, J. (1978). *The Development of Thought*. Oxford: Basil Blackwell.

Piaget, J. & Inhelder, B. (1969). Intellectual operations and their development. In P. Fraisse & J. Piaget (eds), *Experimental Psychology*, vol. 7. London: Routledge & Kegan Paul.

Piaget, J. & Szeminska, A. (1941). *La Genèse du Nombre chez l'Enfant*. Neuchâtel: Delachaux et Niestlé.

Trabasso, T., Isen, A. M., Dolecki, P., McLanahan, A. G., Riley, C. A. & Tucker, T. (1978). How do children solve class-inclusion problems? In R. S. Siegler (ed.), *Children's Thinking: What Develops*? Hillsdale, NJ: Erlbaum.

Winer, G. A. (1980). Class inclusion reasoning in children: A review of the empirical literature. *Child Development*, **51**, 309–329.

Requests for reprints should be addressed to Leslie Smith, School of Education, University of Leicester, 21 University Road, Leicester LE1 7RF, UK.

3
Social and affective development

British Journal of Psychology (1982), **73**, 279–283   *Printed in Great Britain*

Piaget's theory of practical morality

Derek Wright

Piaget's theory of the development of practical morality has been neglected by later theorists. A brief statement of that theory is offered. Since Piaget's original account is in certain respects confused, the account of it involves a measure of interpretation. Specifically, it is concluded that practical morality cannot be heteronomous but is a function of mutual respect relationships.

In his monograph, *The Moral Judgment of the Child* (Piaget, 1932; henceforth referred to as *M.J.*), Piaget offers a theoretical scaffolding with which later investigators can 'erect the actual edifice' (p. ix). So far, this edifice has not been built. The purpose of this paper is to clarify that aspect of the scaffolding which concerns the development of moral obligation and aspiration as a first step towards building the theoretical edifice Piaget hoped for.

The central task of the theory is to explain how the child comes to live autonomously within the moral domain in the sense that: (*a*) he makes, and justifies, his own moral judgements, and (*b*) is impelled, more or less strongly and without coercion, to act in accordance with them. As Piaget puts it, 'For conduct to be characterized as moral there must be something more than an outward agreement between its content and that of commonly accepted rules: it is also requisite that the mind should tend towards morality as to an autonomous good and should itself be capable of appreciating the value of the rules that are proposed to it' (*M.J.*, p. 410).

Theoretical and practical morality

This central distinction is different from, and cuts across, such distinctions as that between judgement and action, or between thought, affect and behaviour.

The child's theoretical morality is his reasoning and judgement stripped of any association with obligation and aspiration for it is dissociated from any need to act. 'This verbal morality appears whenever the child is called upon to judge other people's actions that do not interest him directly or to give voice to general principles regarding his own conduct independently of his actual deeds' (*M.J.*, p. 171).

Practical morality is reasoning and judgement charged with a sense of obligation and aspiration. It is 'effective moral thought', which leads the child 'to form such moral judgements as will guide him in each particular case' (*M.J.*, p. 171). Such judgement represents 'the child's true thought', which 'lies much deeper' than his verbal beliefs, and 'somewhere below the level of formulation' (*M.J.*, p. 67).

Piaget stresses both the distance and the differences between theoretical and practical morality. A theoretical moral problem 'is far further removed from his moral practice than an intellectual problem from his logical practice' (*M.J.*, p. 108).

The differences are of at least two kinds. The first is that in his theoretical morality the child's judgements will be 'devoid of pity and lacking in psychological insight' (*M.J.*, p. 182), whereas in his practical morality his sympathies and antipathies are engaged for 'he is in the presence, not of isolated acts, but of personalities that attract or repel him' (*M.J.*, p. 116). The second is that the theoretical morality will differ from practical as a consequence of the developmental process which produces it, namely conscious realization.

Conscious realization is the active construction at the conscious level of structures of thought which are more or less isomorphic with the 'schemes that have been built up by action' (*M.J.*, p. 112). It depends upon social interaction because 'social life is necessary if the individual is to become conscious of the functioning of his own mind' (*M.J.*, p. 407). It takes time, and probably more than Piaget allowed. It is liable to error both through 'the distortions inherent in the very mechanism of reflection' (*M.J.*, p. 181) and through the very social influences which stimulate it.

In short, practical morality is the indissoluble unity of judgement and obligation and aspiration, it is mainly 'intuitive', and it will be only partially and imperfectly represented by theoretical morality at any one time, and indeed, for many, all the time.

Moral obligation and aspiration

In terms of general theory, 'the real conflict lies between those who want to explain the moral consciousness by means of purely individual processes (habit, biological adaption, etc.) and those who admit the necessity for an inter-individual factor' (*M.J.*, p. 100). Piaget is emphatic 'that two individuals at least must be taken into account if a moral reality is to develop' (*M.J.*, p. 100).

Moral obligation 'intervenes as soon as there is society, i.e. a relation between at least two individuals' (*M.J.*, p. 23); and 'if to the individual conscience rules seem to be charged with obligation, this is because communal life alters the very structure of consciousness by inculcating into it the feeling of respect' (*M.J.*, p. 96).

The implication of these, and many other comments, is that relationships are to be conceived as systems superordinate to the individuals who comprise them. A system may be defined as a set of elements which exist in relation to each other such that the system as a whole exhibits features which are not present in the elements in isolation, nor explicable wholly in terms of some additive accumulation of the features of the elements. The functioning of the elements is constrained, modified and shaped by the system as a whole. Systems are more or less self-conserving, equilibrated, hierarchical, open, and so on.

We can then say that when a child becomes part of an inter-individual relationship system there is generated within him, 'somewhere below the level of formulation', a sense of allegiance to the relationship as such. This allegiance involves, in some degree, both a submission to the demands of the relationship and an aspiration to maintain it which go beyond the straightforward behavioural modification intrinsic to social interaction. 'There must be born of the actions and reactions of individuals upon each other the consciousness of a necessary equilibrium binding upon and limiting both "alter" and "ego"' (*M.J.*, p. 317).

Types of relationship

Relationships will vary widely and it is to be expected that some kinds will be more conducive to the generation of moral obligation and aspiration than others. The dimension that Piaget has focused on is the degree of hierarchical structure with its associated degree of equilibrium. In effect he distinguishes between unilateral respect and the group or collective on the one hand, and mutual respect of the inter-individual on the other.

It is difficult to present a coherent statement of the differences. The closer we study Piaget's exposition the more we come up against obscurities and contradictions. The central problem seems to be that in developing his theory Piaget does not systematically distinguish *concepts* of relationship from actual relationships. Thus he is emphatic that the concepts of unilateral and mutual respect represent idealized ends of a continuum, and do not correspond to actual relationships. Both concepts are in a degree applicable to all relationships. At the same time he uses these terms to refer to actual relationships. Hence many of his theoretical statements about unilateral respect must be interpreted as predominantly unilateral respect but with elements of mutual respect. In the present account the terms will be used for the concepts unless otherwise stated. This necessarily entails an element of interpretation of what Piaget has actually said.

Unilateral respect is essentially a dominance–submission relationship. One person has authority and respect, defines what the other will do, and coerces him into doing it. It is maintained by the assertion of power and control on the one hand, and obedience through 'quasi-physical' fear on the other.

Sympathy and love are not part of the concept, though actual relationships are virtually never without elements of mutual affection. This point can be taken as illustrative of the contradictions in Piaget's own exposition. On the one hand he states that relationships are never 'purely unilateral' because 'a mutual sympathy surrounds relationships that are most heavily charged with authority' (*M.J.*, p. 83), thereby clearly implying that affection is not part of the concept of unilateral respect. On the other hand he defines respect in general as a '*sui generis* mixture of fear and love' (*M.J.*, p. 351).

In mutual respect relationships each individual is respected and valued as an equal. The relationship is characterized by cooperation and reciprocity, and founded on mutual sympathy and affection. Fear, in so far as it is present, is 'the purely moral fear of falling in the esteem of the respected person' (*M.J.*, p. 387). Antipathy is not excluded, for 'the play of sympathy and antipathy is a sufficient cause for practical reason to become conscious of reciprocity' (*M.J.*, p. 229).

The group or collective relationship is subsumed under mutual respect. 'It is no mere metaphor to say that a relation can be established between the individual's obedience to collective imperatives and the child's obedience to adults in general' (*M.J.*, p. 335). In young children's groups 'the individual does not count. Social life and individual life are one' (*M.J.*, p. 97). In a passing remark, he hints that a relationship between two children can have the same deindividuated quality, for he contrasts mutual respect with 'the mutual consent of two individual "selves" capable of joining forces for evil as well as good' (*M.J.*, p. 90).

Conceptually, unilateral and mutual respect are so different as to be antithetical. 'It is impossible to reduce the effects of cooperation to those of constraint and unilateral respect' (*M.J.*, p. 103), and 'if mutual respect does derive from unilateral respect, it does so by opposition' (*M.J.*, p. 93).

In actual relationships there tends to be a gradual development from unilateral to mutual respect as the child grows up. Cooperation is 'the ideal equilibrium to which all relations of constraint tend' (*M.J.*, p. 84). The application of Piaget's concept of equilibration, as he later analysed it, to the development of relationships waits to be done.

Unilateral respect and morality

At this point the confusion mentioned earlier becomes acute. Piaget unequivocally asserts that unilateral respect is the necessary condition for the morality of duty, as mutual respect is for the morality of the good. The problem is that Piaget sometimes seems to be equating duty with moral obligation and sometimes not. The position taken here is that Piaget's theory becomes coherent if, conceptually, we clearly separate the two and understand by duty the essentially non-moral and prudential submission to coercive power.

Several reasons for this position can be given. In the first place Piaget's separation of the moralities of duty and the good is so great as to be *logically* indefensible. Then in his own terms he distinguishes the 'external obedience' of unilateral respect from the 'spontaneous obedience', or 'responding to obligation', of mutual respect. He plainly sees it as desirable that the morality of duty should disappear with age. 'Duties are not obligatory because of their content but because of the fact that they emanate from respected individuals' (*M.J.*, p. 389), and may have nothing to do with morality, may even be immoral. Unilateral respect not only does not foster, but may interfere with, the child's understanding of and commitment to truthfulness (*M.J.*, p. 163) and fairness (*M.J.*, p. 195 and p. 279). It reinforces egocentricity, which is associated with failure to conform consistently to moral prescription.

Unilateral respect may have some ancillary function in moral development since it is 'the first normative control of which the child is capable' (*M.J.*, p. 409). It may, and may not, create in the child regularities of behaviour which make subsequent conformity to moral prescription easier. But it is not the condition under which moral obligation and aspiration as such emerge and develop.

Mutual respect and morality

We are therefore left with the proposition that the child's practical moral life is a function of *the extent to which his relationships are characterized by mutual respect*. If we can separate in Piaget's thinking the influences of Durkheim and Bovet as he understood them, then it can be seen that the whole drift of his own speculation was towards this conclusion. On this view, *practical* morality is not, and cannot be, heteronomous.

The regulation of unilateral respect relationships is determined by the person with authority and power; mutual respect relationships are regulated by the rules that are constitutive of the relationship itself. The concept is of a relationship which embodies the fundamental regulative principles of morality (equal rights, fairness, truthfulness, mutual caring, etc.) as the necessary conditions of its existence. Hence to be party to such relationships is to be living within the moral domain. 'Mutual respect would therefore seem to be possible only with what the individuals regard as morality' (*M.J.*, p. 92); and 'between mutual respect and the rules which condition it there exists a circular relation analogous to that which holds between organ and function' (*M.J.*, p. 93).

Developmentally speaking, 'the earliest social relations contain the germs of cooperation' (*M.J.*, p. 79). Though inevitably the young child's relationships with adults will have elements of unilateral respect, the adult can, if he wishes, go a long way towards creating 'an atmosphere of mutual help and understanding' such that the child finds himself 'in the presence, not of a system of commands requiring ritualistic and external obedience, but of a system of social relations such that everyone does his best to obey the same obligations and does so out of mutual respect' (*M.J.*, p. 134).

Relationships of mutual respect are experienced by the child as desirable and good. They are the context most favourable to the development of self-esteem, confidence, moral and intellectual autonomy, and cognitive development generally. Such relationships never exist in pure form. But in so far as the child consciously realizes the constitutive rules of such relationships, those rules come to form his ideal of the morally good. 'The notion of the good... is perhaps the final conscious realization of something that is the primary condition of the moral life – the need for reciprocal affection' (*M.J.*, p. 173).

The conscious realization of the functional principles of mutual respect relations is a long and slow task. Early steps in the process are the realization that truthfulness and fairness are necessary conditions of such relations. But 'cooperation has to be practised for a very long time before its consequences can be brought fully to light by reflective thought' (*M.J.*, p. 56). 'It is at the end of knowledge and not its beginning that the mind becomes conscious of the laws immanent in it' (*M.J.*, p. 406).

The process is liable to be delayed and distorted by at least two factors. Elements of unilateral respect are built into the very structure of family, school and society generally. They are likely to be more salient in the child's conscious mind than his intuitions of his 'true morality'. Secondly, he may well be exposed to moral teaching at variance with these intuitions. It is to be expected that the coincidence of theoretical with practical morality will be relatively uncommon.

Conclusion

The attempt has been made to present a brief coherent outline of a neglected aspect of Piaget's theory of moral development. Many questions remain, not the least being that of its empirical testing. It is the writer's view that cognitive-developmental theory in this field has suffered from neglecting it. It deserves to be elaborated in more precise detail. And it has consequences for moral education. As Piaget puts it 'our results are as unfavourable to the method of authority as to purely individualistic methods' (*M.J.*, p. 411); and 'the adult must therefore be a collaborator and not a master from this double point of view, moral and rational' (*M.J.*, p. 412).

References

Piaget, J. (1932). *The Moral Judgment of the Child.* London: Routledge & Kegan Paul.

Requests for reprints should be addressed to Derek Wright, School of Education, University of Leicester, 21 University Road, Leicester LE1 7RF, UK.

British Journal of Psychology (1982), **73**, 285–294   *Printed in Great Britain*

Parent–child relations and cognitive approaches to the development of moral judgement and behaviour

Michael Siegal and **Robin Francis**

This paper examines Piaget's cognitive approach to moral development particularly as it relates to the moral behaviour of young children. Research on moral behaviour and moral reasoning or cognition using measures derived from Piaget's theory has indicated only a weak to moderate correlation between the two. However, it is proposed that the correspondence between some domains of moral behaviour and a type of social 'hot' cognition is actually quite considerable. Borrowing from the work of J. M. Baldwin, this cognition consists of thoughts and decisions having a high affective value. These can involve the child's relationships with others and particularly parents. A study is reported in which the rule-violating behaviour of children aged five and six years was observed in a naturalistic situation. While self-initiated rule violations were significantly but modestly correlated with low cognitive development, rule violations as reactions to others' misconduct correlated substantially with a lack of identification with the mother (as indicated by children's verbal responses to questions regarding their relationships with others). The implications of a social–cognitive approach for the study of moral development and behaviour are considered.

The cognitive-development approach has long posited a cognitive–structural stage sequence underlying the growth of moral reasoning. Piaget (1932/1977, 1967, 1971) believed that children's moral development can be characterized in terms of two broad and less than distinct stages: one of adult constraint and the other of mutual respect. These stages of moral development parallel the growth of cognitive development and are closely tied to intellectual ability. For example, children will not progress to the stage of mutual respect until, having reached the stage of concrete operational intelligence, they have relinquished an egocentric view of the world and have developed the ability to take the role of the other. Similarly, the development of moral intentionality, a characteristic of the stage of mutual respect, 'corresponds to the more general cognitive differentiation of objective and subjective, physical and mental' (Kohlberg, 1969, p. 374). The view that intellectual ability contributes to children's moral reasoning is well established (Whiteman & Kosier, 1964; Lee, 1971; Keasey, 1975).

While Piaget (1932/1977) was predominately concerned with the moral judgement of the child and did not directly address the possibility of a relationship between judgement and behaviour, at times he nevertheless suggests that the two are related. He noted that 'the peculiar function of cooperation is to lead the child to the practice of reciprocity, hence of moral universality and generosity in his relations with his playmates' (p. 66) and 'for conduct to be characterized as moral there must be something more than an outward agreement between its content and that of the commonly accepted rules; it is also requisite that the mind should tend towards morality as to an autonomous good and should itself be capable of appreciating the value of the rules that are proposed to it' (p. 390).

However, a number of Piagetian-based studies investigating this relationship with honesty as the moral dimension (Grinder, 1964; LaVoie, 1974; McLaughlin & Stephens, 1974) have found only a weak to moderate correspondence between judgement and behaviour. These results suggest that other factors are implicated in the decision to behave morally or immorally.

0007-1269/82/020285-10 $02.00/0 © 1982 The British Psychological Society

As Blasi (1980) suggests, the particular difficulty of the cognitive–developmental approach in predicting moral behaviour may stem from the assumptions Piaget made about rationality and the nature of moral action. Piaget (1932) theorized that intelligence permits the child to regulate affective impulses. As rationality gains ascendency over affection the individual begins, in conjunction with the development of abilities to reason about causality and motivation, to view the world in terms of the logic of reciprocity and mutual cooperation. Piaget asserted the eventual dominance of cognition and considered that moral judgement (and therefore, by implication, moral action) is primarily mediated by logical development, hence the label 'cool' cognition.

Thus it is important to re-examine more closely the social or normative aspect of cognition in moral development. This seems doubly appropriate since both reasoning and behaviour can be tied to the particular context of the conflict situation.

The complexity of moral conflicts can be categorized within a framework relating to children's social–cognitive development. In this regard, a starting-point is provided from a scrutiny of Piaget's theory even though it de-emphasizes the role of normative influences.

An alternative position is that taken by J. M. Baldwin (1896, 1906) and is one which is undergoing a contemporary revival (Russell, 1978; Broughton, 1981). Baldwin's theory of moral development was a unique hybrid of philosophy and psychology. While it was less than precisely articulated, three clear, consecutive 'refinements' were posited in the relationship between self and others.

For Baldwin, children first have a projective sense of self in which they are stimulated to deny their asocial impulses and desires. They are in the process of accommodating themselves to an ideal self as exemplified in the behaviour of others whom they perceive as good. This process is at first largely non-cognitive in that children do not reflect on the motivations underlying their behaviour. It occurs because the affective component of motivation predominates. Children then enter into a subjective sense of self in which they develop a conscious awareness of this ideal.

The child's strivings to 'identify' with the parents' rules and standards for behaviour now become more cognitive and reflective. Later development culminates in a sense of self which involves reflections upon the discrepancies between actual and ideal selves, producing a synthesis of dialectically based courses of action.

The relationship between moral cognition and moral action becomes clearer when seen in terms of Baldwin's theory. Moral behaviour is seen to be non-spontaneous and, directly or indirectly, has to be taught, usually by significant others. While Baldwin's work was largely devoid of concrete research proposals and in this sense was quite unlike Piaget's, Baldwin recognized the importance of non-cognitive factors in moral development and attempted to illuminate the social aspect of social cognition. This emphasis on social factors together with the cognitive contribution of Piaget may serve toward illuminating the relationship between cognitive processes and moral behaviour.

One possible hypothesis is that identification with parents or with significant others is integral to the hot cognition underlying moral behaviour. It contributes a systematic meaning to moral rules and principles, and characterizes an individual's self-definition with respect to others. Supporting evidence in the case of a clash between a principle and a rule involving adult subjects has been discussed elsewhere (Siegal, 1982). The present study is more directly relevant to Piaget's approach as it examines the relationship of young children's moral behaviour to measures of cognitive development and peer group popularity as well as those of identification.

Here it was assumed that verbal reports of identification provide a roughly accurate indication of the extent to which children consciously strive to adopt a parent's behavioural rules and standards (cf. Ericsson & Simon, 1980; White, 1980). However, the study departs notably from that of early pioneering work (e.g. Hoffman, 1971) which was forced to use indirect measures of children's actual behaviour such as teachers' ratings. More recent work (Bolstad & Johnson, 1977) has shown that, while many teacher ratings can discriminate between rule-following and -violating behaviour, there are clear individual differences among teachers. In fact, some teachers may rate as best behaved those children who are observed as misbehaving the most; others appear to tolerate disruptions as long as students perform well academically, an orientation which may contaminate their ratings. Moreover, precisely what rules the teachers are using as a basis for rating is unclear. Different teachers can rate children on rules which may vary from teacher to teacher both in content, extent of application, and method of enforcement.

Therefore children's behaviour in the present study was directly observed in a naturalistic and commonly occurring situation representative of a clash between a rule and a ritual. Following Piaget, it was expected that rule violations interpretable as ritualistic patterns of behaviour would be associated with a lack of cognitive development. At the same time, it was expected that rule violations would be at least as strongly associated with a lack of identification.

Method
Children

These were 18 children aged 5 years 4 months to 6 years 6 months (mean age = 5 years 9 months). The 14 girls and 4 boys were members of a Grade 1 class of a primary school located in an upper-middle-class district of Brisbane, Australia. One other child was absent owing to illness and was excluded from participation. All the children had two parents present in the home. The study was conducted two months into the school year.

The situation

The situation was selected from pilot work with teachers and pupils. Three Grade 1 teachers (including the subject's teacher) were asked to suggest naturally occurring situations in which there was a conflict between a school rule known to the children and patterns of ritualistic behaviour. The consensus was that children's behaviour during napping or relaxation periods most clearly fitted this description. These napping periods form an integral part of the children's day and are customarily held soon after lunch each afternoon. From the point of view of the present study, this situation had the added bonus that any deviation from a motionless state of napping could be clearly scored either as restlessness or as violating the rule not to engage in disturbing others during relaxation.

To ensure that children themselves perceive this situation as involving a moral rule rather than a social convention, a group of 30 Grade 1 children from another school in the area were asked whether it would be right or wrong to bother others in a school where there was no rule which prohibited disturbances during naptime (cf. Nucci & Turiel, 1978). All except two responded that it would still be wrong indicating in this sense that their own orientation toward the rule was generalized, collective, and moral. (Following the completion of the study, the subjects themselves were asked this question. The verdict was unanimous. All replied that it would still be wrong).

For the purpose of observing the children's behaviour, a wall was installed in one corner of the classroom. Built into the wall was a three foot high trapdoor above which was a one-way mirror. The top of the wall was about eight feet high and was graced by six floral illustrations. A camera lens was concealed in the centre of each flower. One of the lenses was operative and connected to videotape equipment hidden in a space behind the wall. It was positioned high enough to capture a full view of all the children. The wall was unobtrusively present in the classroom and was surrounded by plants and books. It did not attract the children's attention.

The classroom itself was laid out in a traditional plan with four rows of desks. The children were permitted to sit where they preferred.

Procedure

The children's behaviour was videotaped over nine periods within a space of three weeks when all the subjects were present.* Each session took place in the regular time after lunch when the teacher announced 'Time for your nap now, children'. She continued, as was customary, in reciting this rhyme:

> Quiet I shall sit,
> Moving not a bit,
> Feet I shall rest,
> Head on my desk,
> Eyelids downward creep,
> Soon I'll be asleep.

Then she said, 'Remember the rule: it's not fair to disturb the other children during relaxation because they need their rest'.

After two minutes, the session entered its second phase. The teacher told the children that she had to go out for a while and that they should remember the rule about remaining quiet and not disturbing others. When two further minutes elapsed, she reappeared in the room for the third phase of the session and told the subjects to keep napping. The period ended six minutes after it began.

The children were also seen individually by a female experimenter for about half an hour. Each child was given measures of cognitive development (from Form C of the Piagetian-based Concept Assessment Kit, Goldschmidt & Bentler, 1968) as well as the parental identification index items devised by Hoffman (1971). The children were asked to say whom they admire (or think the most of) whom they would want to be like as a grown-up, and whom they take after mostly. If a parent was mentioned along with some other person, the child was given half a point. Otherwise, responses were scored as in the original Hoffman study: each time the mother or father was mentioned alone, the child was given one point for mother or father identification respectively. Finally, as a measure of peer group contact and experience, each child was asked to say which classmates he or she would prefer to play with during freetime.

For each of the three phases in the sessions (adult present, adult absent, adult returns), the children's behaviour was scored in three categories: (1) self-initiated rule violations directed toward disturbing others, (2) rule violations as reactions elicited from others' provocations, and (3) restlessness as behaviour which, although not involving others, did not indicate quiet relaxation with one's head on the desk. All instances of behaviour which did not conform to a motionless state were scored in one of these three categories. Talking, tossing and turning, and touching others were amongst the behaviours scored as rule violations.

The behaviour of each child was scored by two independent observers who did not participate in either the videotaping or testing. One observer scored all the sessions and the second rescored half with an agreement between the two raters of 90 per cent or more on each of the nine measures.

Results

The intercorrelations, means, and standard deviations on the nine behavioural measures are shown in Table 1. As is to be expected, there were significant differences over the three phases of the sessions in the levels of restlessness, initiated rule violations, and rule violations as reactions ($Fs = 6.77$, 7.16 and 10.66 respectively, d.f. = 2, 34, $Ps < 0.01$). On both initiations and reactions, violations increased when the teacher left the room and decreased when she returned (in all cases, $t > 2.25$, $P < 0.02$). The numbers of violations in the latter case were no different than when the teacher was initially present ($t < 1$). While the children's restlessness was unchanged between the present and absent phases ($t < 1$), restlessness also decreased significantly upon the teacher's return ($t = 6.48$, $P < 0.01$).

Of the 36 correlations on the nine measures, 34 were positive. Six of these were significant at the $P < 0.01$ level for a two-tailed test. Restlessness correlated significantly across all three phases of the experiment ($rs = 0.78$–0.86, d.f. = 16, $Ps < 0.01$), as well as with rule violations as reactions in the third phase of the session when the teacher returned

---

* The original plan was to observe children's behaviour over 10 periods. However, one session had to be cancelled owing to a statewide power strike in Queensland.

Table 1. The nine behavioural measures: Intercorrelations, means and standard deviations

Adult:	Restlessness			Initiations			Reactions		
	Present	Absent	Returns	Present	Absent	Returns	Present	Absent	Returns
Restlessness									
Present		0·86**	0·86**	0·35	0·33	0·11	0·16	0·24	0·58**
Absent			0·78**	0·47*	0·40	0·12	0·06	0·36	0·48*
Returns				0·29	0·24	0·06	0·09	0·27	0·49*
Initiations									
Present					0·59**	0·43	0·12	0·15	0·06
Absent						0·05	0·25	0·18	−0·09
Returns							−0·17	0·21	0·07
Reactions									
Present								0·35	0·20
Absent									0·69**
Returns									
Mean	31·56	30·39	25·39	4·78	15·39	5·39	3·67	7·67	3·06
SD	14·28	10·64	9·63	3·75	16·87	3·93	2·96	5·94	2·19

* $P < 0.05$, d.f. = 16, two-tailed test; ** $P < 0.01$, d.f. = 16, two-tailed test.

($rs = 0.49–0.58$, d.f. = 16, $Ps < 0.05$). Initiations when the teacher was present correlated with initiations when the teacher was absent ($r = 0.59$, d.f. = 16, $P < 0.01$), as well as with restlessness during that phase ($r = 0.47$, d.f. = 16, $P < 0.05$), while reactions when the teacher was absent correlated with reactions when the teacher returned ($r = 0.69$, d.f. = 16, $P < 0.01$). None of the relationships between initiations and reactions were significant indicating that the numbers of reactions were not a function of the numbers of initiations.

Intercorrelations, means and standard deviations on the five independent measures are shown in Table 2. None of the relationships was significant at the $P < 0.05$ level for a two-tailed test. However, at the $P < 0.10$ level, mother identification correlated with peer group popularity ($r = 0.42$) and sex correlated with father identification ($r = 0.44$) indicating, not surprisingly, a tendency for boys to identify with their fathers.

With regard to the identification measures, the mother was mentioned at least once by 11 of the 18 children while the father was mentioned at least once by eight children. Table 3 shows the relationships of identification as well as sex, cognitive development and peer group popularity to the behavioural measures.

Table 2. Intercorrelations, means and standard deviations on the independent variables

	Cognition	Mother	Father	Peers	Sex
Cognitive development		+0·25	+0·14	+0·12	+0·11
Mother identification			−0·21	+0·42	−0·24
Father identification				+0·03	+0·44
Peer group popularity					−0·04
Sex of subject					
Mean	4·47	0·44	0·25	2·61	
SD	2.55	+0·43	0·30	1·34	

Table 3. Relationship of the behavioural measures to cognitive development, mother and father identification, peer group popularity and sex of subject

Adult:	Restlessness			Rule violations as initiations			Rule violations as reactions		
	Present	Absent	Returns	Present	Absent	Returns	Present	Absent	Returns
Cognition	+0·21	−0·23	−0·42*	−0·40*	−0·24	−0·02	−0·12	−0·34	−0·26
Mother	−0·27	−0·25	−0·29	−0·16	−0·24	+0·19	−0·44*	−0·64**	−0·46*
Father	−0·21	−0·15	−0·07	−0·20	+0·11	+0·22	+0·22	+0·28	−0·02
Peers	+0·08	+0·01	+0·02	−0·15	+0·13	+0·22	−0·26	−0·24	−0·08
Sex	−0·16	−0·23	−0·16	−0·18	−0·02	+0·05	−0·08	+0·05	−0·20

* $P < 0.05$, d.f. = 16, one-tailed test; ** $P < 0.001$, d.f. = 16, one-tailed test.

Eight of the nine correlations between mother identification and behaviour were negative. Three of these were significant and all involved the reactions measures. The correlation between mother identification and reactions was -0.44 ($P < 0.05$, one-tailed test) when the teacher was present and rose to -0.64 ($P < 0.001$) when the teacher was absent. The latter relationship remained significant ($r = -0.58$, $P < 0.01$) and accounted for 34 per cent of the variance in rule violations as reactions even when the association between mother identification and reactions in the teacher present phase was partialled out. When the teacher returned, the correlation now dropped back to roughly that in the initial phase when she was present ($r = -0.46$, $P < 0.01$). It disappeared almost completely when the association between mother identification and reactions in the teacher absent phase was partialled out ($r = -0.04$, n.s.).

Turning to the relationship of cognitive development to behaviour, eight of the nine correlations here were also negative. Two of these were significant at the $P < 0.05$ level for a one-tailed test. Cognition correlated negatively with restlessness ($r = -0.42$) in the return phase and with initiations in the present phase ($r = -0.40$). On none of the measures did a multiple regression analysis indicate that cognition explained a significant proportion of the variance in behaviour not accounted for by mother identification ($Fs < 1.10$, d.f. = 3, 15). Cognition, unlike mother identification, did not correlate with behaviour spanning two adjacent time phases of the experiment.

Sex of subject, father identification, and peer group popularity did not significantly correlate with any of the behavioural measures. In no case did these add significantly to the variance explained by mother identification or cognitive development, as indicated by stepwise multiple regression analyses.

Discussion

When considering the generalizability of findings from observational studies of this type (Strayer, 1980, p. 819), it should be kept in mind that results such as these are based on a relatively small sample size. However, the children were observed over a reasonably extensive time span.

Initiations and reactions appear to emerge as two independent, uncorrelated measures of rule-violating behaviour. The case of initiations provides some support for the Piagetian focus on the cognitive processes underlying moral development. Rule-following behaviour (i.e. a lack of initiations) correlated with performance on cognitive–developmental tests of concrete operations. The modest magnitude of the correlation (-0.40) was in the same range as that generally reported between measures of cognitive development and moral reasoning (Keasey, 1975; Rest, 1979) and between measures of egocentrism and moral judgement, on the one hand, and those of moral behaviour, on the other (e.g. Rubin & Schneider, 1973). However, in the absent phase, there was no such relationship. Possibly while cognitive development may predict initiations committed under the surveillance of authority, children regardless of their intelligence may violate rules in the absence of authority. This lack of relationship persists even when authority is restored. However, cognitive development correlated negatively with restlessness in the return phase. Possibly intelligence is associated with the lesser likelihood of becoming bored toward the end of the napping periods.

With respect to identification, a lack of mother identification appears in general to account for a significant proportion of the variance in rule violations *as reactions*. It accounted for a sizable proportion of the increased level of rule violations between the present and absent phases of the experiment and for the decreased level of violations in the return phase. Since violations in the absent and return phases were highly correlated, it might be said that a lack of identification (as correlated with rule violations in the absent phase) is an antecedent of the violations which occur when children are put back under surveillance.

These findings are similar to those found by Bixenstine *et al.* (1976) in a study which examined children's conformity to peer-sponsored misbehaviour as indirectly indicated on their responses in questionnaires. A loss in favourableness toward adults was related to children's expressed willingness to succumb to others' misbehaviour. These results also support Hogan & Mills' (1976) observation that children are likely to follow rules which adults endorse if their parents are objects of admiration. It may be, then, that the mother in particular may be the source of a sort of 'ego-strength' which is associated with a resistance against violating rules by reacting to others' misbehaviour.

By contrast, reactions are more social acts than are initiations in that their origin resides in the behaviour of others rather than in the head of the subject. In this connection, it is worth noting that the relationship between conformity behaviour and cognitive measures of moral reasoning such as those of Piaget and Kohlberg is quite minimal (Blasi, 1980, p. 37). Thus the suppression of rule violations as reactions is more highly related to perceptions of important others than to cognitive development. It may embody a push and pull of affective strength toward and away from adults. In this way, identification may serve to promote rule-following behaviour which does not succumb to others' misconduct.

The lack of association between behaviour and either peer group popularity or father identification might be partly due to the age of the children. The study was carried out fairly early in the school year before the children, who were attending school for the first time, would have been able to solidify peer group relationships. The lack of father identification might be attributed to the fact that the mother is still the primary socialization figure in the home for many young children, and the situation itself took place in a primary school setting over which a female adult presided as authority.

The next step is to extend this work as part of a longitudinal study involving larger numbers of children. Identification, cognitive development, and peer group popularity could then be studied as precursors of rule-violating behaviour observed over different periods in time.

For the present, it can be concluded that both cognitive and social factors have a place in the study of moral development. Approaches like Piaget's and especially Kohlberg's*,

* More recent work by Kohlberg (1978) and Nisan & Kohlberg (in press) is headed in this general direction. As questions have arisen about the effects of culture and group norms on the universal nature of stages, attention has been diversified from the study of cognitive stage and role taking to include the study of normative influences on moral development such as those involving group norms or expectations.

which place so much weight on cognition that what is social is squeezed out, are liable to give an incomplete picture of moral development – if manifest moral behaviour is to be subsumed under this heading.

The problem, as Cofer (1981, p. 52) has pointed out, is that cognitive theories imply rationality and that the terms used to describe rational behaviour often have 'cool' connotations. 'Where, in cognitive theory', Cofer laments, 'are the strong urges and the "hot" emotions or passions that have been central to thinking in respect to motivation and emotion for so long?' While Piaget and Kohlberg have emphasized the cognitive aspects of moral development, moral cognitions relating to action are unlikely to exist in some cases unless subsequent to affect and motivation. In this regard, an important part of children's moral behaviour may be based, not on a cognitive awareness of others' perspectives, but on an affective compliance with others and particularly adults as Baldwin initially asserted. Some recent research on adults suggests that affect may often precede and be independent from fully cognitive judgements (Zajonc, 1980; Fiske, 1981).

So without a broader approach which embraces the hot side of cognition, progress in examining many aspects of moral behaviour is likely to be even more difficult than need be. This would require that more attention be devoted to the quality of parent–child relations and to factors affecting children's identification with their parents' behavioural rules and standards. However, it should be emphasized that parental identification is often integral but not synonymous with hot cognition as related to moral behaviour. It is merely one prominent feature; at times individuals may define their moral actions with respect to peers as well as political, literary or cult figures.

Moreover, there is more to investigating children's perceptions of their parents than merely examining the family as a self-contained unit. Clearly, the family is part of larger social systems which may support or create stress within socio-economic and historical contexts. While identification may be enhanced under non-stressful economic conditions, it cannot be assumed that children are necessarily understanding of parental economic hardships (Siegal, 1981). Difficulties in meeting children's basic economic needs may undermine parental authority in the family and mar the quality of parent–child relations (Rockwell & Elder, in press).

Here we tread upon something of an ideological issue (Riegel, 1972). For ironically, like behaviourism, the cognitive–developmental approach has generated a psychology which is quite compatible with the existing ideology and socio-economic arrangements of Western society (Sullivan, 1977). But moral questions often amount to challenges to the *status quo* and its institutions. For this reason, a psychological theory is needed to account for the hot cognitive processes underlying these challenges. Such processes, it may be argued (cf. Bronfenbrenner, 1977; Belsky, 1981) must be seen in relation to rapid changes in the structure of families such as the rising incidence of one-parent families and increases in the rate of maternal employment. These changes may powerfully affect children's perceptions of their parents' power and nurturance (Hoffman, 1979; Santrock & Warshak, 1979), and hence become involved in the translation from hot cognition to overt moral behaviour. This is indeed a tall order and one which, we propose, can only be filled from a social–cognitive viewpoint.

Acknowledgements

This paper was prepared with support from the University Research Grants Committee of the University of Queensland and the Australian Research Grants Committee. Thanks are due to James Chapman, Lyn O'Donoghue, and Carol Thorley for their fine assistance. We are grateful to Graeme Halford and Sharon Winocur for comments on an earlier version of the manuscript.

References

Baldwin, J. M. (1896). *Social and Ethical Interpretations in Mental Development*, 2nd ed. London: Macmillan.

Baldwin, J. M. (1906). *Mental Development in the Child and the Race*, 3rd ed. London: Macmillan.

Belsky, J. (1981). Early human experience: A family perspective. *Developmental Psychology*, **17**, 3–23.

Bixenstine, V. E., DeCorte, M. S. & Bixenstine, B. A. (1976). Conformity to peer-sponsored misbehavior at four age levels. *Developmental Psychology*, **12**, 226–244.

Blasi, A. (1980). Bridging moral cognition and moral action: A critical review of the literature. *Psychological Bulletin*, **88**, 1–45.

Bolstad, O. D. & Johnson, S. M. (1977). The relationship between teachers' assessment of students and the students' act' ' behavior in the classroom. *Child Development*, **48**, 570–578.

Bronfenbrenner, U. (1977). Toward an experimental ecology of human development. *American Psychologist*, **32**, 514–532.

Broughton, J. M. (1981). The genetic psychology of James Mark Baldwin. *American Psychologist*, **36**, 396–407.

Cofer, C. N. (1981). The history of the concept of motivation. *Journal of the History of the Behavioral Sciences*, **17**, 48–53.

Ericsson, K. A. & Simon, H. A. (1980). Verbal reports as data. *Psychological Review*, **87**, 215–251.

Fiske, S. T. (1981). Social cognition and affect. In J. H. Harvey (ed.), *Cognition, Social Behavior, and the Environment*. Hillsdale, NJ: Erlbaum.

Goldschmidt, M. L. T. & Bentler, P. M. (1968). *Concept Assessment Kit*. San Diego: Educational Testing Service.

Grinder, R. E. (1964). Relations between behavioural and cognitive dimensions of conscience in middle childhood. *Child Development*, **35**, 881–891.

Hoffman, L. W. (1979). Maternal employment: 1979. *American Psychologist*, **34**, 859–865.

Hoffman, M. L. (1971). Identification and conscience development. *Child Development*, **42**, 1071–1082.

Hogan, R. & Mills, C. (1976). Legal socialization. *Human Development*, **19**, 261–276.

Keasey, C. B. (1975). Implications of cognitive development for moral reasoning. In D. J. DePalma & J. M. Foley (eds), *Moral Development: Current Research and Theory*. Hillsdale, NJ: Erlbaum.

Kohlberg, L. (1969). Stage and sequence: The cognitive-developmental approach to socialization. In D. A. Goslin (ed.), *Handbook of Socialization Theory and Research*. Chicago: Rand-McNally.

Kohlberg, L. (1978). Revisions in the theory and practice of moral development. In W. Damon (ed.), *Moral Development: New Directions for Child Development*, No. 1. San Francisco: Jossey-Bass.

La Voie, J. C. (1974). Cognitive determinants of resistance to deviation in seven-, nine-, and eleven-year-old children of low and high maturity of moral judgment. *Developmental Psychology*, **10**, 393–403.

Lee, L. C. (1971). The concomitant development of cognitive and moral modes of thought: A test of selected deductions from Piaget's theory. *Genetic Psychology Monographs*, **83**, 93–146.

McLaughlin, J. A. & Stephens, B. (1974). Interrelationships among reasoning, moral judgment and moral conduct. *American Journal of Mental Deficiency*, **79**, 156–161.

Nisan, M. & Kohlberg, L. (in press). Universality and variation in moral judgement: A longitudinal and cross-sectional study in Turkey. *Child Development*.

Nucci, L. & Turiel, E. (1978). Social interactions and the development of social concepts in preschool children. *Child Development*, **49**, 400–407.

Piaget, J. (1977). *The Moral Judgement of the Child*. London: Penguin (originally published, 1932, London: Routledge & Kegan Paul).

Piaget, J. (1967). *Six Psychological Studies*. New York: Random House.

Piaget, J. (1971). *Science of Education and the Psychology of the Child*. New York: Penguin.

Rest, J. R. (1979). *Development in Judging Moral Issues*. Minneapolis: University of Minnesota Press.

Riegel, K. F. (1972). Influence of economic and political ideologies on the development of developmental psychology. *Psychological Bulletin*, **78**, 129–141.

Rockwell, R. C. & Elder, G. H., Jr (in press). Economic deprivation in children's problem behaviour. *Human Development*.

Rubin, K. H. & Schneider, K. H. (1973). The relationship between moral judgment, egocentrism, and altruistic behavior. *Child Development*, **44**, 661–665.

Russell, J. (1978). *The Acquisition of Knowledge*. London: Macmillan.

Santrock, J. W. & Warshak, R. A. (1979). Father custody and social development in boys and girls. *Journal of Social Issues*, **35**, 112–125.

Siegal, M. (1981). Children's perceptions of adult economic needs. *Child Development*, **52**, 379–383.

Siegal, M. (1982). *Fairness in Children: A Social-cognitive Approach to the Study of Moral Development*. London: Academic Press.

Strayer, J. (1980). A naturalistic study of empathic behaviors and their relation to affective states and perspective-taking skills in preschool children. *Child Development*, **51**, 815–822.

Sullivan, E. V. (1977). A study of Kohlberg's structural theory of moral development: A critique of liberal social science ideology. *Human Development*, **20**, 352–376.

White, P. (1980). Limitations on verbal reports of internal events: A refutation of Nisbett and Wilson and of Bem. *Psychological Review*, **87**, 105–112.

Whiteman, P. E. & Kosier, K. P. (1964). Development of children's moral judgements: Age, sex, IQ, and certain personal–experiential variables. *Child Development*, **35**, 843–850.

Zajonc, R. B. (1980). Feeling and thinking: Preferences need no inferences. *American Psychologist*, **35**, 151–175.

Requests for reprints should be addressed to Michael Siegal, Department of Psychology, University of Queensland, St Lucia, Australia 4067.

British Journal of Psychology (1982), **73**, 295–303   *Printed in Great Britain*

Social interaction and cognitive conflict in the development of spatial coordination skills

Nicholas Emler and **Gayle L. Valiant**

In a recent experiment, Doise & Mugny (1979) have shown that pairs of children working on spatial representation tasks make more subsequent progress than children who work alone on such tasks. This appears to lend support to Piaget's claims about the effects of social interaction upon the development of operational thought. In the first of the two experiments reported here the effects of working in pairs on spatial representation problems but from opposing perspectives were examined with respect to subsequent improvement in individual performances. Such paired training resulted in more improvement than solitary practice but was no more effective than training designed to induce intra-individual conflict. The second experiment demonstrated that the effect of working in pairs upon subsequent improvement was related to the amount of disagreement that occurred during training between partners. Again, however, working in pairs was overall no more effective than training based on intra-individual conflict.

In a series of training studies, Doise and his colleagues have sought to provide empirical verification for Piaget's views about the role of social experience in the development of thought (e.g. Doise *et al.*, 1976; Mugny & Doise, 1978; Doise & Mugny, 1979). In his early writings, Piaget (1928, 1932) attached considerable importance to the effects of interaction with peers in breaking down the cognitive egocentrism of young children and in encouraging development of the capacity to decentre thought. Piaget's claim that the thinking of young children is characteristically trapped within the relativity of its own perspective was supposedly demonstrated in their performance on such problems as the 'Three Mountains' task (Piaget & Inhelder, 1956), wherein if asked to predict how a set of objects would appear from some other perspective they respond as if it would correspond to their own. Piaget argued that such 'egocentrism' would be overcome through confrontation with the thought of others, and in particular through the experience of disagreements.

The programme of research reported by Doise & Mugny (1981) appears to provide some support for this argument. They claim that the socialization of thought may not be reducible to the imitation of correct responses; developmental change can result directly from conflicts arising from social interaction. In other words, children need only be confronted with another who disagrees with their particular non-operational solution, rather than by someone who produces or demonstrates a correct solution. In one experiment, Doise & Mugny (1979) found that a difference in visual perspective between two pre-operational children confronted with a 'Three Mountains' type of task may be sufficient to produce conflict leading to developmental change. In the experiments reported here we attempted to verify and extend Doise & Mugny's observations.

Experiment 1

The objective of the first experiment was to determine whether cognitive conflict is sufficient to generate developmental change or whether it must arise through 'social' means to be effective. The experiment took the form of a training study involving the ability to coordinate spatial relations. The tasks used for training and for diagnosis of initial and final levels of performance were similar to those used by Doise & Mugny (1979). They involved making a copy of a model village, but in relation to a reference mark which had been rotated 90° or 180° in relation to the original (see Fig. 1).

0007-1269/82/020295-09 $02.00/0 © 1982 The British Psychological Society

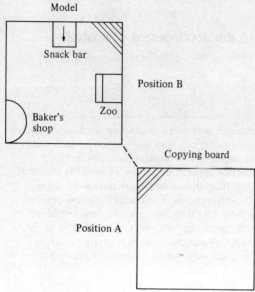

Figure 1. Example of layout of two boards with copying board rotated 180° from model relative to child at position A.

Two separate aspects of the training were varied independently (*a*) whether the child worked alone or with another who occupied an opposing perspective, and (*b*) whether or not the child moved to the opposing position following completion of the task to re-examine his solution. This 2 × 2 design provided four different forms of training. If cognitive conflict is more effective when it arises from disagreement between children, then working with another child should produce more progress than working alone. If this 'social' element is not critical then those children who work alone but examine their solutions from the opposing perspective should progress as much as those working with another.

Method

Children. Eighty children, aged between five and eight years, participated in the experiment. They were drawn from the first three years of three different primary schools located in lower middle- and working-class districts of industrial cities. There were 26 children from first-year classes (mean age = 5·36 yr, SD = 0·29), 30 from second-year classes (mean age 6·34 yr, SD = 0·34) and 24 from third-year classes (mean age 7·57 yr, SD = 0·09).

Test materials. The 'village' consisted of three different buildings placed on a 25 in square piece of card on one corner of which was a blue mark representing a lake. On a table to one side was a second piece of card, identical to the first but with the same set of three buildings placed off the card at the side. The task was to build a village on this second card, identical to the first. The children were asked to imagine a man coming into the village from the lake and to make their copy so that this man would find all the buildings in exactly the same places as in the original.

Design and procedure. There were three phases to the experiment, a pre-test consisting of three reconstruction problems, a training phase involving four problems and a post-test with two problems. Each phase of the experiment was separated from the next by an interval of approximately one week. Of the three pre-test problems, one was a warm-up problem (0° rotation), the others involving 90° and 180° rotations respectively. Initial level of performance was determined on the basis of these latter two problems. The children were then divided between four training conditions. *Direct practice* (mean age 6·43 yr, SD = 0·91), *Intra-individual conflict* (mean age 6·41 yr, SD = 0·88), *Inter-individual conflict* (mean age 6·38 yr, SD = 0·96) and *Combined conflict* (mean age 6·34 yr, SD = 0·99), with 20 children in each condition. The composition of the groups was equated for sex and school of origin.

Training conditions

Direct practice. The procedure here followed that of the pre-tests except that there were four tasks. One involved no rotation of the reference mark, two a 90° rotation and one a 180° rotation. This combination was chosen to allow for the same balance of tasks to be used in all training conditions.

Intra-individual conflict. The children again worked alone but each time, after indicating they were satisfied with their solution, moved around to the opposing position where they were asked again if their copy was exactly like the model. If they demurred, they were asked to make changes to their copies as necessary.

Inter-individual conflict. Pairs of children worked from opposing positions (A and B in Fig. 1) and for each problem were asked to continue until both agreed that the solution was correct. At this stage the experimenter checked with each child that he or she was indeed agreed that the copy was indeed the same as the original. If any disagreement was evident, they were asked to continue until both were satisfied. In this condition one problem involves a 0° rotation for one child (but a 180° rotation for the other), two involve a 90° rotation (but for each child it is a rotation in a different direction), and one a 180° rotation for the first child (but a 0° rotation for the other).

Combined conflict. Here, after it had been established that the pair agreed on a solution, they were asked to exchange positions so that each viewed the model and their copy from the position formerly occupied by the other. They were then again asked if the copy was the same as the original and to agree on the necessary changes if they were not now satisfied.

In these latter two conditions each pair consisted of children whose pre-test performances were at similar levels. The only other restrictions were that pairs were of the same sex and from the same class in school.

The post-tests consisted of two copying tasks similar to the second two used in the pre-test.

Each performance at each stage of the experiment was classified in terms of the following response patterns: egocentric (in which buildings were placed in the correct positions in relation to one another without rotating them as a whole to correspond with the reference mark); position error (in which either one or two buildings were placed in their correct positions in relation to the reference mark); total error (in which all three were placed in the wrong positions but without corresponding either to an egocentric or to a mirror pattern); mirror (a mirror image of the correct solution); correct. Performances were then given a score based on the following convention: total = 0; egocentric = 1; position = 2; mirror = 3; correct = 4.* The pre- and post-training levels of performance of each child were based on the mean of their scores on the two rotation problems in the pre- and post-tests respectively.

Results

The overall effects of training on patterns of response correspond to the ordering on which the scoring was based. Total errors showed the largest decline, followed by egocentric errors, with a slight increase in position errors and a more substantial increase in mirror errors, the post- to pre-test error ratios being 0·44, 0·53, 1·13, and 1·86 respectively.

An analysis of variance was performed on the data with tests (pre vs. post) (2), individual vs. collective (2) and exchange vs. no exchange of position (2) as variables. There was a significant main effect for tests ($F = 78·268$, d.f. $= 1$, 76, $P < 0·001$), i.e. a training effect, but not for the other main effects (ind. vs. coll: $F = 0·005$, d.f. $= 1$, 76; exch. vs. no exch.: $F = 0·00$, d.f. $= 1$, 76). The between-conditions interaction (ind./coll. with exch./no exch.) was also non-significant ($F = 2·933$, d.f. $= 1$, 76). The only other significant effect was the three-way interaction ($F = 9·406$, d.f. $= 1$, 76, $P < 0·005$). The other interactions with tests were non-significant (ind./coll. with tests: $F = 0·501$, d.f. $= 1$, 76; exch./no. exch. with tests: $F = 0·014$, d.f. $= 1$, 76).

* This convention was derived from the results of a separate experiment in which 60 children, aged five to eight, completed a series of spatial coordination problems similar to those used here. The finding that these response patterns occur and in this developmental order was replicated with a further sample of the same size and age range. Details may be obtained from the authors.

As may be seen from Table 1, the pre- to post-test gains in all three *conflict* conditions were greater than those in the practice condition. The Newman–Keuls procedure was used to test for the significance of residual gains in each *conflict* condition over the gain in the *practice* condition. Residual gain was significant in the *inter-individual* condition ($P < 0.05$) but also in the *intra-individual* condition ($P < 0.05$), while it was not significant in the *combined* condition. The mean gains for the *inter-* and *intra-individual* conditions were identical ($\bar{X} = 1.27$). Thus the anticipated greater effectiveness of inter-individual conflict over intra-individual conflict was not confirmed. The same procedure was used to compare gains among *conflict* conditions. Residual gains in both *inter-* and *intra-individual* conditions over those in the *combined* conditions were significant ($P < 0.05$).

Table 1. Mean pre- and post-test scores for different training conditions

Training conditions	Pre-test		Post-test	
	$\bar{X}$	SD	$\bar{X}$	SD
Direct practice (n = 20)	1·25	1·03	1·85	1·08
Intra-individual conflict (n = 20)	1·27	0·92	2·54	1·05
Inter-individual conflict (n = 20)	1·25	0·98	2·52	1·07
Combined conflict (n = 20)	1·23	0·87	1·91	1·27

Figure 2 illustrates the relations between performance on the pre-test, on trials 2 and 4 of the training phase, and on the post-test for each condition. Trials 2 and 4 are chosen because in these the problem involves the same rotation, whichever of the two positions is occupied and whether or not children exchange positions during the task. It can be seen that the *conflict* conditions do result in enhanced performances during the training phase while the *practice* condition indicates a cumulative practice effect. A comparison of the pre-test to training phase improvements in performance between *conflict* conditions and *practice* condition indicates that this improvement was significantly greater in all conflict conditions (*intra-individual*: $t = 2.996$, d.f. $= 38$, $P < 0.005$; *inter-individual*: $t = 2.500$, d.f. $= 38$, $P < 0.01$; *combined*: $t = 2.590$, d.f. $= 38$, $P < 0.01$).

Inspection of the effects of each of the two conflict-based training conditions (*intra-* and *inter-individual*) on changes in the types of errors produced did not reveal any significant differences in the particular type of effect each form of training had.

Discussion

As expected, training based on the creation of conditions for inter-individual conflict was significantly more effective than straightforward practice. However, confronting children with their own solutions from a different perspective appeared to be equally effective. The combination of these two features (*combined conflict*) seemed merely to eliminate the benefits which each provided by itself. While these results do therefore confirm the relevance of cognitive conflict to developmental change, they do not suggest that the circumstances under which such conflict arises are particularly important.

The relation between training phase performance and pre- to post-test changes revealed in Fig. 2 also indicates a reason why conflict produces progress in this situation. The conflict conditions result in better performances in the training phase and these better performances are reflected in post-test gains (except in the case of combined conflict in which the nature of the training seems to disrupt assimilation of these better performances). In other words, conditions conducive to cognitive conflict may result in progress because they allow children to produce more adequate solutions in the training phase.

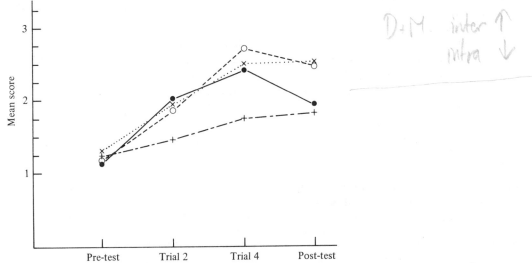

Figure 2. Relations between pre-test, training, and post-test mean performance levels for each training condition. +—·—+, direct practice; × · · · · · ×, intra-individual conflict, ○---○, inter-individual conflict; ●——●, combined conflict.

The most immediate question that arises is why there should be a discrepancy between these results and the findings reported by Doise & Mugny (1979) which indicated a superiority of socially induced conflict over intra-individual conflict. It is possible that differences in details of the training (number of buildings, nature of cues) could account for some of the differences in results. Another possibility, however, is that there are cultural factors which influence the effects of the different forms of training used in these studies. Doise & Mugny (personal communication) have suggested that a cultural emphasis on individualism may increase the effectiveness of intra-individual conflict. The differences between intra- and inter-individual conditions were less marked for the middle-class children in their sample, which if one allows that the middle class have a more individualistic orientation, is consistent with their suggestion. Makie (1980) reported that intra- and inter-individual conflict were equally effective for New Zealand Pakele children who, she argued, come from a culture with a strongly individualistic orientation towards learning. She found inter-individual conflict to be relatively more effective for children from cultures emphasizing cooperation (Samoan and Cook Island Maoris). It is possible that our English and Scottish children had an orientation closer to Makie's New Zealanders and less like her Samoans and Cook Islanders or Doise & Mugny's Spanish Catholic children.

Another question arises from the lack of any direct evidence that the inter-individual conflict training did indeed generate conflict. From informal observations it was clear that disagreements occurred and were sometimes quite intense. The extent of disagreement, however, was not quantified in any way so it was not possible to make a direct check on the reliability of the procedure as a method for generating social conflict. In some pairs there appeared, overtly at least, very little disagreement.

Experiment 2

In the second training study measures of disagreement were taken. Given our assumption that social interaction is a source of developmental change in so far as it produces conflict, it was predicted that the effectiveness of collective training would be a function of the amount of disagreement that occurred. This study was limited to the two forms of training found to be most effective in Expt 1. It thus provided for a further comparison of the relative effectiveness of intra- and inter-individual conflict. It also afforded an opportunity to determine whether children's initial level of performance affected their ability to benefit from training.

In this experiment the length of training was extended in an attempt to increase its effectiveness, and pre- and post-tests were expanded to increase their sensitivity to any changes produced by training. It was recognized that a longer pre-test could itself generate subsequent improvement on the test and so a non-training control group was included.

Method

Children. As in the previous study, five- to eight-year-olds of both sexes were drawn from the first three forms of a primary school, though in this case one with a predominantly working-class catchment area. Selection for the training phase was based on pre-test performances indicating either a low or moderate level of proficiency on the reconstruction task. Those whose errors were predominantly total and/or egocentric were classified as 'low'; those whose errors were predominantly position and/or mirror were classified as 'intermediate'. Those who succeeded on more than one of the three pre-test rotation tasks or who failed to understand the task requirements were eliminated at this stage. Sixty children between five and eight years old were selected for the training phase. A further 30 were selected for the no training control group. Of the total sample, 29 children came from the first year (mean age = 5·62 yr, SD = 0·35), 35 from the second year (mean age = 6·53 yr, SD = 0·36), and 26 from the third (mean age 7·53 yr, SD = 0·26).

Design. Children selected for training were assigned to one of two training conditions, corresponding to the intra-individual and inter-individual conflict conditions of Expt 1. Twenty children (mean age 6·60 yr, SD = 0·91), half classified as low and half as intermediate on the pre-tests, were assigned to the *intra-individual* condition. Forty children (mean age 6·56 yr, SD = 0·86), equally divided between lows and intermediates were assigned to the inter-individual or *collective* condition. This apportionment between conditions was to allow for a further division within the *collective* condition on the basis of the amount of disagreement occurring during training. The no training control group (mean age 6·66 yr, SD = 0·75) was also equally composed of lows and intermediates.

Procedures. The procedure was as for Expt 1 except that pre-and post-tests each consisted of four tasks of which the first in each case was a warm-up problem involving no rotation, while the training phase involved six problems. In the *collective* condition a check was made on disagreements occurring in each pair by noting every instance in which one child made a physical change in a placement made by the other. Again, one week separated each phase of the experiment, two weeks separating pre- and post-test for the no training control. Three children were lost from the final sample as a result of prolonged absence from school during the post-testing period.

Results

The data were submitted to analysis of variance with conditions (3), initial levels (2), and tests (2) as factors. There were significant main effects for levels ($F = 109·97$, d.f. = 1, 81, $P < 0·001$) and tests ($F = 35·13$, d.f. = 1, 81, $P < 0·001$) but not for conditions ($F = 2·71$, d.f. = 2, 81). There was a significant interaction between levels and tests (F = 5·49, d.f. = 1, 81, $P < 0·05$), reflecting a tendency for lows to progress more than intermediates (the simplest explanation for this being in terms of a ceiling effect). There was also a significant interaction between conditions and tests ($F = 5 \cdot 01$, d.f. $= 2, 81$, $P < 0 \cdot 01$), but not between levels and conditions ($F = 1 \cdot 72$, d.f. $= 2, 81$). The three-way interaction also failed to reach significance ($F = 2 \cdot 51$, d.f. $= 2, 81$, $0 \cdot 05 < P < 0 \cdot 10$).

Means for pre- and post-tests in each condition at each level are presented in Table 2. The Newman–Keuls procedure was used to test for the significance of residual gains in the training conditions over the mean gain in the control condition. Residual gain in both the *individual* and the *collective* condition was significant ($P < 0 \cdot 01$).

Table 2. Relationship between pre-test performance levels and post-test improvement for different training conditions

	Initial performance level									
	Low					Intermediate				
	Pre-test		Post-test			Pre-test		Post-test		
Training conditions	n	$\bar{X}$	SD	$\bar{X}$	SD	n	$\bar{X}$	SD	$\bar{X}$	SD
Intra-individual conflict	10	0·83	0·54	1·90	1·11	9	2·26	0·55	2·63	0·84
Collective conflict	19	0·82	0·49	1·52	1·10	19	2·23	0·53	3·07	0·57
No training control	15	0·82	0·47	1·39	1·06	15	2·27	0·63	2·04	0·83

To examine the effects of amount of disagreement on progress in the collective condition, lows and intermediates were first compared with the Mann–Whitney U test. Lows and intermediates did not differ significantly in numbers of disagreements ($U = 167 \cdot 5$, $n_1 = n_2 = 19$). It therefore seemed justified to divide the children in the collective condition into those above and below the median respectively in terms of numbers of disagreements. This gave 18 children in the low disagreement category (mean age 6·55 yr, SD $= 0·88$; 8 lows and 10 intermediates in terms of pre-test levels), and 20 children in the high disagreement category (mean age 6·56 yr, SD $= 0·87$; 11 lows and 9 intermediates). The two categories were then compared in terms of pre- to post-test gains. There was significantly greater pre- to post-test gain in the high disagreement category than in the low disagreement category ($t = 1 \cdot 88$, d.f. $= 36$, $P < 0 \cdot 05$; mean gain for high disagreement $= 0·96$, mean gain for low $= 0·56$).

Discussion

It has proved possible to show in these experiments that development can be induced by training which provides opportunities for the experience of conflict. Whether such conflict must necessarily originate in social interaction, however, is less clear. It would appear from this last experiment that children who have not progressed beyond an egocentric level derive no greater benefit from social than from intra-individual conflicts of perspective. This confirms what we have found in Expt 1, in which the large majority of children would have been classified as 'lows' according to the criteria applied in Expt 2. Thus we have not been able to find evidence that for the children we have been able to sample social interaction is especially crucial in breaking down egocentrism.

From the second experiment an additional reason emerges for the lack of a clear advantage of collective over individual forms of training: collective training does not always result in overt disagreement, and the effectiveness of this training is related to the amount of overt disagreement that occurs. This is consistent with the proposition we set out to examine, namely that social interaction stimulates cognitive development in so far as it confronts the child with experiences of disagreement. But this leaves us with further questions. First, why is it that the opposing points of view do not always produce disagreement, or at least disagreement that is openly expressed? Second, even when disagreement is manifested will it necessarily produce cognitive conflict or developmental change? Answers to these questions will require a deeper probing of the dynamics of children's collective problem solving.

The consequences of disagreement, for instance, may depend on whether children at this age would expect to disagree in such a situation and, furthermore, on how they interpret disagreements. Robinson & Robinson (1976) found that one reason for 'egocentric' communication failures between children (cf. Glucksberg & Krauss, 1967) may be that they do not readily grasp that messages can be inadequate; they tend to blame the listener for failing to understand. Perhaps when children find that others disagree with their solutions, they have difficulty appreciating that they rather than the other may be wrong, or, more subtly, that both may be wrong. They may even fail to see that only one solution can be right, and indeed will even fail to recognize a correct alternative when it is presented. This may underlie the tendency in Expt 2 for the 'intermediate' group but not the 'lows' benefited relatively more from collective performance (see Table 2); it is necessary to recognize that an egocentric response is wrong before the experience of disagreement with another becomes informative. The occurrence of disagreement, however, did not appear to be related to children's pre-test levels of performance. The probability of open disagreement was as high amongst pairs of 'lows' as amongst pairs of 'intermediates'.

Both the occurrence of disagreement and its consequences could well depend on another set of factors that have been relatively ignored in this area of research, those of the relationship that exists between the children who are required to interact. If these children are drawn from the same classes, as is usually the case, there will already exist some relationship between them, whether of friendship, enmity, dominance or only acquaintance. One might predict, for example, that overt disagreements will occur less often between children who occupy different positions in a dominance hierarchy. It may also be that children are more surprised when they find themselves in disagreement with their friends than with others and for this reason, or perhaps reasons associated with the greater facility of interacting with friends, will profit more from such disagreements. Rather than ask whether social interaction as such is essential for cognitive development or whether experience of disagreement is important, we should perhaps in future ask: interaction with whom and disagreement with whom contributes to development?

One question to which we have not been able to provide a clear answer here concerns the significance of cultural differences in intellectual attitudes. It remains possible that such a difference lies at the origin of the disparity between our results and those of Doise & Mugny (1979). None the less, we should not simply confine our attention to the failure of some children to benefit from joint performance. It is also worth emphasizing that many of the children in our experiments who worked alone *did* progress, and this phenomenon deserves further examination. Does this reflect the fact that some children, by virtue of whatever set of factors, are disposed to learn at least as readily from their own experience as from testing it against the experience of others? It would be interesting to examine further the strategies spontaneously employed by children to solve spatial relations problems. For example, would some children examine spatial relations problems such as those we used from different perspectives if they were not encouraged or discouraged from doing so by the experimenter?

References

Doise, W. & Mugny, G. (1979). Individual and collective conflicts of centrations in cognitive development. *European Journal of Social Psychology*, **9**, 105–108.

Doise, W. & Mugny, G. (1981). *Le Développement Social de l'Intelligence*. Paris: Intereditions.

Doise, W., Mugny, G. & Perret-Clermont, A. N. (1976). Social interaction and cognitive development: Further evidence. *European Journal of Social Psychology*, **6**, 245–247.

Glucksberg, S. & Krauss, R. M. (1967). What do people say after they have learned how to talk? Studies in the development of referential communication. *Merrill-Palmer Quarterly*, **13**, 309–316.

Mackie, D. (1980). A cross-cultural study of intra-individual and inter-individual conflicts of centrations. *European Journal of Social Psychology*, **10**, 313–318.

Mugny, G. & Doise, W. (1978). Socio-cognitive conflict and the structuration of individual and collective performances. *European Journal of Social Psychology*, **8**, 181–192.

Piaget, J. (1928). *Judgement and Reasoning in the Child*. London: Routledge & Kegan Paul.

Piaget, J. (1932). *The Moral Judgement of the Child*. London: Routledge & Kegan Paul.

Piaget, J. & Inhelder, B. (1956). *The Child's Conception of Space*. London: Routledge & Kegan Paul.

Robinson, E. J. & Robinson, W. P. (1976). Developmental changes in children's explanation of communication failure. *Australian Journal of Psychology*, **28**, 155–165.

Requests for reprints should be addressed to Nicholas Emler, Department of Psychology, University of Dundee, Dundee DD1 4HN, Scotland.

Gayle L. Valiant is at the University of Leeds.

British Journal of Psychology (1982), **73**, 305–311 *Printed in Great Britain*

Egocentricity in the child and its effect on the child's comprehension of kin terms

Ann Macaskill

Piaget suggested that language acquisition is dependent on cognitive development and this paper presents data which are examined in terms of this hypothesis. As a result of a normative study on the comprehension of kin terms, the author suggested that kin terms could be divided into two categories, child-centred terms and other-centred terms. It was hypothesized that the decline of egocentricity in the child was a necessary development for the comprehension of other-centred terms. Data are presented in support of this hypothesis.

Piaget & Inhelder (1969) rejected the assumption of innate language mechanisms to explain the acquisition of language in the child, arguing instead that cognitive structures, which are built up during the sensori-motor period through interaction with the environment, precede language and are prerequisites for language development. Language is conceptualized as building on and further developing cognitive operations that have already risen during the sensori-motor period. This process is thought to continue throughout development so that for the child to acquire new linguistic forms he must have mastered the cognitive concepts which underlie these linguistic forms.

In a previous paper, Macaskill (1981), normative data on the comprehension of kin terms by children were presented and then examined in terms of the Piagetian hypothesis that language acquisition is dependent on cognitive development. Kin terms were shown to be comprehended by the child in an orderly sequence in terms of the sorts of relationships which were involved, the number of relational components in the terms and the cognitive demands that the comprehension of these relationships made on the child. Macaskill (1981) suggested that kin terms can be divided into two groups, those which define other people's relationship to the child, called child-centred relationships, and terms which define the child's relationship to others, called other-centred relationships. This gave the following division of kin terms:

child-centred relationships: mother, father, grandmother, grandfather, sister, brother, aunt, uncle, cousin;

other-centred relationships: daughter, son, granddaughter, grandson, niece, nephew.

The terms brother, sister and cousin were included in the child-centred category as it was apparent from the acquisition study that, at the age when a child first acquires these terms, he perceives siblings and cousins as something he has rather than as something he is, although on questioning he may admit to the latter. This position was supported in the original study of brother and sister by Piaget (1928) and the replication by Elkind (1962).

The acquisition study by Macaskill (1981) found that child-centred terms were acquired before other-centred terms and it was suggested that the egocentricity of the child could be a crucial factor in this as other-centred relationships require the child to take the role perspective of the other in order to define the relationship which he holds for that person. The study reported in this paper was designed to explore this hypothesis.

Piaget described egocentricity in the young child as consisting of a 'general incognizance of the notion of point of view and hence a lack of awareness of how the child's own point of view may differ from other people's' (Piaget & Inhelder, 1956, p. 196). The young child is, as Piaget put it, 'The unwitting centre of his own universe'. Piaget suggested that because the child is continually a prisoner of his own point of view, his conceptual and cognitive discriminations and also his comprehension and use of language will be adversely affected. This is in accord with the hypothesis put forward in this paper.

In studying the decline of egocentricity in the child, psychologists have looked at both empathic role-taking ability and perceptual role-taking ability. However, the crucial concept underlying both types of perspective taking is the awareness of the existence of other perspectives which may be different from those of the child. Some reliable measure of the decline of egocentricity in the child was required and as perceptual role-taking ability appears earliest, in advance of empathic role-taking ability, it was decided to study the former.

The testing procedure most frequently used in this context is the Piaget & Inhelder (1956) 'Three Mountain Experiment' or some variant on it, so it was decided to use it in this experiment. Success on this task indicates an awareness on the child's part that the viewpoints of others may be different from his own.

Due to some controversy in the recent experimental literature (Feffer, 1959; Feffer & Gourevitch, 1960; Flavell *et al.*, 1968; Borke, 1971, 1972, 1975; Chandler & Greenspan, 1972; Fishbein & Lewis, 1972; Huttenlocher & Presson, 1973; Hoy, 1974; Cox, 1976; Eliot & Dayton, 1976; Marvin *et al.*, 1976; Salatas & Flavell, 1976) two types of test were used in this experiment, the original Piaget & Inhelder test and the modified version suggested by Huttenlocher & Presson. The modification involved subjects rotating a three-dimensional scene identical to the model used in the original Piaget & Inhelder experiment, to reproduce the doll's point of view instead of selecting it from a series of pictures as in the Piaget & Inhelder version. Borke *et al.*; Hoy; and Huttenlocher & Presson reported that this modified procedure resulted in fewer errors than the traditional method of responding and that children were successful on this form of the task at a much younger age.

This experiment was designed to investigate the hypothesis that the decline of egocentricity in the child as evidenced by his awareness of other points of view is necessary for the child to be able to comprehend other-centred kinship terms. Thus for example it is suggested that, because of his egocentricity, it is easier for a child to see a person as his grandfather than for him to see himself as a grandson to his grandfather.

To test the child's comprehension of kin terms a sentence completion test was used. This consisted of a definition for a kin term with the word for the term being supplied by the child. This was the same procedure as used to collect normative data on the acquisition of kinship terms which is reported in Macaskill (1981).

Method

Children

The children were randomly selected from second-year (mean age 6:1) and third-year classes (mean age 7:1) in a primary school. These particular age groups were selected on the basis of the normative data on the comprehension of kin terms previously collected by the author, as a selection of children at different stages of developmemt in their comprehension of kin terms was required. In total 69 children, 33 females and 36 males, were tested. Children were then grouped on the basis of their performance on the Piaget and modified Piaget tests, which, allowing for equal numbers of children per group, gave three groups of 20 children. Four children were dropped from group 2 and five from group 3. This was done randomly. The mean age and standard deviation of each group is shown in Table 1.

Materials

The standard model was used for the Three Mountain Experiment as described by Piaget & Inhelder (1956), although in this case there were two identical models, one of which was placed on a turntable to allow it to be rotated. In addition there was the standard collection of 10 coloured photographs of

Table 1. Mean age of children

Experimental groups	Males		Females		Overall	
	Mean age	SD (months)	Mean age	SD (months)	Mean age	SD (months)
3	6:6	3·6	6:11	6	6:8·5	6
2	6:8	8·4	6:6	7·2	6:7	7·2
1	6:6	6	6:6	8·4	6:6	6·8

the scene taken from different perspectives as in the original experiment and a doll approximately 6 cm high. No features, such as eyes, were visible on the doll's head as their inclusion could have forced the child to consider aspects such as the doll's line of vision, rather than simply its position.

Sentence completion test for the comprehension of kin terms. Each definition was typed on a separate card and the terms used were as follows:

Child-centred terms
The woman who had you as a baby is your..............(MOTHER)
The man who had you as a baby is your..............(FATHER)
The mother of your mother/father is your..............(GRANDMOTHER)
The father of your mother/father is your..............(GRANDFATHER)
A girl/boy with the same parents as you is your..............(SISTER/BROTHER)
Your mother's/father's sister is your..............(AUNT)
Your mother's/father's brother is your..............(UNCLE)
The children of your mother's/father's sisters are your..............(COUSIN)
The children of your mother's/father's brothers are your..............(COUSIN)

Other-centred terms
You are your mother's/father's..............(SON/DAUGHTER)
And a boy/girl would be her/his..............(SON/DAUGHTER)

Note. As subjects seemed to experience difficulty with the double possessive, the questions for granddaughter and grandson were preceded with the following question in its relevant form to ensure that the child was focusing on the appropriate person. Has your mother got a mother, or has your father got a father?

You are your mother's mother's..............(GRANDDAUGHTER OR GRANDSON)
And a girl/boy would be her..............
You are you father's father's..............
And a girl/boy would be his..............
Similarly for mother's father's and father's mother's.
You are your mother's/father's sister's..............(NIECE OR NEPHEW)
And a girl/boy would be her/his..............
You are your mother's/father's brother's..............
And a girl/boy would be her/his..............

Procedure

Children were tested individually in an empty classroom. The experiment consisted of three tests, the original Piaget & Inhelder 'Mountain Experiment', a modified form of this test, called the 'Modified Piaget Test' and the sentence completion test. The order of presentation of the three tests was counterbalanced, giving six possible orders and children were randomly assigned to an order, so that 10 children, five male and five female, completed each order.

The time taken per child varied considerably, but in no case was it longer than 20 minutes.

Piaget & Inhelder Mountain Experiment. Initially the child was shown the model and given a little time to examine it. Next he was shown the set of pictures and it was pointed out to him that the pictures showed the three mountains from various positions around the table. Finally the child was shown the doll and the experimenter explained to him the nature of his task. He was told that the doll was to be moved around the table and that he was to see if he could pick out the picture that showed the same view of the mountains as the doll could 'see' in the position that it was then in. He was asked if he understood and further explanations were given if necessary. The order of positioning the doll was randomized for each child. All the 10 pictures were shown at the same time after each change of position and the children were given as long as they liked to make their decisions. This was the same procedure as that followed in this part of the original experiment.

Modified Piaget Experiment. Here again the child was shown the model and given time to examine it. Then his attention was drawn to the second model and it was pointed out to him that the two models were exactly the same. Next he was shown how one of the models could be turned and he was encouraged to try doing this. Finally he was shown the doll and the nature of the task was explained as in the Piaget & Inhelder experiment, although this time the child was asked to see if he could turn the model round so that the experimenter could see the same scene as the doll could 'see' from the various positions. The experimenter was in front of the model, and she was seated to be at approximately the same level as the doll. In between trials the child was asked to watch where the doll was moving to and the experimenter then moved the doll in the original model and then returned to her position in front of the second model and the child then rotated this model. Again the child was given as long as he required to complete this operation. Positions for the doll were randomized as before and the same positions were used.

Sentence completion test. All children were told that they were to be asked about the various people who made up a family. The experimenter would read them a sentence which described a family member but the name which the person was called was missing and the child was required to supply this word at the end of the sentence. Subjects were then given the following example: 'The people you live with are your FAMILY'. This served as a practice trial and to induce mental set for the remaining questions. It also allowed the experimenter to check that the younger subjects understood the term and further explanations were given if required.

Each definition was then read out to each child and the child's responses recorded. The presentation order was randomized for each child.

Results

On the Piaget & Inhelder Three Mountain Experiment, children were found to behave in ways similar to those described by Piaget & Inhelder. Some responded by giving their own perspective while others, although appearing to be aware that the doll's viewpoint was different from their own, still could not reproduce the doll's view successfully. Others seemed to find the task relatively easy and appeared to have little difficulty in responding correctly. Children were successful at this task at a somewhat earlier age than that reported by Piaget, but this was relatively unimportant as the children's performance still corresponded to the developmental stages described by Piaget.

All those who were successful on the Piaget test were also successful on the modified Piaget test (group 3). Children in group 2 were successful only on the Modified Piaget Test, while those in group 1 could complete neither test. This latter group can be described as still being egocentric in their responses, showing no awareness of the existence of perspectives other than their own.

Next the number correctly completing any of the other-centred kin terms was totalled. This is shown in Table 2. Of the children who were no longer egocentric, that is groups 2 and 3, 26 were able to complete at least one other-centred kin term correctly, while 14 were unable to complete any of the other-centred terms. This is consistent with the Piagetian hypothesis that cognitive development precedes language acquisition, as one would predict that some children would have achieved the cognitive advance without yet having attained

Table 2. Number of subjects in each group completing any of the other-centred terms

Test of egocentricity	At least one term correct	None correct	*n*
Group 1 (unsuccessful on both tests)	3	17	20
Groups 2 (successful only on the modified test)	6	14	20
Groups 3 (successful on both tests)	20	0	20

its linguistic expression. Group 2 children were cognitively no longer egocentric in their responses but 14 of them still had to generalize this ability to their comprehension of language.

On the other hand, group 3 children could all complete some other-centred kin terms, responding with a mean number of 4·2 terms correct out of a possible total of six. These could all complete the more difficult test of egocentricity, demonstrating not only an awareness of the existence of perspectives other than their own but also the ability to mentally manipulate these in a fairly abstract fashion. With this group, their cognitive skills were more advanced as were their abilities to comprehend other-centred kin terms.

Although chi-squared tests of association indicated that the differences between the groups in Table 2 were significant ($\chi^2 = 33\cdot24$, $P < 0\cdot01$), all the group 1 children did not conform totally to the predicted pattern of responses. Seventeen children could not complete any of the other-centred terms as predicted, but three could complete one of the other-centred kin terms despite still apparently being egocentric on the Piaget tests. On the tests of egocentricity, these three gave responses other than the egocentric one although these responses were still incorrect; this suggested that these children could be in the transitional phase, having some awareness of the existence of different viewpoints but unable to conceptualize them precisely. It was also interesting that all three children were female and responded only to the term 'daughter'; previous research by the author found that the term 'son' invariably appeared at the same time as 'daughter'. Indeed the wording of the sentence completion test is such as to facilitate the response 'son' being given; its absence in these cases suggests that the children were still responding in a somewhat egocentric fashion being able to complete the definition, 'You are your mother's daughter', but being unable to take the cognitive step required to complete, 'And a boy would be her . . . . ?'. The second question requires the subject to switch from the personal, 'I am my mother's daughter', to the more abstract, 'A boy is my mother's son'.

An analysis of variance on the data indicated that there was a significant main effect of groups ($F = 65\cdot24$, d.f. $= 2, 57$, $P < 0\cdot001$), with group 3 completing the highest number of kin terms in total, group 2 performing at the next level and group 1 being poorest. The type of term also had a significant main effect ($F = 259\cdot99$, d.f. $= 1, 57$, $P < 0\cdot001$), with overall performance on child-centred terms being at a higher level than for other-centred terms. These results merely served to confirm that the language acquisition data conformed to the normative data previously collected by the author and discussed earlier.

Discussion

When carrying out experiments to relate aspects of the child's cognitive development to his language acquisition it is often extremely difficult to show that the two are definitely causally related. Both are such complex topics. This experiment has however presented some evidence in support of the Piagetian hypothesis that language acquisition is dependent on cognitive development.

With the decline of egocentricity in the child, as measured by his ability to take the role perspective of another, the child could indeed begin to comprehend other-centred kin terms. Not all children who successfully completed the modified form of the Piaget test could define other-centred kin terms and this was as expected, if cognitive development precedes the acquisition of language skills. However, all the subjects who could perform the original and more complex Piaget & Inhelder test could also define other-centred kin terms, indicating that they were at a more advanced stage of development.

With three exceptions, the subjects unable to complete either of the Piaget tests were also unable to define any of the other-centred kin terms, which was as predicted, and as explained previously, it was felt that these three subjects did not seriously damage the case.

The modified form of the Piaget test proved to be a more sensitive measure for ascertaining that children are no longer egocentric than the original Piaget test. This is basically because it is a much simpler test, allowing the child to deal with the problem in a fairly concrete fashion while the original test is a more abstract, cognitive operation altogether.

This experiment then provided support for the hypothesis that the decline of egocentricity in the child, as assessed by his ability to take the role perspective of another, was related to the child's ability to comprehend other-centred kin terms and this is consistent with the Piagetian hypothesis that language acquisition is dependent on cognitive development.

References

Borke, H. (1971). Interpersonal perception of young children: Egocentrism or empathy. *Developmental Psychology*, **5**, 263–269.

Borke, H. (1972). Chandler & Greenspan's 'Ersatz egocentrism': A rejoinder. *Developmental Psychology*, **7**, 107–109.

Borke, H. (1975). Piaget's mountains revisited: Changes in the egocentric landscape. *Developmental Psychology*, **11**, 240–243.

Chandler, M. J. & Greenspan, S. (1972). 'Ersatz egocentrism': A reply to H. Borke. *Developmental Psychology*, **7**, 104–106.

Cox, M. V. (1976). Training perspective ability in young children. Paper given at the Annual Conference of the Developmental Psychology Section of The British Psychological Society, Guildford, September.

Eliot, J. & Dayton, C. M. (1976*a*). Factors affecting accuracy of perception on a task requiring the ability to identify viewpoints. *Journal of Genetic Psychology*, **128**, 201–214.

Eliot, J. & Dayton, C. M. (1976*b*). Egocentric error and the construct of egocentrism. *Journal of Genetic Psychology*, **128**, 275–289.

Elkind, D. (1962). Children's conception of brother and sister: Piaget replication study V. *Journal of Genetic Psychology*, **100**, 129–136.

Feffer, M. H. (1959). The cognitive implications of role-taking behaviour. *Journal of Personality*, **27**, 152–168.

Feffer, M. H. & Gourevitch, V. (1960). Cognitive aspects of role-taking in children. *Journal of Personality*, **28**, 383–396.

Fishbein, H. D., Lewis, S. & Keiffer, K. (1972). Children's understanding of spatial relations: Co-ordination of perspectives. *Developmental Psychology*, **7**, 21–33.

Flavell, J. H., Botkin, P. T. & Fry, C. L. (1968). *The Development of Role-Taking and Communication Skills in Children*. London: Wiley.

Hoy, E. A. (1974). Predicting another's visual perspective, a unitary skill? *Developmental Psychology*, **10**, 462.

Huttenlocher, J. & Presson, C. C. (1973). Mental rotation and the perspective problem. *Cognitive Psychology*, **4**, 273–299.

Macaskill, A. (1981). Language acquisition and cognitive development in the acquisition of kinship terms. *British Journal of Educational Psychology*, **51**, 283–290.

Marvin, R. S., Greenberg, M. T. & Mossler, D. G. (1976). The early development of conceptual perspective taking: Distinguishing among multiple perspectives. *Child Development*, **47**, 511–514.

Piaget, J. (1928). *Judgement and Reasoning in the Child*. London: Routledge & Kegan Paul, 1951.

Piaget, J. & Inhelder, B. (1956). *The Child's Conception of Space*. London: Routledge & Kegan Paul.

Piaget, J. & Inhelder, B. (1969). The gaps in empiricism. In A. Koestler & J. R. Smythies (eds), *Beyond Reductionism*. London: Hutchinson.

Salatas, H. & Flavell, J. H. (1976). Perspective-taking. The development of two components of knowledge. *Child Development*, **47**, 103–109.

Requests for reprints should be addressed to Ann Macaskill, 52 Linden Avenue, Sheffield S8 0GA, UK.

Book review

The Philosophy of Moral Development, vol. I. *By* L. Kohlberg. San Francisco: Harper & Row. 1981.
Pp. 441. ISBN 0 06 064760 4. $21.95.

This is a book whose appearance has been waited for by many for a long time. It is the first of
three volumes by Lawrence Kohlberg, certainly the best known among contemporary investigators of
man's morality and how it develops. Its appearance is rewarding for all those who, in their desire to
know the work of Kohlberg, had no other choice but to search patiently through numerous journals
and books which contain articles written by the author. In this respect, the volume itself and the
impressively long bibliography of Kohlberg's writings attached to its end are a very good guide to
and summary of Kohlberg's central ideas and interests. That is one of the volume's major assets – its
contribution to the study of moral development in general.

   The Philosophy of Moral Development is a collection of essays mostly by Kohlberg although the
names of three other authors play some part as well. This thematically defined collection of essays is
divided into four parts, all of them centred around the stage concept seen in its relationship with
other morally related topics: education, justice, legal and political issues, and problems beyond
justice. Most of the chapters are reprints of papers published between 1967–77 and, for that
reason, probably known to the majority of Kohlberg's readers. The fashion in which Kohlberg has
chosen to organize his *Volume I* reflects at the same time a step-by-step development of the theory
itself. For all that, it seems appropriate to say that the newness of this collection consists, primarily,
in its bookness. What indeed is a relatively novel ingredient of the theory is its addition of a seventh
stage so as to include the religious factor in moral development.

   I remember reading an article a few years ago where this new development, i.e. stage 7, was
announced. Its provisional title was 'Rational Mysticism' and the full account of the stage was only
expected in the 1990s. Its appearance now is a nice surprise to those who have been waiting for it.
How fulfilling this new proposal by Kohlberg is will depend, first and foremost, on one's own
philosophy of life and of the human condition. In other words, Kohlberg's arguments hold only
given certain assumptions along the dimension secular–religious. Before I bring out some of my
comments concerning this new stage and its implications, I shall dwell on some other, almost equally
important aspects of the theory.

   Kohlberg has embarked upon the philosophical inquiry of morality with the aim of providing an
interdisciplinary and comprehensive account of its nature and development. Such an enterprise is
praiseworthy in itself. Kohlberg's interest in education and its problems is genuine. The role he
assigns to the developing cognition in morality is an important one and deserves attention. The
plenitude of problems, questions, and remarks raised by Kohlberg's theory is a compliment to the
author in its own right. All this shows that its author is a man devoted to his field, with eagerness
and zeal to put many things right and to solve some of the most important educational problems.
Yet, this difficult and ambitious undertaking makes Kohlberg simplify the situation by drawing some
rather bold and straightforward conclusions, despite the lack of reasonably convincing evidence or
the lack of evidence other than his own. In fact, Kohlberg's reliance on his own and on his
colleagues' evidence is striking. This is just one of the many examples: 'Although the personality is
unitary, it progresses through stages in a sequential order. Here I draw on my theory and findings
concerning stages of moral development (Kohlberg, 1968, 1969, 1970)' (p. 378). Or, '. . .clear
theoretical and operational distinctions between the two concepts of intelligence have not been made
until recently. Factor-analytic findings now can provide an empirical basis for this distinction
(DeVries and Kohlberg, 1977)' (p. 90). These conjectures and poorly founded statements should not
imply an intellectual arrogance on the part of Kohlberg. He is rather an engaged thinker who
sincerely argues for his cause. Errors are not uncommon in such cases. His occasional passionate
claims and appeals should be taken by the reader with some measure. But, to be fair to Kohlberg,
critical comments such as these should also be taken with some measure, at least until the appearance
of the other two volumes. Only then will a complete evaluation of his theory, as it is now, be
possible. Nevertheless, since each of the three volumes is an independent whole, it is not only justified
but also required to make an independent review of each one of them.

   Kohlberg's inclination to be exclusive with respect to his own research evidence becomes somewhat disturbing as he enters the problems of religious development. The evidence he draws on is not only scarce and more or less anecdotal, but rather bizarre, too. The examples chosen to illustrate the most sublime aspects of the highest stage include a few characters from literature, e.g. Antigone, Othello, Ivan Karamazov, etc., and a few tragic human cases. The purpose of such examples is to show the import of despair and tragedy in religious development, i.e. the limits of rational human morality. One such of Kohlberg's examples resolves her despair by 'committing her life to her mentally ill brother and his fellow sufferers' (p. 405). Another example of the same class defined himself as 'the son of a madman' and had decided he should never marry or have children.

Although one may find that these illustrative cases from literature and various tragic destinies add to the book's vividness, there is something of a greater importance here for a psychologist concerned with the construction of a theory. Making a theory in this manner resembles Freud's constructing of psychoanalysis. A theory with pretensions to explaining human personality in general is based upon a small number of pathological cases.

Kohlberg's style of thinking and writing shows remarkable similarities with Piaget's, which I do not find surprising. Kohlberg's theory of moral development is, in fact, an application and elaboration of Piaget's theory of cognitive development to problems of morality. The same concepts figure as central in both of the theories, such as, stage, equilibration, parallelism, etc., besides their more general common ambition to seek an answer to some philosophical questions of relevance to psychology and education. The connoisseurs of Kohlberg's work are most probably familiar with Piaget's work, too. And if so, then Kant's philosophy of morality must also be strongly associated with these two names. Apart from Kant and Piaget, Kohlberg's major theoretical models include: Socrates (5th century BC), Dewey (1903), Baldwin (1906) and Mead (1934). Kohlberg's effort to provide some justification for this not very up-to-date collection of sources gives the book a slightly apologetic tone. To some of these influences I shall come back later. At the moment, some other comments concerning the book as a whole should be made.

The reader will have to cope with repeatedly outlined categorizations and typologies. This form of communication is usually helpful in presenting some complex and multitudinous material, provided there is sufficient distinction, visual and otherwise. Kohlberg has done that most often in a prose form which makes it a rather difficult task for the reader to follow the argument behind. Moreover, conceptual distinctiveness within these typologies is not always perfect. As an example of this, Kohlberg distinguishes three fundamental approaches to education or ideologies: 'cultural transmission', 'romantic ideology', and 'Dewey's progressivism'. Then, he goes on to distinguish three fundamental strategies for defining educational objectives: 'the bag of virtue', 'industrial psychology', and 'developmental–philosophic strategy'. As you may find some of these terms a little unusual or even extravagant, there are a few more to introduce you to: metaphysical evolutionism, moral musical chairs, paradoxical–consolidative faith stage, qualified attitude reasoning, cosmic law perspective, and many more of the kind.

The stage concept is so widely known among psychologists that there is not much new to add about it except, perhaps, that it almost deserves its own heading – stageology. This concept owes its prominence to Piaget, not to Kohlberg, and has already been seriously challenged on the grounds that there is little empirical support for it, especially among the most recent research evidence. The new research findings suggest continuity of development rather than separate stages. Kohlberg's only mistake with respect to this concept is his failure to mention any of such findings. The stage concept is only a theoretical construct whose unity and distinctiveness is usually overestimated by those who employ it. Kohlberg's use of it, in particular, has already been criticized for the arbitrariness in classifying subjects' answers. Kohlberg himself is aware of this, at least in some cases. The following is such an example: 'Although I classified Socrates' statements to Crito as Stage 5, his statement of his civilly disobedient role as moral educator, quoted earlier, was Stage 6, at least in spirit' (pp. 43–44). The author has provided a truly ample source of evidence obtained from his subjects as well as reasons for assigning them to particular stages. All these examples are selected with the purpose of showing how complex and yet logically coherent the theory is.

According to Kohlberg, the supreme virtue is justice and all moral education should be concerned with it. To make it clear immediately, justice is a form, not a content. If that is still too vague for you to understand, the following quotation may be of some help: 'Although Plato, Dewey, and Piaget each meant different things by *justice* (K.), each recognized justice as the first virtue of a person because it is the first virtue of a society' (p. xiii). The word 'society' used in this context makes it even more obscure. Nevertheless, the question to be asked is: Whom does Kohlberg have in mind? That is, who is to administer justice when it happens to be at stake in a company of those untrained by the Socratic dialogue and who are incapable of it? Kohlberg's philosophical views I do not consider disturbing, at least not for a psychologist involved in empirical research. What I do find disturbing is his neglect of that research. For instance, what about individual differences, cognitive and non-cognitive? A research-oriented psychologist such as Kohlberg should be expected to be more realistic about these matters. An equally vague aspect of the same justice principle has to do with the education for it. Such education is best realized through the Socratic dialogue whose only aim is the development itself. So, the concept without content (justice is a form) ends in becoming a part of an argument without content. This argument becomes even more peculiar when one reads that justice is the supreme principle of morality and even love (agape) has to obey it. Or, as Kohlberg put it, '...if a Stage 7 agape is to be used to resolve moral conflicts, it cannot violate or ignore the basic principles of justice' (p. 309).

I have mentioned the importance of Kohlberg's attempt to bring religion into the study of morality and moral development. The manner in which Kohlberg approaches this problem will not be found satisfactory by all, certainly not by Christian theologians and philosophers of religion, though Kohlberg seems to have had them in mind as potential readers. The immediate impression one gets upon reading this volume is that the religion which Kohlberg advocates is not necessarily theistic, especially not Christian. His rather hostile attitude towards Christianity is revealed in some of his ironical remarks on Christian ethics and its principles. Kohlberg has more sympathy for some sort of pantheism, at any rate, for some sort of religion without God. In Kohlberg's theory, God is a heteronomous agent and therefore any figuring of God in a subject's answer is an indicator of immature development. This is one example which has received Kohlberg's attention as heteronomous, i.e. immature, and therefore was classified as Stage 4. The answer was given by a boy aged 16 in response to the following question: 'Should the doctor "mercy-kill" a dying woman requesting death because of her pain?'

> I don't know. In one way, it's murder, it's not a right or privilege of man to decide who shall live and who should die. God put life into everybody on earth, and you're taking away something from that person that came directly from God, and you are destroying something that is very sacred, it's in a way part of God, and it's almost destroying a part of God when you kill a person. There is something of God in everyone (p. 119).

In spite of my unreserved disagreement with Kohlberg concerning his approach to the relationship between religion and morality, I still consider chapter 9 the most interesting part of his book.

Kohlberg's theory of religious development is not a theory in its proper sense. Kohlberg draws heavily on Fowler's work which, again, has sprung from an enthusiasm for Kohlberg's theory of moral development. The two theories are in the closest relationship possible, each one building upon the other. On p. 323 Kohlberg explains this cooperation in more detail. In his own research, Kohlberg simply adopts Fowler's methodology (not discussed in Volume I) and applies it to a sample of 21 subjects. The findings speak convincingly in favour of a stage-like religious development which shows parallels with both moral development and Fowler's faith development stages. Fowler's method was used with children aged between 4 and 10 who were questioned (interviewed) on various topics among which were those such as: death and afterlife, evil and suffering, freedom and determinism, ideal manhood and womanhood, and the like. I am not at all surprised at the results produced by the method. Suffice it to say that the highest stage was not achieved until the age of 40.

Apart from objecting to Kohlberg's ignoring the philosophy of religion, and Christian ethics as a part of it, one must be worried by those more psychological errors. It begins to seem puzzling whether the word *cognitive* plays any meaningful part in the title of the theory. In other words, there is more 'mysticism', 'despair', 'tragic wisdom', 'contemplating' (Eastern way), 'opening', 'feeling' and the like than *thinking* in Kohlberg's vocabulary when explaining religious development. So, on p. 370 Kohlberg writes: 'The center of the highest state is experiences that are most distinctively religious experiences of union with deity, whether pantheistic or theistic.'

Kohlberg's ambivalent attitude towards the cognitive is of some interest. On p. 60 you can find this statement made by a psychologist with a long-lasting reputation for his research into cognition and its role in moral development. 'For the progressive epistemology, the immediate or introspective experience of the child does not have ultimate truth or reality...' '...it [progressive epistemology] attempts to functionally coordinate the external meaning of the child's experiences as *behaviour* (L.K.), with its internal meaning *as it appears to the observer*' (O.P.).

One of the most ambiguous concepts used in moral philosophy and psychology is autonomy. The real responsibility for introducing it into the study of morality falls upon Kant. Kant, however, being a philosopher and of older times, can be excused for not trying to relate his speculations about human nature to empirical facts. Psychology became involved with the problem of autonomy–heteronomy through Piaget. Kohlberg inherited it from Piaget and adopted it without any questions concerning its meaning and validity. It is one thing to say that a person is autonomous, i.e. freely decides which of the principles of behaviour to adopt, and another thing to say that moral principles are autonomous, i.e. independent of all other domains and created *ex nihilo*. Both of these things can be found in psychology.

The emphasis on reason by Kant, Piaget and Kohlberg is a rather rigorous rationalism required from moral subjects. Such rationalism leads to the deification of reason, as an eminent philosopher of religion put it. The other side of this argument, found in this most recent of Kohlberg's works, is a rather minor role played by the same reason in religious development. It is certainly true that reason should be our ultimate judge and guide in matters of morality, and religion too, but reason should be philosophically and theologically educated.

The Philosophy of Moral Development, volume I, is an interesting book, not always easy to follow, but stimulating in its own way. Judging the theory of moral and religious development formulated by Kohlberg in the light of research findings not included in this volume, the prospects are that Kohlberg's paradigm as it stands now will come to be replaced by a new one as a result of the evidence accumulated so far. Psychology, just as any other scientific discipline, makes progress through discovering its past errors. The theory still develops, however, and this is the reason for optimism with respect to its final form. Looking back to the time when the sixth stage was considered to be an absolute achievement of mature reason, the introduction of the seventh stage, even in its present form, is a very promising development. After all, Kohlberg is aware of this when he says that he has not 'attempted to present a single and final statement' because his views and those of his colleagues are changing and growing. It is to be hoped that this growth will continue so as to include an openness to the evidence outside Kohlberg's own framework.

OLIVERA PETROVICH (Department of Experimental Psychology, South Parks Road, Oxford)

Fowler, J. W. (1976). Stages in faith. The structural–developmental approach. In Th. Hennessy (ed.), *Values and Moral Education*. New York: Penlist Press.

Afterword and acknowledgements

What happens, I take it, in the case of most edited books is that the editor decides on a theme and thinks of the people whom he or she would most like to write about it. Invitations go out, and if enough of them are accepted the book goes ahead. The usual result is a fairly homogeneous collection of contributions which fall roughly or sometimes very smoothly into the mould originally set by the editor. The different chapters, it is true, may represent different points of view and if the editor is judicious there will usually be arguments both for and against this or that hypothesis. But the stamp is the editor's nonetheless: he starts off knowing about the contributors' work and wanting it included in his book.

It is usually a good formula but it is not the only good formula used. This book, perforce, adopted another one. It started as a special issue of the *British Journal of Psychology*, and as is the case with every issue of that journal, any one was entitled to submit a paper. Indeed a general invitation for submissions was published, and in they came from every quarter. I myself asked a few people to write something, but most of the contributions were not invited ones. In fact I could not possibly have asked for many of the papers which I am now very happy to see included in this volume because they described work whose very existence was quite new to me. I had many surprises, most of them pleasant, and I learned a lot.

But the advantage of this formula is not just that it teaches an ignorant editor one or two new things. It also makes it likelier that the structure, which emerges and which is determined more by the contributors themselves than by the editor, does represent the research that is being done quite accurately. So many people are involved to ensure this. Not only were there many submissions, but also a host of referees gave me careful and conscientious reviews of all the papers sent to me. The referees' work was crucial, and my gratitude to all of them is very great. They made it, I hope, an interesting and a worthy volume.

I am grateful too to Max Coltheart for suggesting the volume in the first place and to Michele Benjamin, who administers the BPS journals, for her patient and unruffled advice. A tremendous amount of the burden of sending papers out to referees (and getting them back), of typing the many inevitable letters, and of keeping tabs on what was going on was carried by Betty Hammond. She did it very well and very cheerfully. Maryanne Collis took up that burden extremely efficiently in the final stages.

While I am making my thanks, my thoughts keep straying to the thousands of young children who took part in the research described here. They endure our vanities with good humour. I hope that Piaget's well-deserved influence, to which this book is nothing more than a tribute, and our continuing efforts will in the end help them.

PETER BRYANT
Oxford, April 1982

Index*

---

* Page numbers all refer to the numbering in square brackets at the head of each page.